POPULAR SCIENCE

DO-IT-YOURSELF

ENCYCLOPEDIA

POPULAR SCIENCE

DO-IT-YOURSELF

ENCYCLOPEDIA

. . . *Complete* How-To *Series for the Entire Family* . . .

•

written in simple language

•

with full step-by-step instructions

•

and profusely illustrated

ILLUSTRATED EDITION

Volume 6

Gar - Ins

ACKNOWLEDGMENTS

The editors of this series would like to express their thanks and appreciation to the following companies for their assistance in preparing special sections within this volume, for their technical advice and their permission to use special material, photographs, art and educational charts.

ADJUSTABLE CASTOR CO. AMERICAN COMMUNITY BUILDERS AMERICAN CYANAMID CO. AMERICAN PETROLEUM INSTITUTE ARMSTRONG CORK CO. ASSOCIATED PLAN SERVICE, INC. CLEMSON BROTHERS, INC. CLEVELAND HEATER CO. DAVID BOGEN CO., INC. DE WALT, INC. DOUGLAS FIR PLYWOOD ASSOCIATION DRIER BROTHERS, INC. EFFS POST FEDERAL PURCHASER GENERAL ELECTRIC JENSEN MANUFACTURING CO. KARLSON ASSOCIATES, INC. LIBBY-OWENS-FORD GLASS CO. MASONITE CORPORATION MINNEAPOLIS HONEYWELL REGULATOR CORPORATION MONSANTO CHEMICAL CO. P & G SUPPLY PERMAFLUX CORPORATION PITTSBURGH CORNING CORPORATION PLASTIGLIDE MANUFACTURING CO. RED DEVIL TOOLS ROBERT BRODY CO. RUBBER MANUFACTURERS ASSOCIATION STANLEY TOOLS, DIVISION OF THE STANLEY WORKS SYLVANIA ELECTRIC CO. TACO, INC. THE UPSON CO. UNITED STATES PLYWOOD CORPORATION WASHINGTON STEEL PRODUCTS, INC. YALE & TOWNE MANUFACTURING CORP.

Photograph courtesy of Armstrong Cork Co.

UPRIGHT-FOLIAGE PLANTS

Air Plant or Life Plant (*kalanchoe or Bryophyllum*) grows in bright light or sun. Propagation is by the young plants that form on the edge of the leaf. One kind has flat leaves and another has tubular leaves.

Aloe grows in full sun or shade and doesn't need too much water. Propagation is by small shoots that form near the base of the plant.

Anthericum grows in bright light. Propagation is by young plants that form on the stems.

Boston Fern (*nephrolepis*) grows best in bright light. Propagation is by runners that form new plants when they strike the soil.

Cacti grow in full sun or shade. A sandy soil and not too much water are best. Propagation is by seeds or cutting. (Refer to *Christmas Cactus.*)

Caladiums require bright light and a uniformly moist soil. Propagation is by division of tubers.

Cast Iron Plant (*Aspidistra*) grows under any conditions. Propagation is by division.

Century Plant (*Agave*) requires sun or shade and not too much water. Propagation is by cuttings of the small shoots near the base.

Chinese Water Evergreens (*Aglaonema*) grows well in shade, in soil or water, and in any soil moisture. Propagation is by cuttings rooted in water or sand.

Coleus should be grown in sunlight. Propagation is by terminal cuttings. New plants should replace old ones frequently because of the ungainly growth. The plants require

pinching to cause branching.

Jade Plant (*Crassula*) grows in shade or sun. Propagation is by leaf or terminal cuttings.

Maranta is a creeping plant that grows best in bright light or shade in shallow containers. The soil should be kept very moist.

Peperomia should be grown in bright light or shade. Propagation is by terminal cuttings or by leaf-cuttings.

Pick-a-Back Plant (*Tolmiea Menziesii*) does well in sun or bright light. Propagation is by the young plants that form on the leaves.

Rubber Plants (*Ficus*), many varieties, grow well in bright or poor light. Propagation is by leaf-bud or terminal cuttings.

Silk Oak (*Grevillea*) grows in sun or bright light. Propagation is by seeds.

Strawberry Geranium (*Saxifraga sarmentosa*) grows best in sun or bright light. New plantlets develop on runners.

Velvet Plant (*Gynura*) does best in bright light. Propagation is by terminal cuttings. The plant requires pinching to cause branching.

FOLIAGE VINES

Asparagus grows best in full sun or partial shade. Propagation is by seeds or division.

Baby's Tears (*Helxine*) requires bright or poor light and plenty of water, but watering should be done from below rather than from above. The plant should be grown in a shallow container and the base of the container kept in water, or a wick should be used. Propagation is by division.

English Ivies (*Hedera Helix*), many varieties, grow well in bright light and in very poor light. Propagation is by terminal cuttings.

German Ivy (*Senecio Mikanioides*) needs sun or bright light. It does poorly in the home because of lack of light; it grows best in a window box outside. Propagation is by leaf-bud or terminal cuttings.

Grape Ivy (*Cissus*) grows best in bright light but withstands poor light well. Propagation is by leaf-bud or terminal cuttings. Two kinds are available.

Nephthytis does well in bright light or shade, and needs plenty of water. Propagation is by leaf-bud or terminal cuttings.

Periwinkle (*Vinca major*) is not a good house plant but is good for a window box in sun or shade. Propagation is by leaf-bud or terminal cuttings.

Philodendron can be grown in bright light or poor light. It may be grown in water or dry soil. Propagation is by leaf-bud or terminal cuttings.

Wandering Jew (*Tradescantia or Zebrina*) grows in sun or bright light. Propagation is by terminal cuttings.

Wax Plant (*Hoya carnosa*) grows in sun or bright light. Propagation is by leaf-bud or terminal cuttings.

FLOWERING PLANTS

Achimenes can be grown from the cone-like storage root planted during March to May and placed in a sunny window. They flower during summer. After the plant has flowered, the soil should be allowed

Plants for East or West Windows

African Violets

Begonia

Caladium

Pandamus

to dry gradually and then the plant should be stored in a cool, dark place. Before growth starts again the next year, the old soil should be shaken from the roots and replaced by new.

African Violet (Saintpaulia) does not flower in poor light. During summer, it should be placed in bright light; during winter, in sun. It will not endure summer sun. Afri-

can violet is best watered from below; the wick method is excellent. It can be grown from a leaf-petiole cutting.

Amaryllis (Hippeastrum) bulbs planted about half under soil during November to January flower in early spring. They should be grown in sun. After flowering, they are kept growing in the pot or are planted in a shady place in the gar-

den. They should be protected from frost. They are not allowed to dry.

Astilbe cannot be forced into bloom successfully in the home. Plants in flower obtained from the florist should be watered with a wick or set with the base of the pot in shallow water, and kept in sun or bright light. The plants are hardy and may be planted in the garden after danger of freezing has passed. Propagation is by division.

Azalea (*Rhododendron*) grows in bright light or sun and needs a uniform supply of water. One should buy only plants with many buds and a few open flowers. The buds open in the home. After flowering, the plant may be kept in light where it will grow. After danger of freezing, it may be planted in the pot in the garden and kept moist during summer. Before frost, it should be placed in a cool, well-ventilated room where it does not freeze. A bedroom window is usually good. About January 1, it may be brought into the living room to flower. An acid, peaty soil is required.

Everblooming Begonia (*Begonia semperflorens*) needs sunlight. It can be grown in the window from a cutting from the base of the plant. It may be grown from seeds. It is a good bedding plant.

Calla Begonia (*Begonia semperflorens*) grows in bright light but not sunlight. Propagation is from cuttings only. It is grown primarily for the interest foliage.

Rex Begonia and all rhizomatous forms grow in bright light but not sunlight. Propagation is by leaf cuttings. They are grown for the foliage.

Christmas Begonia (*Begonia socotrana*) is the most showy of the begonias but the most difficult to grow. It should be purchased with many buds, grown in sun, and discarded after flowering because of the difficulty of growing it in the home.

Tuberous-Rooted Begonias are planted in March in moist soil, grow in sun until May, and then in bright light. After they have finished flowering, the plants should be allowed to dry, and then the tubers placed in sand or dry peat and stored over winter in a cool basement. They may be grown from seeds. They are excellent garden plants in a moist, shaded position.

Miscellaneous Begonias include the better varieties of fibrous-rooted forms. They grow best in sun or bright light and are propagated from terminal cuttings.

Butterfly Flowers or Poor Man's Orchids (*Schizanthus*) should be bought in flower and given full sun or bright light. They are annuals and die after flowering. They should not be grown from seeds in the home.

Calceolaria should be bought with many flowers and buds, kept in sun, and at about 50° F at night. The plant should be discarded after flowering.

Calla (*Zantedeschia*), both the yellow and the white, should be grown in sun and given plenty of water. It is dried off during June and kept as cool as possible until August, when the white-calla corm is replanted in new soil and started

Plants for a North Window

African Evergreen

Chinese Evergreen

Ivy

Philodendron

into growth again. The yellow calla must be left in a dry condition until November or later. Propagation is by offsets of the fleshy storage organ.

Christmas Cactus (*Zygocatus truncatus*) grows in sun and where the night temperature during winter is from 60° to 65° F. It should not be kept dry like other cacti and does especially well if the soil is always moist. Flower buds start during Oc-

tober, and the plant will continue to flower during winter and spring. Bud drop occurs when the temperature is too high or the light intensity too low. It can be grown out of doors in summer.

Christmas Pepper (*Capsicum Frutescens*) should be bought in full fruit and discarded after it loses its value as an ornamental because it is an annual. It can be grown for

seed planted during June or July and the seedlings grown in pots in the garden. (See *Jerusalem Cherry*.)

Chrysanthemum plants in the garden may be dug and potted during August to be flowered in the house. They should be kept out of doors as long as possible. They need sun. The varieties obtained from the florist are usually not hardy and may as well be discarded after flowering.

Cineraria should be obtained with buds and flowers, kept in sun, and placed in a room at about 50° F at night. The plant should be discarded after flowering.

Citrus plants grow well in sun if given a good supply of water. They can be propagated from seeds or cuttings.

Cyclamen should be obtained with many flowers and placed in sun at a cool (50° F.) night temperature. The leaves turn yellow and the buds blast if the temperature is too high or the light intensity too low.

After the plant has flowered, the soil may be kept dry until June, when the corm can be removed and planted in new soil and to grow the next year. In a cool bright window, the plant usually flowers again.

Easter Lily needs sun. The bulbs may be planted before Christmas and the plants will flower in the home, but to obtain a plant well budded and watch the buds open is more satisfactory. The plant should be discarded after flowering.

Fuchsia is not a good house plant unless it can be grown in sun. It is best for garden or window box. Flowering stops in summer because

of high temperature. It is propagated from cuttings.

Gardenia should be grown in sun and the night temperature kept near 60° F. The buds drops if these conditions are not maintained. Even though it has no flowers gardenia makes an attractive foliage plant. Propagation is by cuttings.

Genista (*Cytisus*) loses its buds and flowers at a temperature above 60° F. It should not be expected to flower if grown in the home, but makes a good foliage plant. It should be obtained in full bloom.

Geranium (*Pelargonium*) is available in many varieties and some are most valuable for the odor of the foliage. All grow best in sun and all are propagated from cuttings.

Gloxinia (*Sinningia Speciosa*) tubers planted during March or April flower in early summer. They grow and flower well in sun until May, when they should be placed in bright light. They are most satisfactory when watered from below by a wick. After they have flowered the soil can be kept quite dry until the foliage wilts and dies, then the tuber, left in the soil, can be stored in the basement until the following spring when it can be removed from the soil and potted in new soil to start growth again.

Heather (*Erica*) grows in sun or poor light after the buds are nearly open. The soil must be kept especially moist. The plant should be discarded after flowering.

Hydrangea flowers are pink when the soil is slightly acid and blue on the same plant when the soil is very acid. The plant requires

Plants for a South Window

Amaryllis

Cactus

Coleus

Inch Plant

much water and grows best in sun and quite well in bright light. After the plant has flowered, the stems should be cut about 2″ above the ground and planted in the garden. The new shoots flower the next year.

Before September 1 the plant should be dug, potted, and left outdoors in sun until the first light frost. Then it should be stored in a cool, dark place, such as the basement, until January 1, when it can be brought into the living room in a sunny window to grow and flower. The soil must be kept moist in storage as well as during the growing period. Yellow between the veins of the leaves usually is due to an alkaline soil.

Jerusalem Cherry (*Solanum Pseudo-capsicum*) is best obtained from a florist when fruits are ma-

ture. They naturally drop soon. It should be kept as cool as possible and in bright light. It is not advisable to keep the plant for another year because it becomes ungainly and seldom flowers well.

If it is to be carried over, it should be kept growing in sun and pruned severely to obtain the proper shape about May. It can be kept out of doors in summer. They are potted September 1 and kept at a temperature above freezing, preferably in a cold-frame, until near Christmas. (See also *Christmas Pepper.*)

Kafir-Lily (*Clivia*) grows well in the home and flowers in June. It may be kept in the same pot for years. It should be kept cool and in good light during winter, and placed in the garden in a pot during summer. Propagation is by division.

Kalanchoe (*Kalanchoe Blossfeldiana*) is obtained in bud or bloom and kept in sun or bright light. After flowering, it can be con-

tinued in growth and may flower another year. It is best to start new plants from seeds or cuttings. Flowering in the home is questionable because of poor light.

Lily-of-the-Valley (*Convallaria majalis*) pips (rootstocks) are dug from the garden after the foliage dies. They are stored at 30° to 40°F. until January when they can be planted in sand, soil, or moss and forced to flower by merely keeping them wet. They can be grown in bright light. They are discarded after flowering.

Orchids may be grown in a case where the humidity can be kept high, but it is more satisfactory to purchase plants with buds ready to open and let them open in the home. After flowering they are best returned to the greenhouse where better care can be given than in the home. They grow better in sun or bright light. The flowers last several weeks.

Poinsettias (*Euphorbia pulcherrima*) are best obtained in full bloom, grown in sun, and discarded after Christmas. They seldom flower in the home because of the high temperature and the poor light. If one cares to grow them a second year, the soil is dried after flowering and the plants are stored in a cool room. They are cut to 5″ or 6″ from the ground in May and allowed to grow again. They may be planted in pots in the garden in summer and taken into the home September 1. Leaf drop is caused by poor light, high temperature, or improper watering.

Primulas grow in sun and a cool night temperature. The plants are discarded after flowering. They are difficult to continue in growth during summer.

Roses need sun and plenty of moisture. After flowering, the plant should be kept in sun and grown until it can be planted permanently in the garden. They are hardy.

Shrimp Plant (*Beloperone guttata*) grows in bright light. New plants are produced from cuttings.

Slipperwort (*Calceolaria*) is purchased in bloom or with blooms and many buds. It is kept in sun, and discarded after flowering. The foliage yellows if the light is poor.

Snapweed (*Impatiens*) is grown in sun in winter. Its best use is in a window box in shade or in a shady spot in the garden. Propagation is by cuttings.

BULBS FOR FORCING

Tulips, narcissi, hyacinths, and other hardy bulbs can be planted in pots in September or October and kept in a cool basement at about 40° to 50°F. to January, when they can be brought to the living-room window and made to flower. The soil must be kept moist in storage. The plants grow in sun. After the plant has flowered, the foliage should be allowed to grow until it turns yellow when the soil can be dried and the bulbs later planted in the garden. One should not attempt to force the same bulbs in two successive years.

Paper-White narcissi bulbs should be planted in pebbles or soil and placed directly in the sun in the living room. Cold treatment before forcing is of little value.

Garnet Paper

Garnet paper is used for sanding. It is a paper covered with a reddish abrasive, which is fairly hard.

Garnet paper is used for hand finishing of hardwood and softwood as well as composition board and cork.

See *Abrasives*.

Gas Appliances

The selection of the appliances with which gas is used is much more important than is commonly supposed. The American Gas Association, a national organization, has established a laboratory for determining whether appliances offered for sale are so designed that they can be used safely and with satisfaction. Specifications called "approval requirements," with which an appliance must comply before it can be regarded as safe, have been adopted. To receive the approval of the Association, an appliance must pass a number of careful tests. An appliance, whether manufactured by a member of the Association or not, may be submitted for test; and the great majority of models of domestic appliances have been tested. Several thousand models have been approved.

All appliances so approved bear the blue approval star of the Association, and this label is the only certain means available to the average purchaser for distinguishing a safe appliance.

Selecting Appliances

In selecting an appliance for use with propane or butane, make certain that it has been approved for that service. There are important differences between appliances for butane and for manufactured gas, and an appliance made for use with one of them cannot ordinarily be used satisfactorily with the other. In many cases different burners are supplied for manufactured and natural gas. Make sure through the appliance dealer or the manufacturer that you have the right burner.

Even among "approved" appliances which are supposed to be duplicates of the one tested, there may be individual differences or defects which can be distinguished by a well-informed purchaser. Consequently, it is desirable, before accepting a new appliance, to observe it carefully while it is operated under all the conditions likely to exist in service.

There may be difficulties connected with ignition and the uniformity of size and action of the burner "ports," the openings at which the gas burns. All the ports should be clean cut and, unless obviously intended to be different,

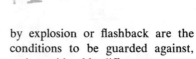

they should be of uniform size and regularly spaced. Any breaking away, even of the surface, of the original casting around a port should subject the burner to rejection. The gas should ignite without delay at all the ports. The flames at all the ports should be of as nearly uniform size and appearance as the eye can detect. When the air shutter is wide open and the flow of gas is varied as much as possible without extinguishing the flame, the flames at the different ports should remain alike in appearance. There should be no noticeable tendency for any flames to flicker, and if the gas rate can be increased until the flames rise from the ports they should all "lift" at about the same rate.

The difficulty of igniting the gas, if any, and the action of pilot lights and accessory controls such as the safety pilots are readily observed. The purchaser of an appliance should make sure that they are fully understood and entirely satisfactory. Uncertain, partial, or delayed ignition of burners followed by explosion or flashback are the conditions to be guarded against, and considerable differences are to be found even among approved appliances.

Installation

The installation of gas appliances should generally be entrusted only to the gas company or a gas fitter of recognized ability. But the householder should make sure that it is so located that it is easy to use. When the appliance is awkward or difficult to operate, accidents are more likely to occur. Appliances should be so located that they are not subject to excessive drafts which might extinguish the flame. There should be no danger of bumping into or stumbling over them or their connections even in the dark. Valves should not be placed where they could be opened by catching clothing on them, where they cannot be easily reached when lighting the gas, not in such a position that a person turning on the gas is forced to stand too near the burner to be safe in case there is a slight explosion. Valves controlling different appliances should be placed far apart if possible. If near together, they should be supplied with handles of such different shapes or material that they can be certainly identified by touch.

Location of appliances in small confined spaces is bad practice; and in extreme cases, for example, where a large water heater is placed in an unventilated closet, the flame may actually be smothered by exhaustion of the oxygen in the air. It is considered dangerous practice to put

water heaters of any kind in bathrooms or bedrooms, or to use heating appliances which discharge the products of combustion into a room in which people sleep. If a bathroom must be heated by an unvented heater, a window or door should be left partly open for ventilation.

In the installation of appliances care must always be taken to avoid any danger of fire. Gas appliances are, in general, much more easily installed properly to safeguard wood floors and walls and other parts of the house or its furnishings than are coal or wood-burning stoves and this has led to a carelessness with gas appliances that is often serious. The risk of fire may be greatly increased by neglect of simple and inexpensive precautions.

Wherever heat is produced continuously for a long period of time, the temperature of nearly combustible materials will be raised dangerously unless there is some provision for removing heat from the space between them and the source of heat. This is equally true whether the heating is done with a solid fuel, electricity, or gas. Usually the transfer of heat is by convection of the air between the stove or appliance and the floor, partition, or other combustible material, but in recent years many appliances have been designed to be used safely when built into or placed snugly in contact with floors and walls even though they are of wood. In every such case, however, a space has been provided within the appliance itself through which cold air circulates and isolates the region of higher temperature. No reasonable amount of "insulating material" will take the place of the free air space. Failure to understand this is the usual cause of fires from gas-burning appliances.

All appliances which receive the approval of the American Gas Association must pass a test which demonstrates that when they are set 6″ from a wooden wall the wall will not be heated to an unsafe temperature. These appliances designed to be built into or set directly against the wall must pass a corresponding test before approval. Unless the appliance is specifically labeled as approved for flush installation, a 6″ space should be left in every case. This applies to lath-and-plaster walls no less than to wooden partitions.

If any appliance must be placed so close to the floor or wall that after long operation the wood or plaster becomes too hot to be comfortably touched with the hand, additional precautions should be taken. Interposing a sheet of metal or asbestos is usually effective, the more so if it is near to or against the appliance rather than the wall.

Floor furnaces and wall heaters must be installed in such a way that every provision made for the circulation of air is fully effective. Stopping any of the vent holes or reducing the clearances provided for are almost certain to result in disaster.

Wooden shelves should not be placed above a stove or heater; but if this is unavoidable they should be carefully protected on the under side from the heat. Such shelves are particularly dangerous if covered with paper.

Curtains hanging too near gas burners, especially gas lighting fixtures, have been a frequent cause of fire.

In many households, spaces behind and around the appliances are used for the storage of brooms, mops, buckets, cloths, and such household necessities. This should not be done, since it is extremely easy for these articles to be set afire.

Adjustment of Appliances

The possible liberation of carbon monoxide from an appliance in which gas is burning presents a problem distinct from that of raw unburned gas which leaks from pipes or burners. In a gas flame to which there is an unrestricted access of fresh air and no sudden chilling, the carbon monoxide is completely burned. When the flame is partially inclosed and brought into contact with an object which takes away some of the heat, the carbon monoxide may not be completely burned.

It is not always easy to tell when an appliance is liberating carbon monoxide through incomplete combustion, but certain things may well be regarded as warnings. Any odor which does not come from grease, varnish, or other material about the flame to which the odor can be definitely ascribed is a cause for suspicion. Of course, carbon monoxide has no odor; but when any odorous substance is liberated from the flame it is pretty safe to assume that carbon monoxide is liberated too. The usual odor accompanying the liberation of carbon monoxide is slightly irritating to the membranes of the nose but is not particularly unpleasant when not too strong. Many people will identify the odor at once as that given off by a plumber's gasoline torch. It has no resemblance to the odor of the unburned gas. Unfortunately, the absence of any odor is not a positive indication that carbon monoxide is not being liberated, even in dangerous quantity.

Another valuable indication is the appearance of the flame. When a flame has a sufficient supply of fresh air its outlines are sharply defined. When, however, the burning gas is surrounded by an atmosphere from which most of the oxygen has already been used, the outlines of the flames are very faint and indefinite and have a wavering or ragged appearance even in the absence of any noticeable air currents.

Most appliances, when correctly adjusted, have flames with distinct greenish "inner cones," the size of which may be a valuable guide to an adjuster familiar with the particular model with which he is concerned; but the inner cones are of little significance, in general, in judging whether combustion is complete. Carbon monoxide may be liberated in dangerous quantities under certain conditions, from flames with bright, well-formed inner cones, while flames without perceptible inner cones may burn the gas completely. It is the size, form, steadiness, and continuity of the pale blue outer boundary of the visible flame which give valuable indications of the safe or unsafe condition of the appliance.

A flame which is depositing carbon (soot) is not necessarily liberating carbon monoxide, but it is to be regarded with suspicion. When the flame flashes back—that is, when the gas burns inside the ports of the burner—carbon monoxide is almost always liberated in dangerous quantity. This condition is usually recognized at once by a roaring noise and a disagreeable odor. Usually there is a distinct pop when flash-back begins.

Whenever any indication of unsatisfactory combustion is observed, notify the gas company, as in a case of leakage. Many gas companies give free service in correcting conditions of this kind and others make only a small charge.

If an appliance is moved from one community to another, or if the character of the gas supply is materially changed, for example, from manufactured to natural or the reverse, it is particularly important that the appliance be adjusted for the new conditions by an experienced man who is entirely familiar with the local situation.

After the adjustment is set, it is

dangerous to change it, particularly to enlarge the orifice at a time of low pressure. If service is unsatisfactory because not enough gas is supplied, the trouble may be caused by a partial clogging of the house piping, of the service pipe connecting with the street main, or of the valve controlling the appliance itself; it may be caused by mechanical difficulty in the meter; or it may be the result of a temporary condition which causes low pressure in the mains which supply the neighborhood.

In none of these cases is the enlargement of the orifice a correct or safe method of remedying the trouble. The only safe course is to notify the gas company and permit it to locate and remove the cause of the difficulty.

Although a change of orifice should never be attempted by the average user of gas, an adjustment of the air shutter may usually be made with safety in the case of ranges, water heaters, and some other appliances, but the adjustment of room heaters not directly connected to flues should be left to an expert. Generally, the small flame at each port on the burner should be distinct, free from yellow, and have a sharply defined inner cone. It is not desirable, however, to open the air shutter so wide as to make the flame noisy, to permit flashing back of the flame when turned down as much as it is likely ever to be in use, or to cause any tendency for the flames to "lift" away from the ports.

Operation and Care

In lighting an oven, a water heater, or other appliance in which a large amount of gas is burned in a partially inclosed space, a few simple precautions should be taken to assure safety. Several arrangements for lighting and flame-control exist. In the simplest of them a lighted match is merely applied to the main burner. The match may be brought to a touchhole from which the flame is communicated by a row of small open tube to the burner. A pilot light may be ignited, after which the gas is turned onto the main burner and the pilot light turned off. There may be a pilot light which burns continuously but without a safety pilot; or there may be a safety pilot which, when cold, prevents gas from flowing to the main burner only, or to both the pilot light and the main burner.

In every case the doors of the burner box and oven or of whatever large space communicates with the combustion chamber should be opened first. If a match is to be applied directly to the main burner or to a tube leading from it, the match should be lighted, then the valve should be opened fully and the match brought to the lighting position about one second later. If the lighted match is held over the burner before the valve is opened, the flame is likely to flash back into the explosive mixture formed with the air initially in the burner. If flashback occurs or if the ignition of the main burner does not occur, close the valve immediately, light another match and try again. If a separately controlled pilot light is provided to assist in the lighting operation, it should be lighted first and the main burner valve opened suddenly. It should then be ascertained that the main burner is actually lighted before turning off the pilot. In case the main burner flashes back when turned on, the gas should be shut off at once and then turned on again before the pilot is extinguished. In case the match flame goes out before the pilot (if any) or the main burner is lighted, the gas should be turned off immediately and another match lighted before the gas is turned on again.

If a safety-pilot is provided which controls the supply of gas to the main burner but not to the pilot, simply light the latter and wait for the safety pilot to warm up and then turn on the main gas supply. When safety-pilot controls the supply of gas to the pilot light as well as to the main burner, instructions as to the lighting of the particular appliance should be obtained from manufacturer or gas company and followed.

In general, the main valve should be opened and heat applied with the flame of a match or taper where it will cause the safety-pilot to open and will ignite the pilot flame. One hand should be on the main burner valve, and another match should be within reach. When the safety-pilot opens, if the gas does not ignite immediately and without flashing back, turn it off at once; then promptly turn it on and apply the match or lighted taper to the main burner as directed for lighting a burner without a pilot. The action must be quick or the safety pilot will cool and again interrupt the gas supply. If failure to light the appliance satisfactorily occurs more than once or twice, the gas company should be asked for advice or assistance.

After lighting but before leaving a burner, the flame should be observed to make sure that perfect ignition has occurred. This applies to burners under the solid or partly inclosed cooking top of a range and to a radiant space heater as much as to an oven, water heater, or furnace.

It sometimes happens that the gas does not light at every port of a burner and unburned gas escapes from those at which there is no flame. Oven burners are especially subject to this trouble. When the gas is lighted, see that there is a flame at every port. If much difficulty is encountered in getting all the ports of the burner to light, something is wrong. Usually the burner needs cleaning, but if cleaning does not remedy the trouble, the burner must be repaired or replaced by an experienced appliance adjuster.

The ignition of flowing sleeves

when women reached over front range burners to light the back ones formerly caused many bad burns. This hazard has been pretty well eliminated by changes in both appliances and clothing but should be kept in mind by women working in the kitchen. The use of catalytic or most friction lighters as a substitute for matches is to be avoided. With such lighters ignition is usually delayed longer than with a match, frequently much longer. Hence, gas may accumulate before ignition to the extent of causing a dangerous flame. The type of friction lighter in which a wheel, rotated by a spring, definitely directs a shower of sparks forward in a narrow stream is the best of these devices and can usually be relied on. It is probably as safe as, or safer than, matches; but the use of many other forms of mechanical or catalytic lighters introduces a distinct hazard.

Appliances should always be kept clean and in good condition. If any part of the appliance appears to be broken, bent, or out of position, you should have an experienced man correct the condition unless the part can be simply replaced, as in the case of the glowers or radiants of radiant heaters.

In all cases safe combustion requires clean burners and unobstructed flue passages. Obstructions in the burner ports or air shutters and accumulations of dirt or soot in the burners modify the design, interfere with the proper mixture of air and gas, and create dangerous conditions. Burners can be easily cleaned by washing in boiling water and soda; they should be dried before

using. After cleaning a burner or displacing it for any other reason, it must be carefully restored to exactly its original position.

Nothing is more dangerous than to close the vent of an appliance either by carelessly placing something over it or by deliberately obstructing it, as is sometimes done by persons ignorant of the dangers, for the purpose of saving heat. The proper way to save heat is to burn the gas only when needed and then at the lowest rate that will accomplish the desired work.

A vessel containing a liquid should be closely watched as boiling begins because the liquid may run over the edge of the untensil, extinguish the flame, and permit unburned gas to escape. The boiling over of cooking foods is the most common cause of clogged burners.

Guard against turning a burner too low, for it may blow out or flash back, and thus cause bad results. Especially after a burner has been turned down, one should be sure the flame is actually burning before turning on more gas.

A caution for housewives—keep flammable materials away from the gas range. For example, the range should not be used to dry clothing. Few housewives need to be warned of the danger of overheating deep fat when making doughnuts, fritters, etc., or the paraffin used for sealing jars; but the great concentration of heat in the gas flame and the rapidity with which materials are heated by gas may catch the cook off her guard.

Gas or gasoline is still employed for lighting to some extent in camps and rural homes. The glassware of gas lamps should be maintained in good condition, for not only may glass falling from a broken globe injure someone but also, if highly heated, it may ignite any combustible material on which it falls. Carbon collecting on the mantle because of dirt in, or improper adjustment of, the lamps is also a serious matter; it decreases the amount of light received and hot pieces of the carbon may fall from the lamp and set fire to furnishings. A lamp or any other appliance showing such carbon deposits should be cleaned and adjusted. Mantles should be replaced as soon as the slightest break appears, because the uneven heating resulting from a broken mantle is the usual cause of broken glassware. It is uneconomical as well as unsafe to neglect broken mantles.

Accessories on Appliances

Accessories that may alter the character and size of the flame, or the access of air to the burner and the escape of products of combustion from it, should never be pur-chased. Particularly to be avoided are the "solid tops" or plates to be placed on a stove designed for the use of a grate top, and the miscellaneous devices sold from house to house and alleged to save gas when placed on other appliances. Meritorious solid top stoves, built as such, are in use but they must be particularly well designed to be safe and reasonably economical. Placing a solid cover on a range not designed for it interferes with the admission of air around the flame and with the escape of the products of combustion through the open grates as intended by the designer.

An attachment which should be strictly avoided is one alleged to filter or purify the gases escaping into the room from an oven or space heater and installed on the vent of the appliance. An open elbow turned away from the wall, or other equivalent deflector, is useful to prevent the streaking of the wall behind an appliance, and may prevent local overheating; but the householder should never allow steel wool or other metallic shavings, perforated plates, or porous material of any kind to be introduced into the vent or flue passages of an appliance.

Flexible Tubing

Considering its limited importance and application, flexible tubing has, without doubt, been the cause of a far greater number of serious accidents than anything else for which there is legitimate use in connection with the burning of gas. Several types of accidents have been common: (a) Cracking or breaking of the tubing itself, allowing gas to

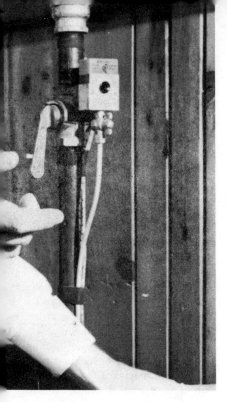

fireplaces, and all other appliances which are to be used in one location for a considerable period of time should always be connected with rigid and permanent piping. There is little difference in cost, considering the fact that the flexible connection may have to be replaced repeatedly during the life of the appliance.

If flexible connections must be used, as in the case of a gas iron, the best tubing obtainable should always be secured. The best available evidence that the tubing is safe is the approval of the American Gas Association, which subjects tubing to a series of rigorous tests to determine its safety from each of the more common hazards. Tubing should always have the connectors at both ends permanently attached at the factory. Always take the utmost care in connecting the tubing. See that the ends are as tight as they can be made and that they will not loosen with a strong pull. See that no part of the tubing is left in a position in which it may become overheated. The gas should always be shut off the appliance at the inlet end of the tubing, never at the appliance. For this reason it is unsafe to use a flexible tubing with an appliance which has a shut-off.

When tubing which has been in use shows the first sign of leakage or other serious deterioration, throw the piece away and get new tubing. Successful repairs are almost impossible to make. The very best repairs lengthen the life of the tubing so little that the saving effected is negligible. Many deaths have resulted from attempted repairs of this kind.

Also see *Gas Hazards*.

escape; (b) the pulling off of the tubing from the appliance or from the gas outlet to which it is connected; (c) the separation of the tubing itself from the connectors which attach it to gas outlet or appliance; (d) the momentary kinking or collapsing of the tubing (when stepped on, for example) which extinguishes the flame or causes it to flash back; and (e) the overheating of the tube or its connectors, which results in leakage.

Burners at which backfiring has occurred usually get extremely hot, and the rubber connectors sometimes melt or burn off. Even the flexible metal tubing with metal connectors usually depends for tightness on a thread of rubber packing and will leak if overheated.

The best precaution against the dangers of flexible tubing is to avoid its use whenever possible. Hot plates, radiant heaters installed in

Gas Furnace

See *Heating Systems.*

Gas Hazards

Like many other sources of energy, gas must be used carefully, for in careless hands it is a source of great danger. However, nearly all gas accidents are readily preventable by the observance of simple precautions.

Several types of gas are used in American households. The more important of these are commonly classified in the gas industry as manufactured gas, natural gas, mixed gas (natural and manufactured), and liquefied petroleum gases (also popularly referred to as bottled gas) which are mainly propane, butane, or their mixtures.

Types of Accidents

In the utilization of gas in the household, five kinds of accidents may occur: (a) Asphyxiation by unburned gas; (b) asphyxiation by the gas resulting from incomplete combustion; (c) burns to persons; (d) destruction of property by fire; and (e) explosions, which may or may not be accompanied by fire or injury to persons.

Asphyxiation by unburned gas occurs only when manufactured or mixed gas is used. Natural gas and liquefied petroleum gas are almost always practically free from poisonous constituents and are not likely to be breathed in sufficient quantity to cause asphyxiation. The possibility of asphyxiation by the products of incomplete combustion is equally serious in households using either natural or manufactured gas, and is by no means limited to gas-burning appliances. Wherever fuel is burned this hazard may exist.

Many hazards would be avoided if gas users would more frequently seek the advice and assistance which every gas company is glad to render. Usually the company has special facilities for dealing with every difficulty likely to arise; and it has as great an interest in safe and satisfactory service as the consumers have. In particular, the gas company should be promptly notified in any case of serious trouble and should be consulted before any unusual change is made in the equipment used. No accessory made by one manufacturer for use with an appliance should be used on another appliance without the advice of the gas company.

Meters and Regulators

Flammable materials and rubbish should not be placed near the gas meter, since a fire in such material would be likely to melt the soldered seams of the meter or its

connections and the flame of the escaping gas might greatly increase the extent of the fire.

The gas meter should never be tampered with or subjected to strain. It is generally one of the weakest parts of the piping system because it is usually constructed of light sheet metal and the breaking of its case will cause the escape of gas. The householder should, therefore, allow the company to install the meter where, in its judgment, it will be safe from mechanical strains, falling objects, and other harmful conditions such as excessive heat, cold, or moisture. Meters are frequently placed on shelves or other supports to take the weight off the connections. Such support should never be removed.

The installation of so-called house governors or regulators, except those installed on the inlet side of the meter by the gas company, or those supplied as a part of the regular equipment of a house-heating furnace or other appliance requiring unusually accurate control, is seldom justified for residential service. The gas company is responsible for the delivery of gas to the user at pressures suitable for the operation of all ordinary appliances, and the obligation is usually met, often with the aid of governors. When expert service is regularly employed for the care of appliances, the use of regulators will, of course, be left to the judgment of the expert.

Turning Gas On and Off

The practice of some gas users of partially closing the shut-off valve at the meter is not advisable; it rarely, if ever, saves gas and may unfavorably affect the operation of appliances already adjusted to give the most economical and satisfactory service. With adequate piping and open valves, the use of one appliance affects another scarcely at all, but if the meter valve is closed enough to affect appreciably the gas supply to one burner, the operation of another will reduce the supply available to the first, possibly to the extent of introducing a hazard from the flashing back or extinction of the flame. Even if there is only one burner on the line and it burns gas at too high a rate, the remedy is the adjustment or replacement of the burner orifice, not interference with the gas supply.

It is well, however, to know the location of the meter shut-off cock and to have a wrench handy with which to close it in case of necessity; but having once been shut off, the gas should not be turned on again by the householder. The gas company should be notified and requested to turn on the gas. This precaution is so important that in some cities even experienced gas fitters are not allowed to turn on the gas unless actually in the employ of the gas company.

Prepayment meters, once very common in the poorer sections of cities and in resort towns, are now fortunately almost nonexistent in this country. If one must be used and if the flow of gas has stopped, the householder should never put another coin into the meter until absolutely certain that there are no open burners.

Leaks

Any leakage of gas, no matter how small, may be dangerous. Although the quantity of gas escaping may appear to be insufficient to cause asphyxiation or explosion, it is never possible to be sure of this without a chemical analysis of the mixture. Hence, one should never regard an air-gas mixture as safe, and when even a slight escape of gas is noted, shut off any equipment using the gas and immediately provide as much ventilation as possible.

"Manufactured" gases all possess distinctive odors. Strong, unpleasant scents are added to all liquefied petroleum marketed for domestic use, and much of the natural gas, but not all of it, is similarly odorized. Leakage of gas is usually first detected by odor, which is noticeable when the room is first entered even though the amount of gas present is very small. However, if a person for any reason remains in a room containing gas, he soon loses to some extent the ability to judge by the odor whether or not the air is

heavily charged with it. Therefore, anyone who persists in staying in the room after the gas is smelled may in a little while not suspect that he is running any risk, even at the moment when he is on the point of losing consciousness.

Even at the start it is difficult to judge from the intensity of the odor how much gas is leaking. Therefore, it is never safe to disregard the odor of gas. The very first thing to do is to ventilate the room and then search for the leak, which will usually be at a gas cock or a joint in the connections. If this is quickly located by odor, sound, or by applying soap solution, and it is evident that the leakage is so small as not to permeate the room, no other precaution need be taken than the temporary use of soap to stop the leak and a notification to the gas company, so that a permanent repair may be made. Tubing that is cracked or that has loose ends, even though leaking very slightly when first noticed, should be put out of use immediately.

Never search for a gas leak with a match, candle, lantern, or with the aid of any other ordinary lighting appliance. Even the switch operating an electric light may cause a spark which will ignite an explosive mixture and thus cause disastrous results. Never try to locate the point of leakage by igniting the escaping gas, for unexpected "pockets" of explosive mixtures may exist, as between joists, beneath stairways, or close to the ceiling, and these explode without warning. It is safer to open the windows or take other precautions—in the dark, if need be—having someone outside the affected room on the watch to render assistance if necessary. Not only is there danger of explosion, but the use of a lighted match near a lead meter connection or at the soldered seams of a meter may cause a tiny unseen flame at a point of leakage, which can melt the lead or solder, causing a larger leak and eventually a serious fire.

If the odor of gas seems to permeate the room, and the actual leak cannot be located quickly, the gas may be coming into the room through the floor or walls. No time should be lost in extinguishing all flames or fire, in opening the windows, and in seeing that all persons leave the room or, if necessary, leave the house altogether. These precautions should be taken on the bare suspicion that a serious leak may be present and before any investigation of basement or adjoining rooms is undertaken.

Do not wait for a second impression or for confirmation that the odor is not increasing or is dying away. Remember that the nose loses its sensitivity in a short time in a gas-contaminated atmosphere.

If on opening a door into the basement or an adjoining room, the odor there seems stronger, it is safer not to enter. If there is no fire or flame burning in the room, and if it is unoccupied, it is safer to close the door and leave the premises, if necessary, to wait until someone from the company arrives. If the basement or room must be entered to extinguish lights or to rescue persons

sleeping or unconscious, no light should be carried except an electric flashlight which should be turned on and off only outside the room. A watcher should be stationed outside to summon aid in case the person who entered first should lose consciousness.

Gas sometimes travels for a considerable distance; it may be found at points far removed from the real source of leakage. Gas in dangerous quantities may pass through the foundation walls of buildings, as from the street under frozen ground into the basement, or from the basement of an adjoining building, and also through partition walls and through floors, as from the basement to first floor rooms.

The hazard from gas which has traveled underground is likely to be underestimated for several reasons. The odorous constituents of the gas mixture are strongly absorbed by many soils; the familiar odor is likely to be disguised by the removal of some of its components and by the addition of others; and finally the development of the odor is likely to be so gradual as to escape notice in a familiar environment.

Even the slightest odor of gas, the source of which cannot be definitely located, should be immediately reported to the gas company.

In no other case is attention to the first indication of escaping gas so important as that of a buried reservoir containing liquefied petroleum gases. The fuel is in the dense form of a liquid under high pressure (for a gas distribution system) and can escape at an excessive rate through a very small opening. The escape of gas is likely to be the result of corrosion, and without inspection the extent of the corroded area cannot be estimated. A leaking tank must not be uncovered for inspection while under pressure because the removal of the supporting soil from corroded metal frequently results in opening relatively large areas.

The only thing to do is to notify the company supplying the fuel to remove what is already in the tank and make the necessary inspection and replacement or repair immediately. If expert service is not obtainable at once, gas should be burned from the system at a safe place rapidly enough to materially reduce both the temperature of the liquid and the pressure in the reservoir. The leak is not then likely to be enlarged until the fuel supply is exhausted, after which an inspection can be made safely.

Appliances

The installation and use of gas appliances requires care to avoid accidents, too. Refer to the section on *Gas Appliances* for further information.

Gasket

Made of paper, metal, rubber, plastic or other composition material, a gasket performs a function similar to a hose washer. It is set between two parts, usually metal, to prevent leaking at the joint.

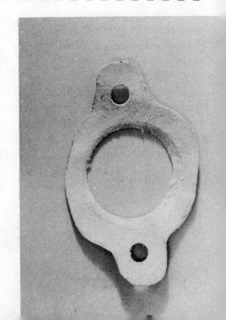

Gate Valve

The action of this valve depends upon the motion of a wedge-shaped disc or gate between the inlet and outlet pipes. Of all valves it offers the least amount of resistance to the flow of water, for the opening in the valve itself is the same diameter as the pipe with which it is used.

Gate valves offer about half the resistance to the water flow of an elbow and are recommended for use in areas where water pressure is low. However, the handyman cannot repair a gate valve once it starts to leak. The disc or gate is made of metal and is not easily replaced. The rubbing of the gate against dirt, grit or sand will wear the metal and make the valve leak.

This valve can be installed in any position. The stem or handle, however, should point upward when the valve is installed in a system which has to be drained for the winter. If the stem or handle points downward, some water will remain in the bonnet, or the section just under

the handle. This water, when subject to cold weather, will freeze and expand. It may cause the upper section of the valve to crack. If it is necessary to install the valve in this position, it is essential that the bonnet be removed when the line is drained. In this way, the water will be removed from the bonnet and the valve can be re-assembled and left without danger of splitting in freezing weather.

Generator

This term is applied to machines used for the transformation of mechanical energy into electrical energy. Generators are used in power plants to produce electricity.

More common to the handyman is the generator in the car. It is used to recharge the car battery while the motor is in operation.

Another form of generator is found on bicycles. It is attached to

An automobile generator.

A generator used on a bicycle.

the front wheel of the bike and, as the wheel turns, the generator pro- duces the current needed to light the headlight and tail light.

German Silver

This is an alloy of copper, zinc and nickel. It is used in handicraft work and also as a solder to join certain metals together.

Gimlet

This small wood-boring tool has its handle attached at right angles to the bit. It is not used frequently today.

A gimlet is used to bore small holes.

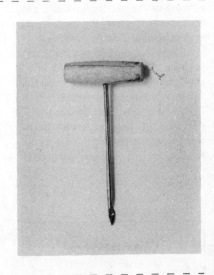

Gimp Tack

This is a small upholstery nail with a round head; it is used to tack cloth gimp to furniture.

Glass

Glass—How To Buy It

A homeowner can get a lot for his money or a little when he buys glass for windows, doors or partitions. But if he knows which glass will do what, and how to buy it, he won't pay double or triple prices for plate glass when he could have used heavy sheet glass, nor will he waste money by ordering glass by the sheet when he could have used a case.

Window glass, also called *sheet glass,* is the most commonly used in the house. In fact before glass walls and picture windows were used it was usually the only kind. It comes in two thicknesses, single strength and double strength; and in two qualities, A and B.

Grades A and B differ only in the number of small defects and waves. However, the difference is not ordinarily noticeable, and many dealers don't even stock A quality because they do not believe that it is worth a 25% premium.

Whether to use single or double strength depends mainly on window size. A good rule to follow is to use double strength for anything over about two feet square. How large can double strength glass be? If winds don't exceed 70 m.p.h., double strength glass may be used in sizes up to 38"x48", or 34"x72".

The next price jump to crystal sheet or plate glass is very sharp. If you want a window wall consider

Economical way to buy window glass is by the case. This way it is much cheaper and easier to handle. Except in very large sizes, a case contains approximately 50 square feet—for example, eight 24"x36" sheets.

the possibilities of working it out using the indicated dimensions of double strength instead of plate glass. This can be most attractive and at about one-fourth the cost. Go right across the room with 30"x72" double-strength glass placed vertically. The distance of approximately 30" to the floor can be plain wall or used for built-in bookcases, cabinets or ventilating louvers.

Case Lots

Buying window glass by the case is one way to save money. Glass by the case doesn't cost much more than half as much as by the sheet. It's also easier to handle. At economical prices you can afford to use glass liberally in anything you build or remodel or enclose. And, buying by the case does not mean

Plate glass top finishes this table handsomely. To order glass for rectangular one, dimensions are enough. An irregular shape should be traced on sheet of stiff paper.

Inside, looking out—Note the frost-free double glass window at left with pair of ordinary plate glass units. Inset shows the sealed air space that is built into double-glazed units, providing valuable heat insulation and preventing condensation.

you're stockpiling it for years to come. Usually a case of window glass is whatever number of sheets comes nearest to totaling 50 square feet. Cases of very large sheets contain 100 square feet.

Crystal sheet, which is heavy window glass of good quality, is the economical thing to buy when the opening is too big for double strength.

Plate glass, which is polished to optical perfection, may be ⅛″ thick or for a big view window, ¼″ thick. If you have a long-distance view through your window, you will need plate glass. Otherwise you can use crystal sheet; for short distances you will never notice the slight waviness.

For plate and usually crystal sheet, in sizes too big for you to handle and too expensive for you to risk breaking, you must figure on

Heat-absorbing plate glass makes windbreak for terrace of seashore home. Panes of this type, slightly tinted, filter out sun's infrared rays.

paying a higher installed price, which includes an expensive labor cost.

Heat-absorbing plate glass, while no substitute for air conditioning, does screen out approximately 29% of the sun's heat. It is used in west windows of seaside homes, as well as in car windows. It costs about 2½ times as much as regular plate glass.

Obscure glass is used where you want light but no visibility. For example, a wall of it might be just the

Use patterned glass wherever light without transparency is desired. There are many patterns; wide and narrow corrugations, stipples, ribs and diamond designs.

thing for a basement recreation room where part of the basement is used as a garage or workshop. For this you would need the thick kind, say ⅜″. Thinner figured glass serves for entrance panels, cupboard doors and shower enclosures.

Transparent mirror glass is often used for one-way vision in entrance doors. Ready-made it is extremely expensive, but a glass dealer who makes mirrors can usually prepare it for you at about half the price.

Insulating glass is the modern, superior replacement for ordinary windows plus storm sash. Like any insulation, it usually pays for itself over the years in fuel savings as well as comfort. It consists of two or three panes sealed in units, with air spaces between the panes. A typical double glazed unit has two sheets of ¼″ plate glass with a ½″ air space between. Originally all insulating units were made of plate glass, but it is now made in window glass as well. Unless you need large windowpanes, you can save about one-third by using the window glass kind.

Glass Blocks

In the long list of building materials, glass blocks rank as one of the most versatile. They can be used for exterior as well as interior walls or for partition walls that do not go entirely to the ceiling.

Glass blocks provide light plus privacy. They come in many sizes and shapes and there are special blocks made to control the sun. Furthermore, glass blocks are easy to maintain and special units are available to provide ventilation through glass block walls.

Glass blocks can be installed within a wooden frame or in a bed of mortar. Once you understand how to set glass blocks in mortar—

a project you might want to undertake to replace an existing basement window with glass blocks—then you will be able to handle glass blocks within a frame inside the house. Literature on interior framing of glass blocks is readily available from glass block manufacturers.

Glass blocks make an attractive entrance to a contemporary designed home.

Photograph courtesy of Pittsburgh Corning Corp.

Glass blocks are an ideal way of enclosing the lower half of a porch with louver windows used above. Exterior lighting illuminates the porch at night as the light shines through the glass blocks.

Light and privacy are assured in this glass block wall bathroom. A window is set into the glass block wall for ventilation.

It's possible to get more light in the kitchen by adding a glass block wall above the kitchen sink work area.

Here glass blocks are used to add wall space between the two rooms. The large archway is made narrower by adding translucent walls.

How To Work with Glass Block

The proper mortar materials and mix are important whether for laying bricks or glass blocks.

The proper mortar materials are Portland cement, hydrated lime, sand, water, and waterproofing compound. The addition of an integral waterproofer of the water-repellent type is an added measure to insure watertight joints. Manufacturer's specifications concerning the use of this material should be followed very closely. Where a waterproof masonry mortar is used, no additional waterproofer should be added to the mix. For better results, accelerators and antifreeze compounds should not be used.

ACCURATE MEASUREMENT

The accurate measurement of materials is important. Generally a 1–1–4 mortar mix is satisfactory. However, reasonable variations from the mix are permitted and allowable limits are covered by manufacturer's specifications.

MORTAR CONSISTENCY

The consistency of the mortar mix has a direct bearing on the strength and weather-proofness of the joints. Since glass blocks have no suction like bricks, the mortar must be drier . . . it should not flow or have too much slump. Too wet a mix makes it extremely difficult to get proper alignment of block joints, and cleaning time is greatly increased. The mix should be not too dry, not too wet, but just right. Here is a good thing to remember: Do not re-temper mortar after the initial set has taken place.

1. The sill is cleaned of dirt or foreign materials. The next step in preparing the opening to receive glass blocks is the application of a heavy coat of asphalt emulsion to the sill . . . only to the area to be covered by the mortar bed joint. The emulsion must be dry before the mortar is applied. This generally takes two hours.

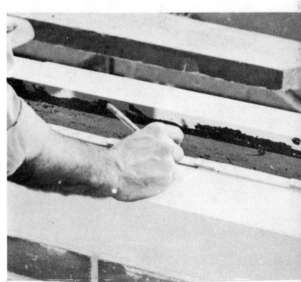

2. Check the dimensions of the opening, then mark off the spacing for the courses of block at the jambs and sill. Glass block sizes are modular. This modular coordination with other building materials makes it easy for the mason to lay out his work. Proper marking of courses eliminates any need for fudging joint thickness in the last courses laid. Where practical, story poles can be used for joint spacing.

3. For panels of glass block over 25 square feet in area, expansion spaces are required at the side jambs and heads of the openings. To prevent mortar bridging the expansion space, strips of expansion joint material are placed at these points and held by gobs of asphalt emulsion on the back of the strip. The first strip must be placed tight against the sill, and as the panel goes up, additional strips are placed. If desired, these strips can be applied for the entire panel prior to the blocks being laid. The expansion strips are 4⅛" wide, 25" long and ⅜" thick.

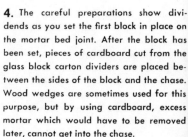

4. The careful preparations show dividends as you set the first block in place on the mortar bed joint. After the block has been set, pieces of cardboard cut from the glass block carton dividers are placed between the sides of the block and the chase. Wood wedges are sometimes used for this purpose, but by using cardboard, excess mortar which would have to be removed later, cannot get into the chase.

5. To insure plumb and level work, work to a guide line. A block is set in the middle of long panels to prevent line sag.

The accurate squareness and thickness of all glass blocks helps you get a plumb level job with good joint alignment.

Note rubber crutch tip on the mason's trowel. This avoids any possibility of chipping the glass when the mason taps the block to get alignment of joints.

6. To insure weather-tight joints all bed and head joints should be full of mortar. Full joints can be obtained by slightly crowning the mortar.

To get a full joint at the corners of the blocks, the mortar should be cut off square at the ends . . . as it is placed on the block. The heavy application of grit on the mortar bond coating prevents slippage of the mortar from the block.

7. When you furrow the bed and head joint mortar, voids are caused. Driving rain often forces itself into these voids. These voids or channels in the mortar joints provide an easy passage for any water which has penetrated through cracks at the face of the joint. The final result is a leaking panel. Remember, don't furrow mortar joints.

We all know that a full mortar joint is necessary to keep water out. Here is what happens if you furrow the bed and head joint mortar. The block in this picture has been removed from the panel. See the void caused by furrowing . . . it will provide an easy passage for water.

8. Properly crowned mortar joints are shown in photograph 6. With the mortar slightly crowned, a full joint will be obtained without voids. This will result in a water-tight panel.

Here is what happens when the head joint mortar is not furrowed.

Look at the mortar on the edge of this block taken from the panel. The full impression of the key-lock edge profile on this block shows that the joint was full.

9. Wall ties are placed in horizontal joints of the panel according to building code requirements. Generally, the spacing is every 24" regardless of block size.

Wall ties . . . 1) Should be used immediately below and above openings in panels . . . 2) Should not bridge expansion spaces . . . 3) Should lap minimum of 6" when more than a single length is used . . . 4) Should not touch glass. To avoid this . . . lay half bed joint . . . press wall tie in place . . . complete bed joint. Wall ties are welded galvanized wire mesh 8' long, 2" wide with cross wires spaced every 8".

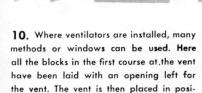

10. Where ventilators are installed, many methods or windows can be used. **Here** all the blocks in the first course at the vent have been laid with an opening left for the vent. The vent is then placed in position on a mortar bed, plumbed and levelled.

As these units are generally small, no expansion space is required and mortar is tamped solidly between the vent and blocks. Wall ties are used in the joints at the sill and the head of the ventilators.

11. The panel is now ready for the last block. First install the block at the jamb, then butter the block edges of the opening. The last block is buttered, tilted up and shoved into place. The joints are then pointed so that no voids will occur.

12. Final appearance and weather-tightness depend on the care with which you tool the joints. The joints should be concave and smooth to provide best protection against water penetration. Pressure on the tool reveals joints which are not full; these joints should be tuck pointed as tooling progresses.

13. Cleaning should be done before the mortar reaches its final set. If proper mix and amount of mortar are used, cleaning will be simple: fiber brush to remove excess mortar, a rag to clean the surfaces.

14. The final result of care in selection and preparation of materials, and of good masonry workmanship is strong weather-tight joints.

Note the smooth concave mortar joints which reveal the block edges as sharp, clean lines.

15. Free movement of the panel with support against wind loads is provided by tightly packed oakum between the chase and panel. A space should be left for calking.

16. The final step in the installation is the calking of the panel perimeter. When this is done, the panel will withstand satisfactorily the weather and wind loads to which it will be exposed over the lifetime of the building.

PANELS OF GLASS BLOCK 35 SQ. FT. OR LESS

In this type of construction the maximum area is 35 square feet with maximum width 5' and height 7'. The general practice is to use an expansion space at the side jambs of all glass block panels. However, for small panels as illustrated here the blocks can be mortared in solid at the side jambs. It is necessary, however, to keep a finger space between brick withes about ¾" deep. This allows the mortar to key in at jamb and secure panel.

Glass block panels, regardless of area or size, are nonload bearing and require space at the head to take care of expansion and lintel deflection.

Sketch courtesy of Pittsburgh Corning Corporation.

PANELS OF GLASS BLOCK BETWEEN 25 AND 100 SQ. FT.

Where it is desirable to show the full face of the block panel, chases cannot be used for lateral support. Proper support can be obtained by using wall anchors if the area is not over 100 square feet and neither panel dimension is over 10'. The wall anchors should be spaced 24" apart—and occur in the same joint as the wall tie. To permit free movement of the panel, the anchors are crimped or bent in the expansion space. As a space for calking must be provided, a standard expansion strip is easily cut to 3" width to be inserted between the anchors with gobs of asphalt emulsion. Local code authorities in some areas may restrict the use of wall anchor construction.

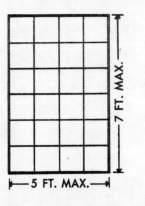

7 FT. MAX.

5 FT. MAX.

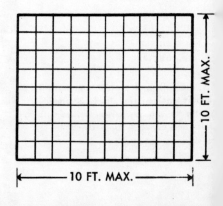

10 FT. MAX.

10 FT. MAX.

Glass Cutter

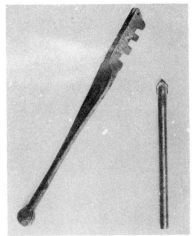

This tool is used to cut glass to size. Usually, a glass cutter has a small rotary wheel or diamond set in the handle.

There are also glass cutting bits for drilling holes in glass. These special bits require the use of a lubricant while cutting. It is best to make a 'well' or 'dish' around the spot to be drilled by using putty to form the walls. Then pour a little turpentine or oil into the 'dish' to lubricate the bit while it is cutting through the glass.

On the left is a glass cutter most frequently used by the handyman. On the right is a glass drilling bit to make holes in glass.

- -

Glass Cutting

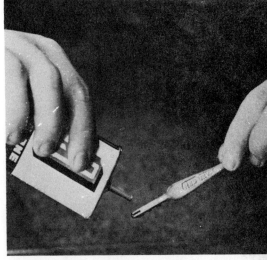

While you can usually buy glass cut to size, there are times when it is necessary to cut the glass yourself. When you watch an expert cut glass, it looks easy enough. Well, here's how to cut glass like an expert.

All you need is a quality glass cutter, a straightedge and some lubricating oil.

It is essential that the glass be perfectly clean. Wipe the surface off with a clean cloth for any dirt or a film over the glass will prevent the glass cutter from making a uniform cut. Now follow the simple step-by-step procedure.

1. Lubricate the wheel of your glass cutter using any household oil, such as 3-in-One. This lubricating of the wheel reduces friction between the glass and the edge of the wheel.

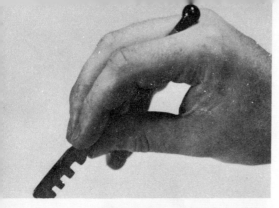

2. Here's how to hold the glass cutter correctly. The right way is between the first and second fingers with your thumb on the under side of the handle. Do not squeeze too hard.

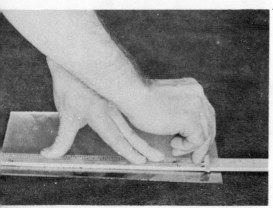

3. Rest the glass on several sheets of newspaper or a piece of felt. If you use a yardstick as a straight edge, moisten the bottom so that it won't slip on the glass. Gently, but firmly, press the cutter to the glass, holding it upright. Start about ⅛" from the edge farthest from you. Make a straight, even and continuous stroke across the whole surface and off the very edge of the glass.

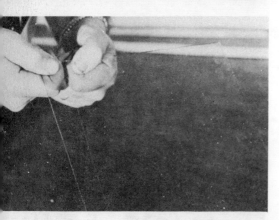

4. To break the glass, hold it firmly on opposite sides of the cut line. Then give a quick bending motion away from the cut. Keep your fingers and thumbs as close to the cut line as possible. Be careful . . . hold firmly. Always break right after cutting so that the cut does not get "cold."

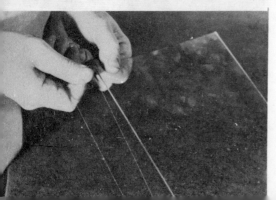

5. Here's what not to do! This shows how hesitation during cutting stroke leaves an uneven spot. This causes the break to curve from the straight line. An even, firm, positive cutting stroke avoids this result.

6. The slots in the end of the glass cutter are used for breaking off narrow strips. If you have to break off a narrow strip, hold the glass in one hand and the cutter in the other. A firm movement will separate the glass at the cut. Tapping the underside of the glass, immediately after making the cut, may make the glass separate more easily.

Fancy Glass Cutting

Once you have learned how to cut a straight line, you might feel adventurous and try some fancy glass cutting. Free-form lines and circles are not too difficult if you have the proper tools and knowledge. There are available circle cutters for glass which will cut circles from 2" to 24" in diameter.

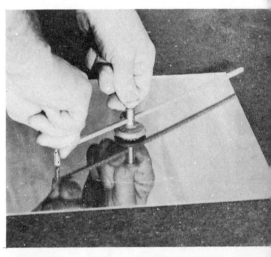

1. A circle cutter is used in the same manner as a regular cutter. Set the glass on a proper base and place the rubber suction cup in the exact center of the circle. Swing the cutter around but do not overlap at the end of the circle. Hold the glass in your hands and press with your fingers to impress the circle right after cutting so that the etched line won't get "cold."

2. The glass surrounding the circle must be cut with a regular cutter to free the circle. Make several straight cuts from the circle to the edge of the glass and then break away the circle.

Photographs courtesy of Red Devil Tools.

Glass Tinting

To prevent sun glare, as well as reduce the heat from the sun, you can buy a clear, invisible plastic to wipe on the glass of your automobile windshield. It comes in several different colors, and may be used not only for the car, but on the screen of the television set and in cases where special colorful window effects are desired. The plastic coating dries in about half an hour; it leaves no streaks on the glass, and does not wash off.

A quart of this material covers about 50 sq. ft. of glass; with it comes a special applicator and manufacturer's directions for its use.

Glazier's Chisel

This is a wide but thin chisel. It is used for removal of window trim and molding.

Because of the thin blade, it is usually possible to remove the trim or molding with this chisel without any appreciable damage to the painted surface.

It can also be used for removal of the shoe mold of the baseboard or even crown molding along the ceiling without marring the surfaces.

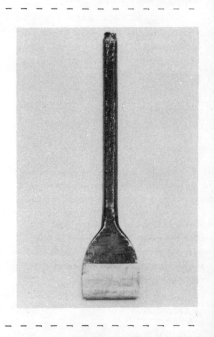

A glazier's chisel.

Glazier's Points

These are small, flat, triangular metal pieces which are used in addition to putty to hold the glass window pane in place. For information on the way they are used, see the section on *Glazing—Windows*.

Glazing— Windows

It's easy to replace a broken window pane.

Photograph courtesy of Libbey . Owens . Ford Glass Co.

A broken windowpane can be replaced without much difficulty. It is usually advisable to remove the sash which contains the broken pane, especially an upstairs window, and lay it on a flat surface such as table or workbench, although if the window is on the ground floor, the pane may be replaced with the aid of a stepladder.

Materials Needed

You will need: chisel or jack-knife for removing putty and for driving in glazier's points; putty knife; rule to measure size of glass needed; small flat paint brush; glass cutter (if you intend to cut glass); yardstick or steel square; glass of the same thickness as the broken pane; glazier's points; putty; raw linseed oil to soften the putty and be

used as a primer; and matching paint for the putty after it has hardened. Good putty suitable for ordinary household use can be made by mixing the best grade of whiting and pure raw linseed oil, or may be obtained already mixed from hardware and paint dealers.

Removing Old Glass and Putty

Broken glass should be removed from the sash and the old putty chipped off with a chisel or jack-knife. Glazier's points should be pulled, and the wood where the new glass is to rest should be scraped well with an old jackknife or similar tool. The wood should then be given a coat of thin paint or linseed oil to act as a primer and prevent the oil in the putty from being absorbed by the wood and the putty from drying out and crumbling.

Measuring for New Glass

Measure accurately the size of the needed glass and give the dimensions to the hardware or paint dealer, letting him cut the pane to the proper size, if you prefer not to cut the glass at home. All four sides from wood to wood in the sash should be measured and $1/8''$ to $3/16''$ deducted to allow for expansion and irregularities. Measuring the four sides is advisable because some sashes are not true and do not form a perfect rectangle. Most of the window glass stocked by dealers is designated as "double strength clear American."

Setting Glass

A thin coat of putty, about $1/16''$ thick, should be spread on the rabbet or groove in the sash for the glass to rest in, and the pane placed in the sash. Care should be taken to have the putty evenly distributed so that unfilled gaps will not appear between the sash and the glass. By pressing gently on the glass to imbed the edges of the pane in the putty, the pane can be made watertight and the cushion of putty thus formed will reduce the possibility of cracking the glass when glazier's points are put in.

1. To protect your hands, wear gloves when removing the broken pieces of glass. This is best done from the putty side.

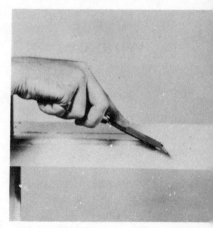

2. Use an old chisel to remove any old putty. If it's hard, you can use a soldering iron to soften the putty or else tap the chisel lightly with a hammer, or preferably with a mallet.

3. Use a rule or a steel tape to measure rather than a cloth tape. Measure the exact height and width of the opening on the outside of the sash.

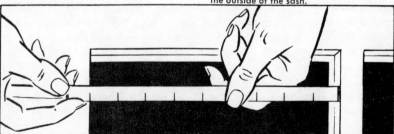

Glazier's points are small, flat, triangular metal pieces used in addition to putty to hold the glass in place. They should be laid on the glass, about three or four to a side, on the long sides first, and forced into the sash with the side edge of a chisel or screw driver by sliding the tool over the surface of the glass. If the glass is still loose after the points have been set, remove those which do not fit well and replace them, pressing the glass more firmly against the bed of putty during the process.

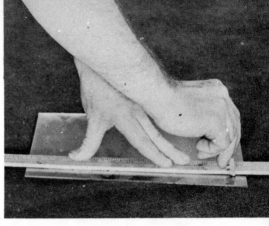

4. Buy the glass cut to size or cut it yourself. It's best if the pane of glass is ⅛" to 3⁄16" smaller than the vertical and horizontal measurements of the window.

Use of Putty

Putty is usually purchased in a can with a lid which provides an airtight seal. To prepare the putty for use, it should be kneaded on a nonabsorptive surface such as a glass plate until the mass is pliable. Putty that remains in the can after use may be kept for some time by pouring a thin film of linseed oil over it to keep it pliable and by placing waxed paper or foil immediately on top of the oil as a seal. Upon removing the waxed paper or foil, and kneading the putty, it will again be ready for use.

For application to the sash, a small piece of putty should be rolled out between the palms of the hands to form a pencil-shaped roll. The rolls should then be laid end to end on the glass where it abuts the sash, one side at a time. The putty should

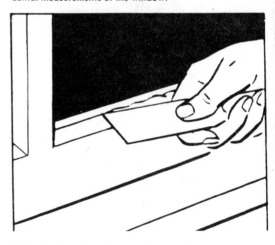

5. Before inserting the new glass, apply a thin layer of putty in the rabbet of the sash where the glass will rest. Apply with a putty knife.

6. Lay the glass in putty bed and press against sash. Then drive or press glazier's points into wood. Use three or four to a side, starting with a long side.

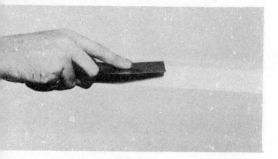

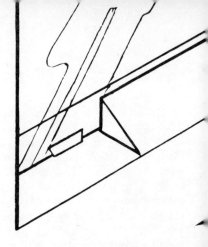

Photograph courtesy of Red Devil Tools.

Sketches courtesy of Libbey.Owens.Ford Glass Co.

7. After points have been applied, roll some putty in your hands and press another layer on over the glass and the sash, doing one side at a time. Smooth with putty knife.

8. This is the way the smoothed putty should look against the window pane. A portion has been removed in this sketch so that you get a cross-sectional view. Finally, paint the surface.

be pressed down firmly but gently with a putty knife, drawing it along the sash from one end to the other. To lessen the danger of breaking the glass by strong pressure, the putty should be soft and pliable. The putty knife should be held at an angle, guided by the glass and sash, to form a smooth bevel. Excess putty spreading beyond this bevel should be cut off and used to fill any depressions that have occurred. Care should be taken not to spread the putty far enough over the surface to show on the inside of the window. The same procedure should be followed for the other sides of the sash.

Putty stains may be removed from the glass with a cloth moistened with turpentine or gasoline. After a day or two, when the putty has hardened, it should be painted to match the window sash.

Metal Sash

Most metal sash are constructed so that the glass may be replaced with little difficulty. There are many kinds of metal sash, however, and the steps to be taken may vary to some extent. The manufacturer usually issues instructions for using his particular product, which should be followed. In case of an emergency, where no such information is at hand, one of the following methods may be used:

The tools and materials needed are screw driver, putty knife, and small flat paint brush; double-strength glass or plate glass; putty made of whiting and white lead; and enough paint of the same color as the sash for covering the top coat of putty.

Some windows are glazed on the outside, while others are glazed on the inside of the sash. In either case, the old putty and broken glass should be removed and the metal sash scraped clean where the new glass is to rest. If wire spring clips were used to hold the glass, they will have to be removed before the glass can be taken out. The new glass should then be imbedded in putty to prevent it from being in direct contact with the metal. The putty should be spread over the metal where the glass is to rest and the glass pushed firmly into place so that putty fills every crevice. The glass can then be fastened tightly with wire spring clips, placed in the holes which have already been bored through the sash. When the glass is thus firmly secured, putty may be applied in the same manner as for wooden sash. After the putty has thoroughly hardened, it should be

painted the same color as the sash.

In some other types of metal windows, the broken glass may be taken out by unscrewing and removing the metal beading or glazing strips and scraping the old bedding putty from the sash. The new glass can then be imbedded in putty, as described in the foregoing. When it has been placed, the metal beading or glazing strips should be refastened tightly against it. These strips will form a neat frame around the glass, which is usually held in place by brass screws.

See *Glass Cutting*.

Glides, Casters and Rests

Adjustable casters and glides have been gaining in popularity because it has been realized that many of our furniture faults—sticky drawers, doors that refuse to stay

Glides are metal, plastic, or rubber plates, discs or cushions used under the legs of furniture to protect the floor. They are needed to prevent indentations in resilent flooring materials, scratching, staining and sometimes indentation of wooden floors and the flattening of carpets and rugs.

Casters are wheel or ball-bearing units used to make furniture easily movable. They are attached to the bottom of the leg in place of a glide.

Rests serve the same function as glides but are not attached to the furniture. They are placed under the furniture leg between it and the floor.

Photograph courtesy of Robert Brady Co.

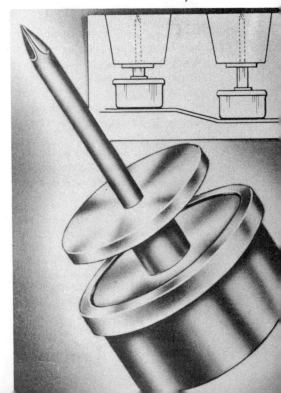

closed, etc.—are caused by uneven settling of the furniture on uneven floors.

The symptoms of uneven floor troubles are an everyday experience to most people. Without stretching one's memory, we can vividly recall the wobbly restaurant table with a wad of paper or matchbook shoved under a leg, a wobble-dancing washing machine, a sticky door or drawer, that wobbly TV set partly on and off the rug. All of these are in need of controlled support, and we probably blame the manufacturer for making faulty furniture when the underlying cause is uneven floor condition.

Why are there so many uneven floors? The answer is that even the best floors will wear unevenly or settle unevenly. What makes floors settle and become uneven? Underground water, leaky water mains, weathering of building materials, traffic vibrations, earth tremors all have a part in creating uneven floors. Articles placed on such floors either wobble or settle.

Wobbling jars mechanisms of motorized equipment. Appliances, TV sets and phonographs serve better without this jarring.

When furniture settles on uneven floors, their frames are twisted out of line. This causes doors and

This modern caster with on-the-spot finger adjustment for easy leveling on uneven floors is designed for use on TV sets, washing machines and other household furniture.

This tiltable base glide is designed for use on heavy pieces where slope or worn spots on uneven floors would cause one edge of the glide to dig into the floor covering. Tiltable feature prevents bends of the stem by assuring broad supporting surface on glide base regardless of floor conditions.

Photograph courtesy of Adjustable Caster Co.

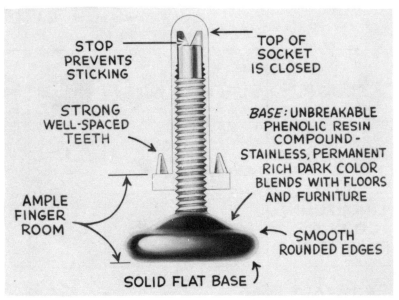

STOP PREVENTS STICKING

TOP OF SOCKET IS CLOSED

STRONG WELL-SPACED TEETH

BASE: UNBREAKABLE PHENOLIC RESIN COMPOUND— STAINLESS, PERMANENT RICH DARK COLOR BLENDS WITH FLOORS AND FURNITURE

AMPLE FINGER ROOM

SMOOTH ROUNDED EDGES

SOLID FLAT BASE

Sketches courtesy of Adjustable Caster Co.

How an adjustable glide as well as caster works: threaded section inside outside sleeve enables finger-tip adjustment for height.

Here are several types of glides and rests. The one in the upper left is designed for use with metal tubular furniture. After it is inserted into the tube, the parachute washer expands and prevents it from coming loose. On the right (top and bottom) are rests designed for round and square furniture legs.

1- LEG UNSUPPORTED - CRACK CLOSED (BEFORE SETTLING)

2 - SETTLING LEG OPENS CRACK -

3 - GLIDE SUPPORTED LEG - *CRACK CLOSED!*

WHICH GLIDE

FLOOR				
WOOD				
LINOLEUMN, CORK OR PLASTIC TILE				
ASPHALT TILE				
CARPET & RUGS THICK PILE				
CARPET & RUGS SHORT PILE				
FLAGSTONE OR CERAMIC TILE				
MASONRY OR TERRAZZO				

STER TO USE

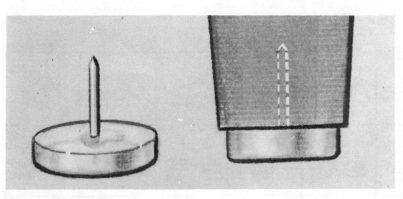

Clear plastic is sometimes used for glides. The button type with a nail in the center is hammered into the chair leg.

drawers to rub. If they rub hard enough, they stick and cannot be closed or locked. Unclosed furniture doors and drawers invite dust.

Furniture is frequently moved around in the home so that it is subjected to settling anew each time it is moved. These frequent settlings over a period of time result in loosened glue joints.

Photograph courtesy of Plastiglide Mfg. Corp.

It is plain that a modern caster and glide with controlled support helps to protect furniture and equipment placed on uneven floors. The old concept of protecting floors from furniture legs is now supplemented by the important idea of protecting valuable pieces from uneven floors.

Another way to protect floors from metal tubular furniture is by means of special glides or crutch tips, which fit over the metal.

Globe Valve

A globe valve resembles the standard kitchen faucet in operation. It is closed by forcing a washer down upon the valve seat by turning a handle.

Globe valves are made with a composition washer or a metal disc. The latter is used for hot water and steam lines. A globe valve with a composition washer is easily repaired, but the type with a metal disc is not.

When installing a globe valve, you should set it on the pipe so that the flow of the water is up through the orifice or opening and the washer is moved against the flow of the water when closing.

The globe valve is used widely in household plumbing despite the fact that it markedly reduces the flow of water through the pipes. Its main advantage is the fact that it is easy to change washers in this type of valve. A globe valve offers about eight times more resistance than an ordinary pipe elbow and about 16 times more resistance to the flow of water than a gate valve. See *Valves*.

A globe valve is commonly used in household plumbing. It should be installed so that the inlet pipe allows water to flow through the orifice and up against the washer.

Gouge

This is a special wood-cutting chisel with either a concave or convex cutting edge, that is, with the bevel ground either inside or outside the curved edge. Gouges are used not only in general woodworking, but also in wood turning and wood carving.

Glossary of Building and Woodworking Terms

The building trades have a special vocabulary all their own; in ordering materials and reading plans or blueprints, these terms will be of use to you:

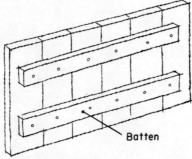

Batten

Anchor—Irons of special form used to fasten together timbers or masonry.

Backing—The bevel on the top edge of a hip rafter that allows the roofing boards to fit the top of the rafter without leaving a triangular space between it and the lower side of the roof covering.

Balloon frame—The lightest and most economical form of construction, in which the studding and corner posts are set up in continuous lengths from first-floor line or sill to the roof plate.

Baluster—A small column used to support a rail.

Balustrade—A row of balusters with the rails, generally used for porches, balconies, etc.

Band—A low, flat molding.

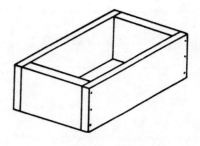

BUTT

Base—The bottom of a column; the finish of a room at the junction of the walls and floor.

Batten (*cleat*)—A narrow strip of board used to fasten several pieces together.

Batter board—A temporary framework used to assist in locating the corners when laying out a foundation.

Beam—An inclusive term for joists, girders, rafters, and purlins.

Bedding—A filling of mortar, putty, or other substance in order to secure a firm bearing.

Belt course—A horizontal board across or around a building, usually made of a flat member and a molding.

Bevel board (*pitch board*)—A board used in framing a roof or stairway to lay out bevels.

Board—Lumber less than 2 inches thick.

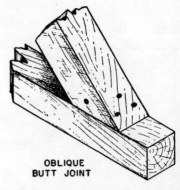

OBLIQUE BUTT JOINT

BEVEL

Board foot—The equivalent of a board 1 foot square and 1 inch thick.

Boarding in—The process of nailing boards on the outside studding of a house.

Braces—Pieces fitted and firmly fastened to two others at any angle in order to strengthen the angle thus treated.

Bracket—A projecting support for a shelf or other structure.

Break joints—To arrange joints so that they do not come directly under or over the joints of adjoining pieces, as in shingling, siding, etc.

Bridging—Pieces fitted in pairs from the bottom of one floor joist to the top of adjacent joists, and crossed to distribute the floor load; sometimes pieces of width equal to the joist and fitted neatly between them.

Building paper—Cheap, thick pa-

STOP CHAMFER

per, used to insulate a building before the siding or roofing is put on; sometimes placed between double floors.

Built-up timber—A timber made of several pieces fastened together and forming one of larger dimension.

Carriages—The supports of the steps and risers of a flight of stirs.

Casement—A window in which the sash opens upon hinges.

Casing—The trimming around a door or window opening, either outside or inside, or the finished lumber around a post or beam, etc.

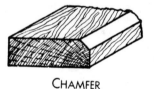
CHAMFER

Ceiling—Narrow, matched boards; sheathing of the surfaces that inclose the upper side of a room.

Center-hung sash—A sash hung on its centers so that it swings on a horizontal axis.

Chamfer—A beveled surface cut upon the corner of a piece of wood.

Checks—Split or cracks in a board, ordinarily caused by seasoning.

Clamp—A mechanical device used to hold two or more pieces together.

Clapboards—A special form of outside covering of a house; siding.

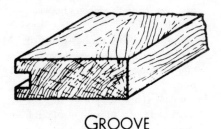

GROOVE

Columns—A support, square, rectangular, or cylindrical in section, for roofs, ceilings, etc., composed of base, shaft, and capital.

Combination frame—A combination of the principal features of the full and balloon frames.

Concrete—A combination of sand, broken stone, or gravel, and cement used in foundations, building construction for walks, etc.

Conductors—Pipes for conducting water from a roof to the ground or to a receptacle or drain; downspout.

Cornice—The molded projection which finishes the top of the wall of a building.

Counterflashings—Strips of metal used to prevent water from entering the top edge of the vertical side of a roof flashing; they also allow expansion and contraction without danger of breaking the flashing.

Deadening—Construction intended to prevent the passage of sound.

Drip—The projection of a window sill or water table to allow the water to drain clear of the side of the house below it.

Fascia—A flat member of a cornice or other finish, generally the board of the cornice to which the gutter is fastened.

Flashing—The material used and the process of making watertight the roof intersections and other exposed places on the outside of the house.

Flue—The opening in a chimney through which smoke passes.

Flush—Adjacent surfaces even, or in same plane (with reference to two structural pieces).

Footing courses—The bottom and heaviest courses of a piece of masonry.

Foundation—That part of a building or wall which supports the superstructure.

Frame—The surrounding or inclosin woodwork of windows, doors, etc., and the timber skeleton of a building.

Framing—The rough timber structure of a building, including interior and exterior walls, floor, roof, and ceilings.

Full frame—The old-fashioned mortised-and-tenoned frame, in which every joint was mortised and tenoned. Rarely used at the present time.

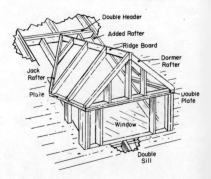

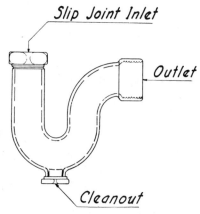

Slip Joint Inlet

Outlet

Cleanout

Furring—Narrow strips of board nailed upon the walls and ceilings to form a straight surface upon which to lay the laths or other finish.

Gable—The vertical triangular end of a building from the eaves to the apex of the roof.

Gage (*gauge*)—A tool used by carpenters; to strike a line parallel to the edge of the board.

Gambrel—A symmetrical roof with two different pitches or slopes on each side.

Girders—A timber used to support wall beams or joists.

Girt (*ribband*)—The horizontal member of the walls of a full or combination frame house which supports the floor joists or is flush with the top of the joists.

Groove—A long hollow channel cut by a tool, into which a piece fits or in which it works. Carpenters have given special names to certain forms of grooves, such as dadoes and housings. A *dado* is a rectangular groove cut across the grain the full width of the piece. Dadoes are used in sliding doors, window frames, etc. A *housing* is a groove cut at any angle with the

grain and partway across the piece. Housings are used for framing stair risers and treads into a string (not stringer). Grooving is used largely in the fastening of boards together or in the prevention of warping and twisting of wide boards or boards glued together. In doing this it is necessary to prevent the warping but to permit the free swelling and shrinking due to changes in the humidity. Various simple devices are used, such as hardwood batten, tapering key, or iron rod. Grooving is required in the first two.

Ground—A strip of wood assisting the plasterer in making a straight wall and in giving a place to which the finish of the room may be nailed.

Ground floor—The floor of a building on a level with the ground or nearly so.

Header—A short joist supporting tail beams and framed between trimmer joists; the piece of stud or finish over an opening; a lintel.

Headroom—The clear space between floor line and ceiling, as in a stairway.

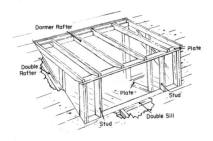

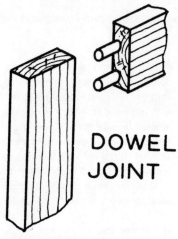

DOWEL JOINT

Heel of a rafter—The end or foot that rests on the wall plate.

Hip roof—A roof which slopes up toward the center from all sides, necessitating a hip rafter at each corner.

Jack rafter—A short rafter framing between the wall plate and a hip rafter.

Jamb—The side piece or post of an opening; sometimes applied to the doorframe.

Joints

    Butt—Squared ends or ends and edges adjoining each other.

    Dovetail—Joint made by cutting pins the shape of dovetails in which fit between dovetails upon another piece.

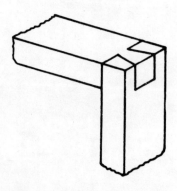

Drawboard—A mortise-and-tenon joint with holes so bored that when a pin is driven through, the joint becomes tighter.

Fished—An end butt splice strengthened by pieces nailed on the sides.

Halved—A joint made by cutting half the wood away from each piece so as to bring the sides flush.

Housed—A joint in which a piece is grooved to receive the piece which is to form the other part of the joint.

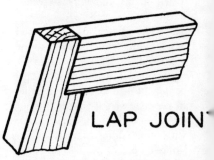

LAP JOIN

Glue—A joint held together with glue.

Lap—A joint of two pieces lapping over each other.

Mortised—A joint made by cutting a hole or mortise, in one piece, and a tenon, or piece to fit the hole, upon the other.

Rub—A flue joint made by carefully fitting the edges together, spreading glue between them, and rubbing the pieces back and forth until the pieces are well-rubbed together.

Scarfed—A timber spliced by cutting various shapes of shoulders, or jogs, which fit each other.

DADO

Joists—Timbers supporting the floor boards.

Kerf—The cut made by a saw.

Laths—Narrow strips to support plastering.

Lattice—Crossed wood, iron plate, or bars.

Ledgerboard—The support for the second-floor joists of a baloon-frame house, or for similar uses; ribband.

Level—A term describing the position of a line or plane when parallel to the surface of still water, an instrument or tool used in testing for horizontal and vertical surfaces, and in determining differences of elevation.

Lintel (header)—The piece of construction or finish, stone, wood or metal, which is over an opening; a header.

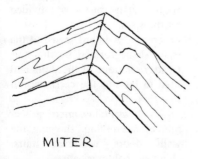

MITER

Lookout—The end of a rafter, or the construction which projects beyond the sides of a house to support the eaves; also the projecting timbers at the gables which support the verge boards.

Louver—A kind of window, generally in the peaks of gables and the tops of towers, provided with horizontal slots which exclude rain and snow and allow ventilation.

Lumber—Sawed parts of a log such as boards, planks, scantling, and timber.

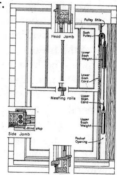

Matching, or tonguing and grooving—The method used in cutting the edges of a board to make a tongue on one edge and a groove on the other.

Meeting rail—The bottom rail of the upper sash, and the top rail of the lower sash of a double-hung window. Sometimes called the check rail.

Miter—The joint formed by two abutting pieces meeting at an angle.

Molding

   Base—The molding on the top of a base board.

   Bed—A molding used to cover the joint between the plancier and frieze; also used as a base

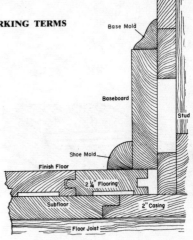

molding upon heavy work, and sometimes as a member of a cornice.

Lip—A molding with a lip which overlaps the piece against which the back of the molding rests.

Rake—The cornice upon the gable edge of a pitch roof, the members of which are made to fit those of the molding of the horizontal eaves.

Picture—A molding shaped to form a support for picture hooks, often placed at some distance from the ceiling upon the wall to form the lower edge of the frieze.

Mortise—The hole which is to receive a tenon, or any hole cut into or through a piece by a chisel; generally or rectangular shape.

Mullion—The construction between the openings of a window frame to accommodate two or more windows.

Muntin—The vertical member between two panels of the same piece of panel work. The vertical sash-bars separating the different panes of glass.

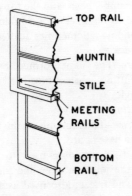

Newel—The principal post at the foot of a staircase; also the central support of a winding flight of stairs.

Nosing—The part of a stair tread which projects over the riser, or any similar projection; a term applied to the rounded edge of a board.

Piers—Masonry supports, set independently of the main foundation.

Pilaster—A portion of a square column, usually set within or against a wall.

Piles—Long posts driven into the soil in swampy locations or whenever it is difficult to secure a firm foundation, upon which the footing course of masonry or other timbers are laid.

Pitch—Inclination or slope, as of roofs or stairs, or the rise divided by the span.

Pitch board—A board sawed to the exact shape formed by the stair tread, riser slope of the stairs and used to lay out the carriage and stringers.

Plan—A horizontal geometrical section of a building, showing the walls, doors, windows, stairs, chimney, columns, etc.

PLOW

Planks or lumber—Material 2 or 3 inches thick and more than 4 inches wide, such as joists, flooring, etc.

Plaster—A mixture of lime, hair, and sand, or of lime, cement, and sand, used to cover outside and inside wall surfaces.

Plate—The top horizontal piece of the wall of a frame building upon which the roof rests.

Plate cut—The cut in a rafter which rests upon the plate; sometimes called the seat cut.

Plumb cut—Any cut made in a vertical plane; the vertical cut at the top end of a rafter.

Ply—A term used to denote a layer or thickness of building or roofing paper as two-ply, three-ply, etc.

Porch—An ornamental entrance way.

Post—A timber set on end to support a wall, girder, or other member of the structure.

Plow—To cut a groove running in the same direction as the grain of the wood.

Pully stile—The member of a window frame which contains the pulleys, and between which the edges of the sash slide.

Purlin—A timber supporting several rafters at one or more points, or the roof sheeting directly.

Rabbet or rebate—A corner cut out of an edge of a piece of wood.

Rafters

   Common—Those which run square with the plate and extend to the ridge.

   Cripple—Those which cut between valley and hip rafters.

   Hip—Those extending from the outside angle of the plates toward the apex of the roof.

   Jacks—Those square with the plate and intersecting the hip rafter.

   Valley—Those extending from an inside angle of the plates toward the ridge or center line of the house.

Rail—The horizontal members of a balustrade or panel work.

Rake—The trim of a building extending in an oblique line, as rake dado or molding.

Return—The continuation of a molding or finish of any kind in a different direction.

Ribband—(See *Ledgerboard*.)

Ridge—The top edge or corner formed by the intersection of two roof surfaces.

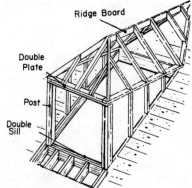

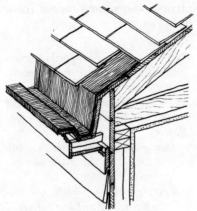

Ridge Cut—(See *Plumb cut.*)

Rise—The vertical distance through which anything rises, as the rise of a roof or stair.

Riser—The vertical board between two treads of a flight of stairs.

Roof—The covering or upper part of a building.

Roofing—The material put on a roof to make it wind and water-proof.

Run—The length of the horizontal projection of a piece such as a rafter when in position.

Saddle board—The finish of the ridge of a pitch-roof house. Sometimes called comb board.

Sash—The framework which holds the glass in a window.

Sawing, plain—Lumber sawed regardless of the grain, the log simply squared and sawed to the desired thickness; sometimes called slash or bastard sawed.

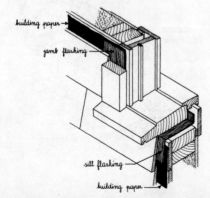

Scaffolding or staging—A temporary structure or platform enabling workmen to reach high places.

Scale—A short measurement used as a proportionate part of a larger dimension. The scale of a drawing is expressed as $\frac{1}{4}'' = 1$ foot.

Scantling—Lumber with a cross section ranging from 2"x4" to 4"x4".

Scarfing—A joint between two pieces of wood which allows them to be spliced lengthwise.

Scotia—A hollow molding used as a part of a cornice, and often under the nosing of a stair tread.

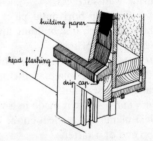

Scribing—The marking of a piece of wood to provide for the fitting of one of its surfaces to the irregular surface of another.

Seat cut or plate cut—The cut at the bottom end of a rafter to allow it to fit upon the plate.

Seat of a rafter—The horizontal cut upon the bottom end of a rafter which rests upon the top of the plate.

Section—A drawing showing the kind, arrangement, and proportions of the various parts of a structure. It is assumed that the structure is cut by a plane, and the

section is the view gained by looking in one direction.

Shakes—Imperfections in timber caused during the growth of the tree by high winds or imperfect conditions of growth.

Sheathing—Wallboards, roofing boards; generally applied to narrow boards laid with a space between them, according to the length of a shingle exposed to weather.

Sheathing paper—The paper used under siding or shingles to insulate the house; building papers.

Siding—The outside finish between the casings.

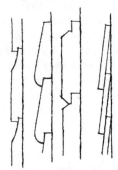

Sills—The horizontal timbers of a house which either rest upon the masonry foundations or, in the absence of such, form the foundations.

Sizing—Working material to the desired size; a coating of glue, shellac, or other substance applied to a surface to prepare it for painting or other method of finish.

Sleeper—A timber laid on the ground to support a floor joist.

Span—The distance between the bearings of a timber or arch.

Specifications—The written or printed directions regarding the

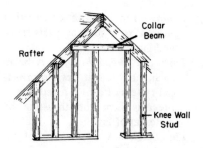

details of a building or other construction.

Square—A tool used by mechanics to obtain accuracy; a term applied to a surface including 100 square feet.

Stairs, box—Those built between walls, and usually with no support except the wall strings.

Standing finish—Term applied to the finish of the openings and the base, and all other finish necessary for the inside of the house.

Stucco—A fine plaster used for interior decoration and fine work, also for rough outside wall coverings.

Studding—The framework of a partition or the wall of a house; usually referred to as 2x4's.

Threshold—The beveled piece over which the door swings; sometimes called a carpet strip.

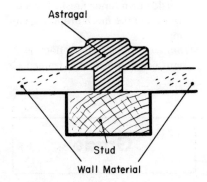

Timber—Lumber with cross section over 4″x6″, such as posts, sills, and girders.

Tie beam (collar beam)—A beam so situated that it ties the principal rafters of a roof together and prevents them from thrusting the plate out of line.

Tin shingle—A small piece of tin

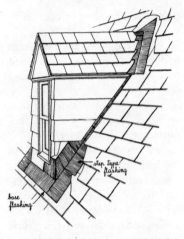

used in flashing and repairing a shingle roof.

To the weather—A term applied to the projecting of shingles or siding beyond the course above.

Tread—The horizontal part of a step.

Trim—A term sometimes applied to outside or interior finished woodwork and the finish around openings.

Trimmer—The beam or floor joist into which a header is framed.

Trimming—Putting the inside and outside finish and hardware upon a building.

Valley—The internal angle formed by the two slopes of a roof.

Verge boards—The boards which serve as the eaves finish on the gable end of a building.

Vestibule—An entrance to a house; usually inclosed.

Wainscoting—Matched boarding or panel work covering the lower portion of a wall.

Wash—The slant upon a sill, capping, etc., to allow the water to run off easily.

Water table—The finish at the bottom of a house which carries the water away from the foundation.

Wind ("i" pronounced as in kind)—A term used to describe the surface of a board when twisted (winding) or when resting upon two diagonally opposite corners, if laid upon a perfectly flat surface.

Wooden brick—Piece of seasoned wood, made the size of a brick, and laid where it is necessary to provide a nailing space in masonry walls.

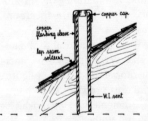

Grade

This architectural term refers to the level of the ground around a building.

Grain

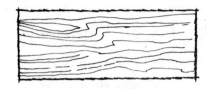

In woodworking, this refers to the direction of the wood fibers. When working on a piece of wood longitudinally, you may be working with or against the grain. When working transversely, you are working cross grain.

Graphite

Carbon, either natural or artificial, can be used as a lubricant. It can be purchased in powdered form or in a colloidal solution, and used to lubricate hinges, moving metal parts and, in particular, cylinder locks.

Grass

For a guide to the selection of the proper type of grass seed, see *Lawns*.

Grease Trap

A grease trap is installed in a drainage system for the purpose of separating grease from waste water so that large quantities of grease are not discharged into the sewer. Grease traps are not used in the average household, but in some communities, grease traps or catch basins are required by law. With a septic tank, it is best to use a grease trap so as to avoid difficulties with the tank.

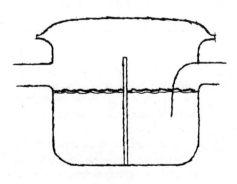

A grease trap.

Green Lumber

Timber from which the sap has not been removed either by natural seasoning or by kiln drying is called green lumber. As this wood dries, it tends to shrink and warp.

It is not economical for the handyman to use green lumber in any construction because of the difficulties that are bound to arise later when the lumber ages or dries. It is better to purchase seasoned lumber for any project except temporary braces or shoring.

Grindstone

Generally made of natural sandstone, a grindstone comes in the shape of a wheel. It is used for sharpening tools and for abrading metal which has rough edges or surface.

See *Sharpening*.

Here a grindstone is attached to the saw arbor and used with a homemade jig to sharpen a chisel.

Photograph courtesy of DeWalt, Inc.

Grommet

These metal fittings are used to reinforce holes in fabric, such as awnings, which are laced to a framework. Grommets come in various sizes and types.

One type of grommet, see accompanying photograph, is set through a hole punched in the fabric and the end is peened over with a special grommet tool.

Another type of grommet is shaped like the one in the photograph, but a special metal ring is set over the male end on the opposite side of the fabric. When the end is peined over, it is forced over this ring. This makes a more secure fitting.

Groove

A groove is frequently called a dado. Actually, a groove is a cut along the edge of the wood.
See *Dado*.

Groove Joint Pliers

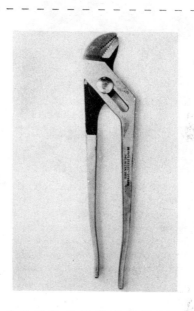

Also known as a parrot-head or pump pliers, the groove joint pliers have adjustable jaws with serrated edges. It is possible to grip varying sizes of nuts, bolts and other parts with this type of pliers. In an emergency, this type of pliers can also be used to hold smaller diameter pipe. The groove joint pliers come in several different sizes which determine the maximum opening of the jaws.

Ground Covers

If you wish to use ground covers around the exterior of the house, you will find suggestions for your selections in the section on *Landscaping*.

Grounding, Tools and Appliances

Whether it be for the power tools of your workshop, or the household appliances such as the washing machine, or the television set, a necessary safety measure is proper grounding. This actually means forming an electrical connection to the ground, or earth, to save you from receiving a shock should you come into contact with an exposed wire in the house. The grounding causes the fuse to blow; this in turn cuts off the electric power immediately, and thus you are rescued from the "live" current and any minor or severe shock you might otherwise undergo.

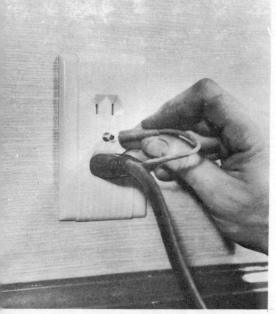

Grounding portable electrical tools is usually done by attaching the "pigtail" to a special type of screw which is set in the cover plate of the receptacle. This technique works with BX cable and with Romex if the cable has a third wire properly connected throughout to ground the system.

Method of Grounding

Grounding is done with a single electrical wire. The first step is to loosen a bolt on the appliance or tool. Then scrape the insulating covering off the end of the grounding wire, and insert this end under the bolt by turning it a couple of times. Next, tighten the bolt again. If any rust or dirt is on the metal surface or bolt, clean it off thoroughly before retightening the bolt.

The other end of the wire (the grounding end) is connected to a metallic electric cable or to a water pipe. In order to do this, you use a grounding clamp. You can buy such clamps at an electrical supply or hardware store; they have a bolt or some other device to tighten the

ground end of the wire to the pipe, also a screw for making the wire secure.

Should you not have a pipe near the appliance or the power tools, you can accomplish the grounding by turning the end of the wire (the insulating covering scraped off the tip) over a screw which is on the plate of the outlet where your electrical appliance or tool it now plugged in. This presupposes, of course, that the wiring system of your home is properly grounded throughout.

Portable Electric Tools

The shock hazard may be great-

The newer power-tool cords come with a special three-prong plug made to fit a special receptacle. In this way, you automatically ground the tool whenever you connect it. There is no possibility that a pigtail will be left unconnected.

er with portable tools, as they are sometimes used in damp places or outdoors. These tools are often provided with a ready-made grounding method—a wire with a very small socket at its end, and a screw with a special tip which is used instead of one of the usual screws on the outlet where the tool gets plugged in. Just by pushing the small socket end over the special-tipped screw, you accomplish the grounding of the portable tool.

If your new power tool comes with the special three-prong plug and you want to use it in an outlet without the special receptacle, there is an attachment you can buy which plugs into the outlet. The extra wire is attached to the screw holding the cover plate on the outlet box.

Grout

This is a mixture of Portland cement, lime and sand with sufficient water to make a consistency that will flow easily without the separation of the ingredients. It is used to fill the spaces between ceramic and other types of tiles used on walls or floors. When combined with gravel it can also be used in setting posts for fences, filling voids or holes in concrete blocks when building regulations require solid masonry construction.

Gutters and Downspouts

It has been estimated that 5,000 gallons of water fall on the roof of the average house in this country during a year. Running down the sides of the house, this water will leave black streaks. Seeping through the brickwork, framing or masonry, it will rot the beams and ruin the interior walls. Striking the ground, it will dig holes in flower beds and gather in the basement.

The only real protection is a system of gutters and downspouts.

The gutters are made of wood, galvanized metal, aluminum or copper. While the latter two are generally more expensive than the others they require less maintenance and wear longer.

Basic Parts

In the accompanying illustration are a number of downspouts, gutters and fittings. If you examine your roof, you will undoubtedly find many of these used.

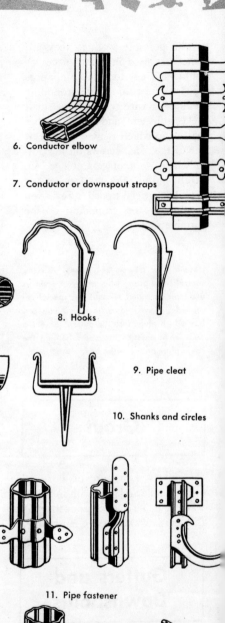

6. Conductor elbow

7. Conductor or downspout straps

8. Hooks

9. Pipe cleat

10. Shanks and circles

11. Pipe fastener

12. Gutter hanger

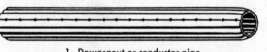

1. Downspout or conductor pipe

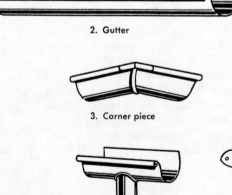

2. Gutter

3. Corner piece

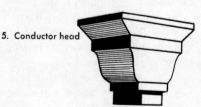

4. End piece, caps and outlet

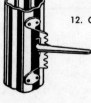

5. Conductor head

Keeping Gutters Clean

Difficulty may arise from the accumulation of leaves, rubbish, and birds' nests in gutters. Such debris, if not promptly removed, may stop up the opening to the downspout and cause water to back up and flow over the edge. This overflow may cause considerable damage if the gutters are built into the cornice, for water can find its way down inside the walls of the house. Unsightly streaks and stains on the exterior wall surfaces may also result if the overflow is not stopped.

To prevent leaves and other refuse from being washed into the downspout, it is advisable to place a basketlike strainer over the gutter outlet. Strainers are usually kept in stock by hardware dealers and are inexpensive. Even when there is no stoppage or overflow, it is advisable to keep gutters clean, because rotting leaves will eventually cause the metal to corrode and leak if allowed to remain. Fine ash and dirt should be removed regularly, as cinders in contact with metal will set up a corrosive action. When dirt of this kind is removed, the gutter should be flushed with clean water to remove all traces of acid.

These conditions may be avoided if the householder will remember to clean out the gutters regularly, especially in the autumn after the leaves have fallen.

It is also advisable to remove unusually heavy snow and ice from gutters to aid roof drainage and prevent damage to gutters or their

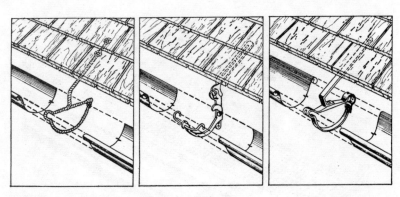

Typical gutter hangers.

fastenings by the excessive weight of such masses. The life of downspouts and metal gutters may be extended considerably by painting them occasionally with good metal paint.

Repairing Metal Gutters

Metal gutters may be half-round or shaped like a cornice but repairs are similar for both types. To correct a buckle or fold in the metal it may be necessary to remove the gutter. The crease can then be hammered out with a soft-faced hammer and a block of wood shaped like the gutter. The hammer head should be of wood, fiber, or plastic to keep it from marring the surface of the gutter.

Small holes may be repaired with a drop of solder and large ones patched with a piece of sheet metal of the same kind as the gutter. The metal must have a clean bright finish or the solder will not adhere. A temporary patch may be made with a piece of roofing felt or cotton duck fastened with flashing cement. The patching material should be thoroughly clean and dry, and both sides of the patch should be given a liberal but even coating of cement.

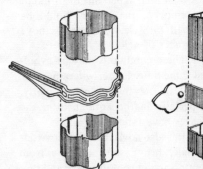
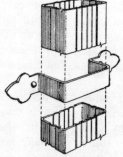
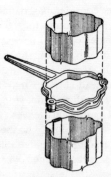

Typical downspout fasteners.

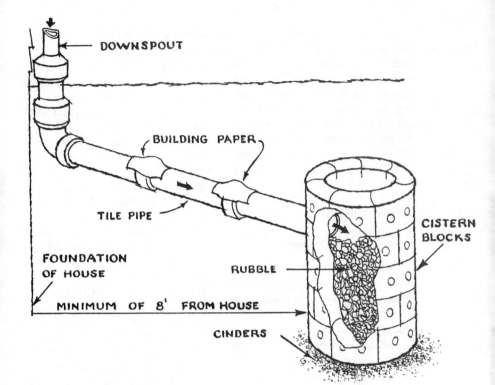

DOWNSPOUT

BUILDING PAPER

TILE PIPE

CISTERN BLOCKS

FOUNDATION OF HOUSE

RUBBLE

MINIMUM OF 8' FROM HOUSE

CINDERS

Repairing Wood Gutters

If a one-piece molded wood gutter has sagged, it should be forced back into place with a heavy hammer and block of wood and renailed in the proper position. Nails should be set, holes puttied, and unpainted spots touched up. The trough may then be treated with linseed oil or given a coat of asphalt paint.

If there is a split in a wood gutter, it can be repaired by patching with sheet metal. Coated iron, copper, or aluminum sheets can be used. Galvanized iron nails should be used for iron sheets, copper nails for copper sheets, and aluminum nails for aluminum sheets.

The metal should be shaped to fit the gutter and should be wide enough to cover the inside surface of the gutter and the tops of both edges. The area to be patched should be thoroughly cleaned, painted with asphalt paint, and covered with a layer of flashing cement, applied with a putty knife. The metal patch should then be pressed into the cement, nailed at intervals of 1½″ along all edges, and another coat of cement applied to seal the edges, cover the nail holes, and protect the metal. If patches are over 10″ in length, additional lines of nails should be used, spaced about 8″ between lines.

The lining of box or trough-type gutters, that is, wood lined with metal, should be examined for cracking. When ice forms in a gutter trough which is deep and narrow, it may expand and force the wall of the trough to loosen or break and the metal to split. For this reason, shallow and wide box gutters are advisable since they permit ice to expand over the edge of the gutter without injuring the box. Box-type gutters should be lined with rustproof metal. If other metal is used, the inside of the gutter should be swabbed with bituminous material or painted with metal paint.

Repairing Gutter Hangers

Metal gutters are attached to the eaves by means of straps of sheet metal, long spikes, twisted wire rope, or adjustable or nonadjustable metal brackets. These hangers may break or pull loose from their fastenings, permitting the gutter to sag and prevent proper drainage. If this occurs, broken straps or hangers should be replaced and adjusted so that the gutter will slope downward with a uniform grade to the outlet end. If supports are too far apart, it may be necessary to install additional hangers to insure a uniform slope for the gutter.

Downspouts (or Leaders)

Downspouts require less attention than gutters, but a certain amount of upkeep is necessary. Slush working down into pipe elbows may freeze, forcing seams and folds to open and allow water to leak through or drip. A leak is more common where leaders are not corrugated to allow for expansion. When a leak starts it should be checked promptly; otherwise the defect may increase until the whole elbow is broken. Recurrent freezing and thawing of a metal leader tube that fills with water because of stoppage may cause it to split. Small splits or bulges can be pressed back into shape and soldered. However, if a downspout is badly broken or rusted, it may be necessary to replace the entire section. The method of removal will depend upon the type of fastening used. The leader pipe comes in sections which fit into each other. To insert a length of pipe, the upper section should be slipped into the lower so that water will flow on the inside and not leak out. To make the installation more secure the sections should be soldered together at the joints.

See *Dry Well*.

Guy Rope

While any rope or wire used for bracing against the wind is called a guy wire or guy rope, technically, a guy rope is a galvanized rope. It consists of 6 strands of 7 wires each with a hemp core.

Gypsum

This is a raw material usually associated with a type of board. Actually, it's hydrous sulphate of calcium, chemically treated to remove some of the water. The handyman uses this product in the form of plaster of Paris.

See *Wallboards*.

H Beam

This is a steel beam, sometimes used in residential building, whose section, or end view, is like the letter H.

Hacksaws

If the metal is too thick or too hard to cut with snips, you'll find that a hacksaw will do the job. The common hacksaw has a blade, a frame, and a handle. The pistol-grip type usually is adjustable to take two or more blade lengths. The straight-handled saw generally is not adjustable.

Hacksaw blades have holes in both ends. They are mounted on the frame by means of pins attached to the frame. There's only one right way to mount a hacksaw blade. Many a beginner has made the mistake of putting the blade in backwards. Always mount the blade with the teeth pointing away from the handle. For ease in mounting, put the blade on the back pin first. Tighten the blade with enough tension to hold it rigidly between the pins, and then the tool is ready.

Selecting Blade

Blades are made of high-grade tool steel or tungsten or molybdenum steel, and are available from 6″ to 16″ in length. There are two types—one is the all-hard blade and the other is the flexible blade. Only the teeth of the flexible type are hardened.

Selecting the best blade for a job is a question of finding one of the right type and number of teeth per inches. An all-hard blade is suitable for sawing brass, tool steel, cast iron, rails and heavy cross-section stock. A flexible blade is usually best for sawing hollow shapes and metals having a light cross-section, and for work which cannot be held firmly in a vise, as cutting conduit or BX on the job.

The pitch of a blade indicates the number of teeth it has per inch. Pitches of 14, 18, 24 and 32 are available. Which pitch you use depends upon the material being cut; see table.

You must also consider the "set," when you select the blade. Set means simply that some teeth are pushed sideways in one direction and the same number in the opposite direction, according to definite patterns. The set provides clearance for the blade so it won't jam and stick, and it also prevents overheating the blade.

The average blade is only .025" thick but the set causes it to make a cut about twice that width. Three types of set are "undulated,"—more commonly called "wave" set—"alternate," and "raker."

Using the Hacksaw

Before you start a hacksaw cut, check again to see that you have the

Selecting the Proper Number of Teeth for the Job

NUMBER OF TEETH PER INCH	FOR CUTTING	USAGE	
		CORRECT	INCORRECT
14	1" or thicker . . . cast iron, machine steel, brass, copper, aluminum, bronze, slate.	PLENTY OF CHIP CLEARANCE	FINE TEETH, NO CHIP CLEARANCE, TEETH CLOGGED
18	¼" to 1" sections of annealed tool steel, high speed steel, rail, bronze, aluminum, copper, and light structural shapes.	AMPLE CHIP CLEARANCE	TEETH TOO FINE NO CHIP CLEARANCE, TEETH CLOGGED
24	⅛" to ¼" angle iron, steel, brass and copper tubing, wrought iron pipe, drill rod, conduit, metal trim.	THREE TEETH OR MORE ON SECTION	COARSE TEETH STRADDLES WORK STRIPS TEETH
32	⅛" or thinner stock of the same materials for which a 24-pitch blade is used.	THREE OR MORE TEETH IN EACH WALL SECTION	PITCH TOO COARSE TEETH STRADDLE WORK

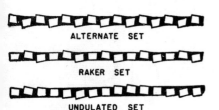

ALTERNATE SET

RAKER SET

UNDULATED SET

The amount of "set" given a saw blade is highly important because it determines the ease with which the saw can be worked. It also insures accuracy of cutting and helps to keep the teeth sharper for a longer period. Pictured here are three types of sets used with blades.

proper blade, and that its teeth point away from the handle. Check and adjust the blade tension.

Secure the stock in a vise, or with clamps, if it's not already anchored to something. It must be held firmly to prevent the blade from "chattering" and twisting. Saw alongside a scribed line and stay just outside that line. The blade will start more easily if you file a V-shaped nick at the starting point. Hold the saw at an angle that will keep at least two teeth cutting all the time—otherwise the blade will jump and individual teeth will be broken.

Start the cut with a light, steady, forward stroke. At the end of the

Starting a cut in hard material is easier if there is a guiding notch made with a file or the saw. To start an accurate cut, use your thumb as a guide and saw slowly with short strokes. Keep the blade nearly parallel to the surface to be cut.

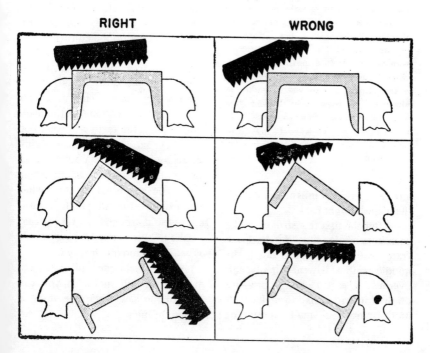

RIGHT   **WRONG**

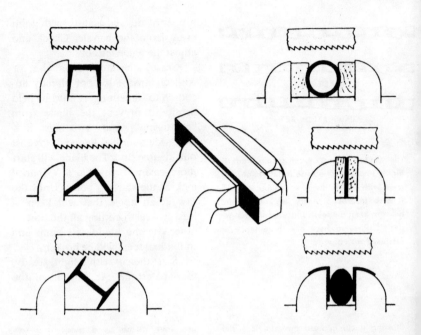

Holding the work is part of good cutting technique. It is best to fasten the work in a vise if it is not already attached to some structure. If the work is not rectangular or square, clamp it so as to allow cutting with as many teeth as possible in the cut. When holding circular or oval pieces, use a special vise or use wood, leather or aluminum jaw covers over the vise. Thin pieces of metal have to be sandwiched between two pieces of wood to make cutting easier and to avoid stripping the blade teeth.

stroke, relieve the pressure and draw the blade straight back.

After the first few strokes, make each one as long as the hacksaw frame will allow. If you don't, the middle teeth will wear rapidly and overheat. Use just enough pressure on the forward stroke to make each tooth remove a small amount of metal. Don't use any pressure on the back stroke. Remember that the teeth point forward, and that the forward edges do the cutting.

After the cut is started, use long steady strokes and do not speed—hold the pace down to 40 or 50 strokes per minute. That may seem slow but if you go too fast the blade will get hot, the teeth will round off and "lose set," and you'll have difficulty sawing straight. You may even break off some of the teeth or cramp the blade and break it. And when you examine the cut, you'll find it is ragged and crooked. So take it easy —about 90% of hacksawing trouble is caused by too much speed.

As you near the end of the cut slow down still more, so you can control the saw when the stock is sawed through.

Conventional hacksaw—this model is adjustable to take both 10" and 12" blades simply by sliding the cam-action lever on the bottom of the handle.

Photograph courtesy of Clemson Bros., Inc.

A hacksaw which has two blades—one fine-toothed for light work and the other coarse-toothed for heavier work—set within the dual frame. Single turnbuckle at end of saw tightens both blades.

Photograph courtesy of Dreier Brothers, Inc.

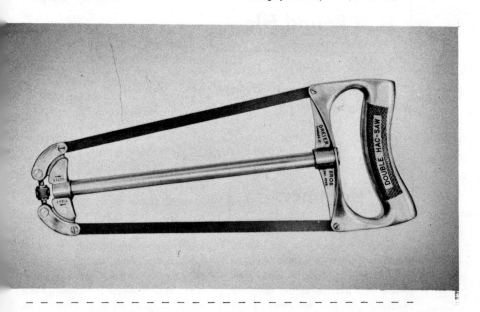

Hairline

Very narrow cracks in painted or varnished surfaces are usually referred to as hairlines. Very narrow cracks in plaster or concrete are termed hairline cracks.

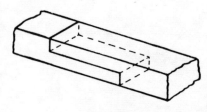

Half-lap Joint

This is a simple joint used in structural work. It is made by cutting away half the thickness at the ends of two pieces so that when united, the joint is flush although the pieces overlap. To cut a half-lap, measure an equal distance from the end of each board and cut half-way through them across the grain. Then

A half-lap joint.

Sketch from "Tool Guide" courtesy of Stanley Tools

mark half the thickness of the boards and cut with the grain up to the cross cut to form a stepped end. See *Joints*.

Half-Round File

This type of file has one side flat and the other curved. The amount of the convexity never equals a semi-circle.

The flat side of the file is always double cut. The rounded side is double cut too except for all smooth and 4″ and 6″ second cut files, which are single cut.

See *Files*.

Hammers

Whoever conceived the idea of cracking a nut with a rock unknowingly invented a tool. When a later genius tied a stick to the rock, he invented the first hammer. There have been a lot of improvements since that humble beginning.

Types of Hammers

Metal-working hammers can be divided into two classifications—hard-face and soft-face. The hard-face hammers are made of forged tool steel. One of the best general-purpose hammers is the ball-pein hammer, often called a machinist's hammer. The ball-shaped end is known as the peining end.

The ball-pein hammer has a couple of cousins known as straight-pein and cross-pein. Both have wedge-shaped peining ends. The face end is the same for all three hammers.

Most metal-headed hammers are classed according to the weight of the hammer head, without the handle. The 4-ounce and 6-ounce sizes are used for light work, such as tap-

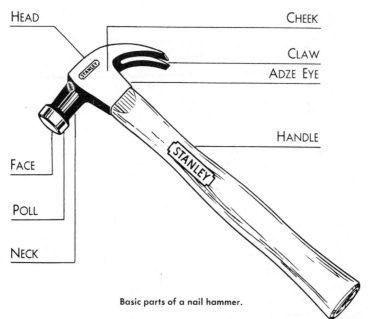

HEAD

CHEEK

CLAW

ADZE EYE

HANDLE

FACE

POLL

NECK

Basic parts of a nail hammer.

ping a prick punch or a small drift punch. The 8-ounce, 10-ounce and 12-ounce sizes are best for general utility work; the 1-pound and heavier types are for heavy-duty jobs. For chipping castings with a cold chisel, you'll normally use the 1-pound ball-pein to pound the chisel head.

A riveting hammer is used for forming metal as well as for driving rivets. And if you're forming sheet metal seams you'll also need a setting hammer, which is designed for getting into tight corners and for forming metal at right angles.

Here's a version of a hammer used with brads. The brad is set into the hole in the end, held by a magnet, and pushed into the wood by pressure on the handle. Once the brad is part way in the wood, the handle is used as a face of a hammer to drive it in the rest of the way.

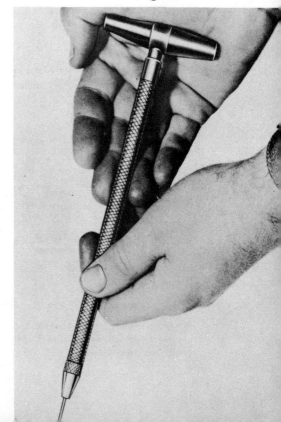

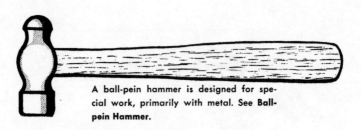

A ball-pein hammer is designed for special work, primarily with metal. See **Ball-pein Hammer.**

Soft-face hammers have pounding surfaces made of wood, brass, lead, rawhide, hard rubber, or plastic. (The plastic often comes with replaceable tips or faces.)

Metal workers use them to form soft metals such as copper and aluminum. They are for driving close-fitting parts together or for knocking them apart. The face may be damaged easily, so don't use a soft-face hammer for rough work. It's not made for striking punch heads, bolts, or nails.

Mallet

A mallet is a hammer-like tool made of wood, rawhide, or rubber.

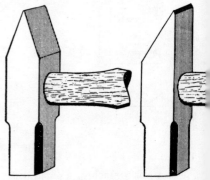

Riveting hammer and setting hammer are specialized tools used for rivets and grommets.

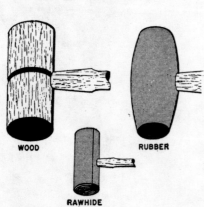

WOOD

RAWHIDE

RUBBER

Mallets are another form of hammer. They are used to drive dowels, pins and when working with wood chisels.

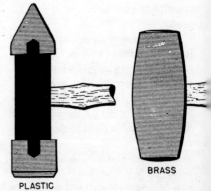

PLASTIC

BRASS

Soft-face hammers are used to prevent marring the surface of the work. There are special faces to add to standard claw hammers as well as the soft-face hammers.

It's used for flattening sheet metal seams and for shaping sheet and strap metal; it will not dent the metal as a steel hammer would. Use a wood mallet to pound a wood chisel or a gouge.

Nail Hammer

You'll drive nails and brads with a nail hammer—sometimes called a claw hammer. Standard nail hammer heads weigh from 10 to 16 ounces, but there are many other weights. The face of the head must be kept smooth and true or it will slide off nail heads and cause the nails to bend. Don't use a nail hammer to work metal, to pound cold

How To Handle a Hammer

1. Always grasp the hammer firmly near the end of the handle. This will permit the swing of the hammer to drive the nail. Holding the hammer nearer the head will make you "push" the nail in with your arm.

2. When nailing, the blow is delivered through the wrist, the elbow and the shoulder—one or all are brought into play, according to the strength of the blow to be struck. It is best to rest the face of the hammer on the nail, draw the hammer back and give a light tap to start the nail and to determine the aim.

3. Strike the nail squarely with the face of the hammer so as to avoid marring the wood or bending the nail. If the nail bends, it is often best to draw it out and use a new one in its place. The cheek of the hammer is its weakest part; you should not try to strike with it.

Sketches from "Tool Guide" courtesy of Stanley Tools

4. In all fine work, it is best to drive the head of the nail below the surface of the wood. Use a nail set to do this job—rest the nail set on the nail head and to prevent it from slipping off, rest your little finger on the work and press the nail set firmly against it. Set nails about $\frac{1}{16}$" below the surface of the wood. See **Blind Nailing.**

chisels, or to drive rivets. Use it only to drive nails and brads.

When you drive brads and other small-headed nails, drive them so that the heads stop $\frac{1}{8}''$ to $\frac{1}{16}''$ from the surface. Then drive the heads flush or below the surface with a nail set. Avoid leaving hammer marks on the surface of the wood, no matter what kind of nails you're driving.

To pull a nail, place the claws of the hammer so that they embrace the nail, then raise the handle. If the nail is so long that adequate leverage is hard to obtain, place a block of wood under the hammer to act as a fulcrum.

Using a Hammer

You know what happens when you "choke" a baseball bat. It reduces the power of your swing. When you grip a hammer handle too close to the head, the same thing happens. The force of the blow is reduced and it's harder to hold the hammer head in the proper position. Grip the handle close to the other end, where it's shaped to fit inside your hand.

When you use a hammer, grasp the handle as if you were shaking hands. Try it to see how well-balanced it feels. When you strike a blow, use your elbow as a pivot point —not your wrist. If you use your forearm as an extension of the handle, the blow will be more effective; you'll have a better chance to strike the work squarely because the radius of your swing is longer.

Whenever possible, strike the object with the full face of the hammer, and with the hammer face par-

How To Draw or Remove a Nail

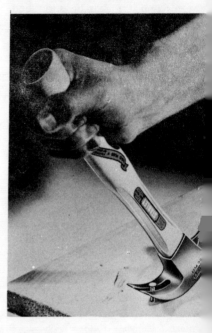

1. To draw a nail, slip the claw of the hammer under the nail and pull until the handle is nearly vertical and the nail partly drawn.

2. If the pull is continued, unnecessary force is required. This will bend the nail, mar the wood, and may even break the hammer handle.

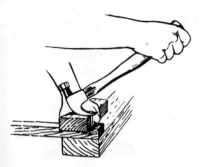

allel to the work. This spreads the force of the blow over a greater area and avoids ·damaging the edge of the hammer face. It also prevents unnecessary denting or marking of the stock. "Hammer marks" are an indication of improper hammer use.

Hammer and mallet handles should be securely fastened in the eye or hole of the head. Never work with a hammer that has a loose head. When you discover a loose head, fix it. If you don't you're inviting serious injury to yourself or someone who may be in your working area.

Keep the handle tight. The eye (or hole) through the hammer head has a slight taper in both directions

3. Slip a piece of wood under the head of the hammer to increase the leverage and to relieve the strain on the handle. It may be necessary to use several blocks of varying thickness, depending upon the size of the nail.

Sketches and photographs courtesy of
Stanley Tools

4. Pulling or drawing a nail from the pointed end is not advised if you wish to keep the wood smooth. For rough framing or temporary woodworking, this technique can be used if it is not possible or too difficult to draw from the head side of the nail.

5. What happens when you draw a nail from the pointed end. A common nail with its head splinters the wood as it is pulled through. A finishing nail, with a head virtually the same diameter as the nail body, leaves an enlarged hole.

from the center. After the handle is inserted in the head, drive a corrugated steel wedge in the end of the handle. This expands the wood so that it fills the eye. If the wedge comes out, or is lost, replace it before you use the hammer again.

Hammer and mallet handles ordinarily are made of tough wood. They can take a lot of hard use, but if misused, they split easily. Hammers are also made with all metal or Fiberglas handles. Don't pound with the end of the handle, and never use it for prying. It's easily broken that way. Keep your hammers clean, and every so often give them a coating of light oil to prevent rust.

Magnetized Hammer

A magnetized hammer is useful for upholstery work. The hammer also serves other purposes where a magnet is desired; for example to hold a nail when starting it if it is inconvenient to hold the nail with your other hand.

Hand Drill

A drilling tool operated by hand. The drill bit in the chuck is revolved by a pinion and speed gear actuated by a crank and handle.
See *Drills*.

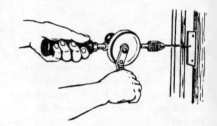

A hand drill used to make holes for screws which will hold hinges in the door frame.

Hand Rail

For added safety when walking up or down stairs, either inside or outside the house, there should be a hand rail. It can be made of wood or metal and should be securely fastened. Some decorative hand rails are made of rope, but these are not advised with small children.

The hand rail should be 2' 10" high for adults and 2' 2" high for children.
See *Stairs*.

Hand Scraper

A hand scraper is used for the final smoothing of a wood surface before you use sandpaper or steel wool. It removes the slight ridges left by a plane. The hand scraper is also used to smooth surfaces that are difficult to plane because of an irregular or curly grain.

There are two types which you can use for fine cabinetwork and in furniture making. One is a rectangular piece of metal, about 3"x5", and the other is a twin-handled tool, somewhat like a spokeshave, and is called a cabinet scraper.

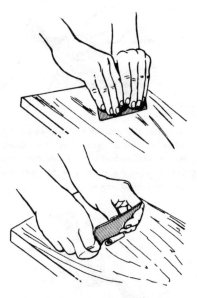

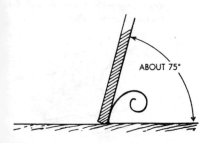

The hand scraper is held firmly between the thumb and fingers at about a 75° angle and sprung to a slight curve by pressure of the thumbs.

The hand scraper can be either pushed or pulled as the grain of the wood demands or whichever is more convenient.

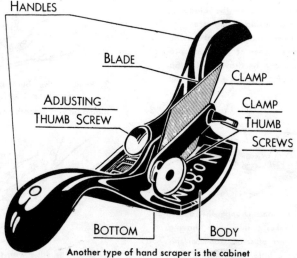

Another type of hand scraper is the cabinet scraper with the cutting blade held at an angle and with two handles, making it easier to use.

How To Sharpen a Scraper

To adjust the cabinet scraper, loosen the adjusting thumb screw and the clamp thumb screws. Insert the blade from the bottom with the bevel side towards the adjusting thumb screw.

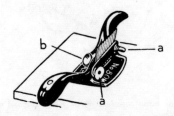

Bring the edge of the blade even with the bottom of the scraper body by standing it on a flat surface and pressing the blade lightly against the wood. Tighten the clamp thumb screws "a." Bow the blade by tightening the adjusting thumb screw "b" to make it project enough to take a thin shaving. If one corner of the blade projects too far, it can be drawn in by tapping the side of the blade near the top.

Try the scraper and change the adjustment until it takes a thin, even shaving; better use a piece of scrap wood for this. Hold it turned a little to the side to start a cut. The scraper is usually pushed but it can be pulled.

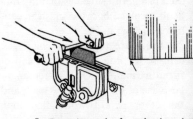

1. Dust, instead of a shaving, in a dull scraper. To sharpen a hand s file the edges square and straig drawfiling with a smooth mill file. round the corners slightly.

2. Whet the blade, holding the square to the surface of an oil ston may prefer to hold the scraper sq the edge of the oil stone.

3. Remove the burr by whetti scraper flat on the oil stone. The should be very smooth and sharp.

4. Draw the edge with three or f strokes of the burnisher held flat scraper.

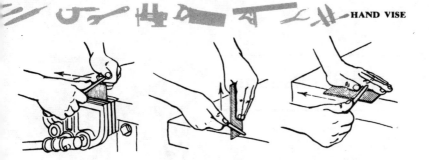

5. Turn the edge with a few strokes of the burnisher. The scraper can be held in any of the three ways shown here. Draw the burnisher toward you the full length of the blade, using a sliding stroke.

Sketch from "Tool Guide" courtesy of
Stanley Tools

Hand Screw

Although clamps of all types were called hand screws, currently, only the clamp with two wooden jaws and two screw handles is called a hand screw. Hand screws are sometimes called wood clamps as well as Jorgenson clamps.

See *Adhesives and Clamps.*

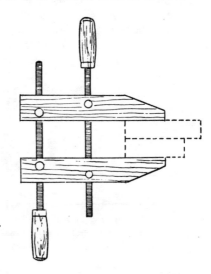

A typical hand screw.

Hand Vise

A small vise used for clamping small, light work is held in the hand.

A hand vise.

Handle Repairs

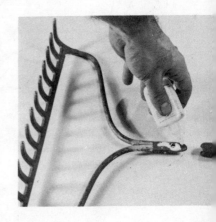

Frequently, too much pressure on a garden hoe or rake or other wooden handle tool causes the wood to split. If the break is major, a new handle should be used to replace the old one.

However, the more common break is merely a split along the grain of the wood. There are several ways to repair wooden handles—gluing the crack is the best and when finished, it's difficult to find the repaired section. However, there are other techniques you can use, depending upon the location of the crack and the normal pressure exerted at that point of the handle.

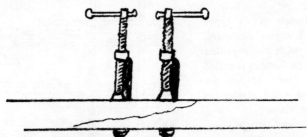

Use a quality glue and force it into the crack. Then clamp the handle. Protective wood blocks often are not necessary for the handles are made of hardwood and the clamp pressure is light.

Wrapping the handle with tape—glass filament mending tape, friction tape or even masking tape—will often permit you to put the handle and tool back into service quickly.

If you have tubular aluminum of a diameter to fit snugly over the handle, slip it into place. The metal tubing should extend about 2″ to 3″ beyond the edges of the crack. Fasten the tubing to the wood handle with round head screws.

Nuts and bolts can also be used to mend a split in a wooden handle. Use round head bolts through pre-drilled holes.

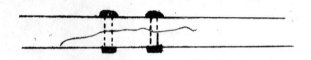

Hanger Bolt

This is a special type of bolt which has a machine bolt thread on one side and a lag screw on the other.

It is used for attaching hangers —metal supports—to wood. It is also used occasionally in furniture construction. The lag screw end is threaded into the wood. The metal hanger is secured at the nut end.

A hanger bolt.

Hard Oil Finish

This is a cheap substitute for varnish, sometimes used for interior work and inexpensive furniture. It is made of rosin or copal or both, melted into drying oil and thinned with turpentine. Because of the wide variety and low cost of varnish today, it is seldom used now.

Hard Water

See *Water Softeners.*

Hardboard

This term is used to cover a whole family of materials, primarily panels, that are made by exploding wood chips into fibrous state, refining the fibers and compressing them into dense, rigid panels in heated hydraulic presses. The fibers are permanently bonded with the natural lignin, which was the original bonding agent in the tree.

Hardboards resemble wood in many respects. They have many advantages not found in natural wood; for example:

- there is no grain to rise or check and mare the surface
- equal strength in all surface directions
- will not split, splinter or crack
- available in large panels
- easily worked with ordinary woodworking tools

Types and Sizes

Hardboard comes in many different sizes and types. It is often called Masonite, but this is the name of only one company making this material. Some are 'tempered,' making them highly resistant to moisture so that they can be used outside as well as inside the house.

Normally, hardboard comes with one side smooth and the other textured similar to a cloth weave. This is natural because of the webs used in the manufacture of the product. Some hardboards are available with simulated leather grain, scored

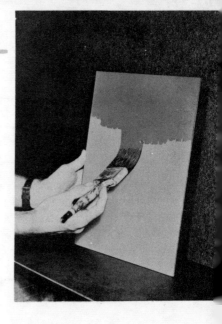

Prime-coated hardboard is ready to take any type of paint. The finished coat, light or dark, enamel or lacquer, can be applied with a brush or roller.

Photographs courtesy of Masonite Corp.

tile patterns and also perforated.

See *Walls*.

Generally available in ⅛″, 3⁄16″ and ¼″ thickness in panels 4′x8′, hardboard also comes as thin as 1⁄10″ and as thick as ¾″ in panels 3′x4′ to 4′x12′.

Fastening Techniques

Hardboard 3⁄16″ or thicker can be fastend directly to studs, furring strips, joists or other framing members spaced not more than 16″ on center or directly over solid backing of wood, hardboard or plaster. Panels ⅛″ or thinner, however, can be applied over solid backing only.

It is possible to use nails, bolts, rivets, staples, screws, toggle bolts and adhesive to secure hardboard to a surface. Here are some hints for nailing:

1. Use the type and size nail recommended by the manufacturer for the specific panel you purchase. Any lumber dealer will help you or you can write directly to the manufacturer for literature.

2. Provide a solid, continuous support behind every joint.

3. Always nail perpendicular to the surface; do not toe-nail.

4. Do not use hardboard as the surface to which you are nailing another hardboard panel.

5. Do not nail into the panel edges.

6. When nailing a panel in place, always nail the center of the panel before nailing along the outside.

7. Do not nail closer than ¼″ from the edge, preferably ³⁄₁₆″.

8. Casing or finishing nails may be set below the surface and the holes filled.

9. Screws of adequate size can be used instead of nails. It is best to drill holes through the hardboard first, countersinking for the head, if flathead screws are used.

Bending Hardboard

While hardboard cannot ordinarily be formed to compound curves, such as dish-shaped, the panels can be readily bent to simple, one-direction curves. Such bent shapes fall into two general types:

1. those which must be supported with a permanent framework,

2. those which are self-supporting.

Cold dry bends—Hardboard may be bent with no preparatory treatment around a permanent framework by fastening the board along one end and then attaching it as it is bent around the supporting members.

Cold moist bends—to make a sharper radius bend, or a bend without permanent framework, it is necessary to moisten the panels thoroughly by dipping them in water for 40 minutes to several hours. The panels can be prepared, if dipping is not possible, by scrubbing cold water into the screen or textured side of each panel with a stiff broom or brush until the color turns dark

Hardboard is also available with specially-tempered surfaces for use as forms with concrete. The hardboard is used as a surfacing material over a plywood core. Because of its special surface, it can be reused a number of times without injury to the surface.

Bending Hardboard				
The minimum bend you can figure for hardboard for thickness and grade				
STANDARD	⅛″	³⁄₁₆″	¼″	⁵⁄₁₆″
Minimum bending radii for cold				
dry bend, smooth side out	12″	18″	26″	40″
smooth side in	10″	12″	22″	28″
for cold moist bend, smooth side out	8″	12″	18″	28″
smooth side in	4″	6″	14″	16″
TEMPERED				
Minimum bending radii for cold dry				
bend, smooth side out	9″	13″	24″	36″
smooth side in	6″	10″	18″	24″
for cold moist bend, smooth side out	4″	8″	16″	24″
smooth side in	3½″	5½″	10″	14″
PATTERNED HEADBOARD				
Minimum bending radii for				
cold dry bend	14″			
for cold moist bend	10″			

Perforated hardboard is sometimes used to make attractive walls in a room. See **Walls** and **Perforated Wallboard**.

Photographs courtesy of Masonite Corp.

chocolate brown. Stack the panels with the screen sides together and cover with a tarpaulin. Allow the panels to stand for at least 24 hours for ⅛″ board to a minimum of 48 hours for ⁵⁄₁₆″ board. This applies to standard and tempered hardboards. The special types, such as the leather-grain, require at least 72 hours.

Finishing

Some hardboard panels come with surfaces prepared for final finish coat. Others must be prepared in the same manner as raw wood. Any type of paint or finish can be used over hardboard once the surface has been prepared.

Hardboard can also be used for house exteriors, if it is specially treated during the manufacturing process. Quarter-inch hardboard was used for this home, applied in 4′ sheets over insulating board sheathing.

Hardwood

Any lumber that is dense and heavy is classed as hardwood. Some common hardwoods used by the handyman are: mahogany, reddish brown and open grained; walnut, chocolate brown and open grained; maple, very light brown and fine grained; oak, flesh color and coarse grained; birch, reddish-brown and medium grained.

See *Lumber.*

Hasp

This is a door fastening which can be secured by a peg or padlock.

A hasp.

Hatchets and Axes

These are usually sturdy tools, but they need to be given good handling and care since their edges may bcome nicked and dulled. Following are good procedures for the maintenance of the tools.

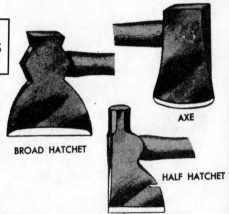

BROAD HATCHET

AXE

HALF HATCHET

Types of hatchets and axes.

Grinding Edges

Remove nicks by holding horizontally against abrasive wheel. Move back and forth across stone.

Grind cutting edge of hatchet to bevel. Cool frequently in water. Move from side to side across face of grinding wheel.

Careless grinding will ruin any ax through heat caused by friction, or by making the edge so thin it will not stand up under the force of a swinging blow. Do not use a high speed dry grinding wheel. An ax ground on a dry wheel is likely to be ruined. Grind slowly on a wheel kept very wet.

When regrinding, start to grind from 2″ to 3″ back from the cutting edge and grind to about ½″ from edge. Work for fan-shape effect, leaving reinforcement at corners adequate for sufficient strength. Then "roll off" on a convex bevel.

Remove all scratches with whetstone or hone. A scratch on highly tempered steel will sometimes cause material to break where it is scratched.

Sharpening

Straight-edged tool—Place tool

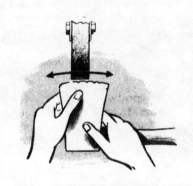

Removing nicks in the blade on a grindstone.

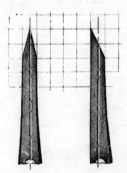

FOR GENERAL USE   FOR HEWING TO A LINE

Proper hatchet bevels—top view looking down on the hatchet.

RIGHT

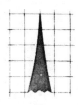

GROUND
CONCAVE

WRONG

GROUND
STRAIGHT

WRONG

on a lightly oiled oilstone. Tilt tool so bevel lies flat on stone. Exert slight pressure on tool. Hold right wrist rigid (no sidewise twist), and move tool back and forth on stone a few times. If tool is ground with a double bevel, turn tool over and repeat operation.

Curved-edged tool—Hold tool stationary. Place stone flat on bevel. Apply light pressure and move stone with a circular motion. Place stone on other bevel (if any) and repeat operation. If only one bevel is used, place stone flat on other side of tool head and remove wire edge with a circular motion.

Common Misuses

Do not strike heavy blows when tool is very cold. Breakage may result because frost makes steel brittle. Warm hatchet or ax before using in cold weather.

Sharpening the cutting edge for a single or double bevel with a grindstone. If your grip is steady enough and your eye alignment good, you have no problem. Otherwise, use a jig to insure proper angle for the bevel.

Hatchet bevel ground with a convex "roll off"—note correct shape. The concave and straight ground edges are not recommended.

A hatchet can be sharpened with an oil stone. Move cutting edge along the stone maintaining the proper angle for the edge bevel.

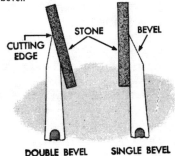

CUTTING
EDGE

STONE

BEVEL

DOUBLE BEVEL   SINGLE BEVEL

Hawk

This is a plastering tool usually used by professionals and infrequently used by the handyman. It is a small, square board with a handle underneath. Plaster or mortar is placed on the surface of the board. The hawk is held in one hand and the plaster or mortar is taken from the top of the board and applied with a trowel held in the other hand.

Hazards in Home, Check List

The following check list is a means of finding out if any potentialities for accidents exist, and an incentive to elminate them as soon as possible. The answers to these and similar questions will give you a good idea of the prevailing safety conditions in or about your home.

1. Are all stairs provided with railings?

2. Is there sufficient headroom on all stairs?

3. Are stairs adequately lighted?

4. Are there any loose rugs at foot of stairs or at places where sharp turns are frequently made?

5. Are floors or steps too highly waxed or polished?

6. Are steps cluttered with loose material or articles?

7. Is bathtub provided with handhold?

8. Are porches provided with railings?

9. Are chairs or unsafe substitutes used in place of ladders?

10. Are sharp tools left where children may handle them?

11. Is there a fire extinguisher in the home? What kind?

12. What type of matches are used?

13. Are matches kept where children cannot play with them?

14. Are plenty of ash trays provided for smokers?

15. Is kerosene ever used to light fires?

16. Are kerosene lamps ever filled while lighted?

17. Is gasoline used in the home for dry cleaning, etc.?

18. Is stove polish used? What kind?

19. Are combustible materials kept away from stoves and out of contact with stove pipes?

20. Is there a screen for the open fireplace?

21. What disposition is made of wastepaper?

22. Is rubbish allowed to accumulate in attic, basement, or elsewhere?

23. Are gas pipes or fixtures used to support clothes lines, clothing, or utensils?

24. Are gas cocks adjusted to turn smoothly but not too easily?

25. Are gas connections made with tubing? Is it in good condition?

26. Where are poisonous drugs kept? Are all bottles properly labeled?

27. Are any of the electrical circuits over-fused or improperly fused by pennies, etc.?

28. Is the frame of the electrical washing machine grounded?

29. Is portable cord for electric appliances or lamps badly worn?

30. Is portable cord of an approved type?

31. Is a stand provided for the electrical iron?

32. Are there any metal pull-chains without insulating links?

33. Are electric lights in bathroom controlled by wall switches?

34. Are portable electric heaters or other portable electric appliances used in the bathroom?

35. Is the outdoor radio antenna

equipped with a lightning arrester?

36. Is the automobile engine ever run in the garage with the garage doors and windows closed?

37. Are first-aid materials at hand?

38. Are porches, walks, and sidewalks kept in good repair and free of ice, snow, etc.?

39. Are cooking utensils on the stove kept and so used that a person will not be burned by steam or hot liquids?

40. Are the toys of the children maintained and used in a safe manner?

41. Are firearms kept in the home? If so, are they kept where children cannot have access to them?

42. Do you keep tubs or other containers filled with hot water where a child will not fall or stumble into them?

43. Are the laundry appliances so guarded that no one will be injured in their use?

44. Do you from time to time instruct the children in the prevention of injuries to themselves or their playmates?

Headboard

With an increased number of Hollywood type beds and those made by placing a foam rubber mattress over a flush door, there is renewed interest among homeowners in headboard making. It's a simple job to make your own headboard.

The headboard can be attached to any bed with screws through the headboard into the bed frame or with brackets fastened to the headboard with screws and to the bed with nuts and bolts. Examine your bed and decide upon the more convenient method for you.

There are innumerable headboards you can make. Many of them will fit into any room's dec-

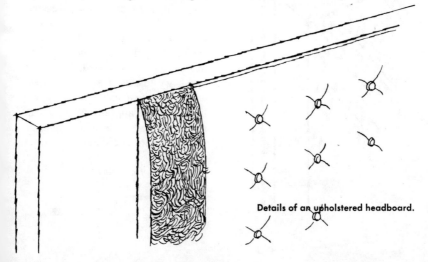

Details of an upholstered headboard.

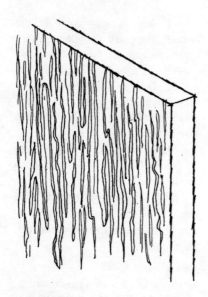

Decorative patterns can be "etched" into the wood's surface.

Perforated metal or hardboard can be set within a 2x3 frame.

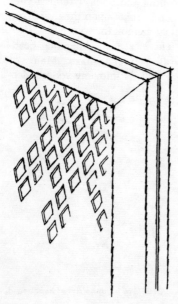

orating scheme, while others are purely contemporary or period.

For headboards with built-in features, see *Furniture—Plans*.

Here are 6 different headboards which Mr. and Mrs. Handyman can make. They can be built with simple tools and many of them can be made in just a few hours.

Upholstered Headboard

An upholstered headboard can be covered with any type of a fabric. If you use vinyl plastic, however, you will be able to clean the cover without removing it from the headboard. Just soap and water is all that's needed.

Use a piece of ¾" plywood, harboard or Novoply for the base. It should be as wide as the bed; its height depends upon your own taste. As a guide, your headboard should be about 4" to 6" higher than a pillow resting on end on the top of the mattress.

Cover the face or visible side of the headboard with a batting material or foam rubber. This can be glued to the wood to make the application of the vinyl material easier.

Cut the plastic large enough so that it can be nailed to the back of the headboard. If it is nailed to the edges of the ¾" board, it will be necessary to attach an edging strip with decorative nail heads. To relieve the flat appearance, you can use decorative nails in the face of the headboard and create an attractive pattern.

Also see *Furniture*.

Etched Pattern

You can use fir plywood or a

hardwood-veneered plywood, ¾"
thick, for the headboard. For the
technique of treating the raw edge
of the plywood see the section on
Furniture.

Select an attractive pattern or
design or purchase one from your
local dealer. Trace the pattern on
the plywood and rout out the upper
surface of the plywood so that the
pattern is "etched" into the wood.

Apply a finish—stain or natural
—to the wood surface. When this
has dried, use a thin artist's brush or
striping tool and paint the pattern in
a color that is best for the room's
color scheme and which produces
the best contrast with the wood finish.

Perforated Headboard

Another unusual headboard is
one made with a 2x3 frame and perforated metal or hardboard. Make
the frame with mitered corners at
the top two corners and a rail—or
cross piece—about 2" below the
top of the mattress. The rail is set
between the two side uprights with
either a butt joint held by blind dowels or two dado joints cut into the
side uprights.

A groove, however, is cut on the
inside face of the 2x3, into which a
piece of perforated steel or aluminum or perforated hardboard is
placed. See section on *Furniture* for
working details.

The 2x3 wood frame can be
made of hardwood and then stained
and finished or of select pine or fir,
which is sanded smooth, the holes
filled and then the entire surface
painted.

The perforated hardboard is

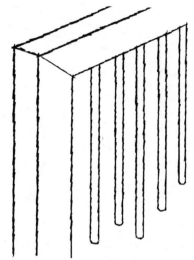

Dowels, either ¾" or 1", can be combined
with a wood frame to make an unusual
headboard.

Floor tiles—asphalt, rubber, cork, vinyl—
can be glued to the headboard base to
produce an attractive headboard.

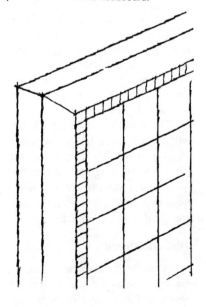

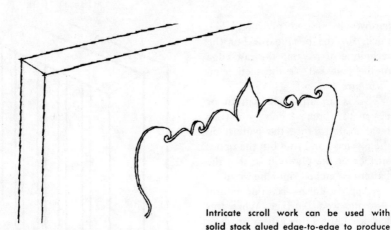

Intricate scroll work can be used with solid stock glued edge-to-edge to produce a striking headboard.

available in colors or can be painted. Perforated steel should be finished by applying an undercoat suitable for metal and then painted with enamel. Perforated aluminum can be left just as it's bought in the store.

Dowel Headboard

This is a variation of the perforated headboard. Dowels, either ¾" or 1" in diameter, are set vertically inside the 2x3 wooden frame. It is best to drill the holes in both the top and bottom cross pieces at the same time to make certain that they are aligned perfectly.

The dowels should be set into half the thickness of the wood and glued in place. The unit can be finished by staining the wood and painting the dowels. Or you might want to paint the frame in one color and the dowels in another.

Tiled Headboard

A striking headboard can be made by cementing floor tiles to the headboard base, which can be made of ¾" plywood, Novoply or hardboard. It is best to apply a 1" hardwood frame to cover the edges of the tile and plywood or Novoply.

You have an unlimited choice of tiles—types, sizes and colors. You can use two-toned cork tiles, rubber tiles, vinyl tiles or even asphalt tiles. Either all the tiles can be of one color or you can make a pattern similar to those used on floors or ceilings.

Scroll Design

If you prefer intricate designs, you can make cut-out patterns. A scroll design, copied from available plans, can be made by removing sections of the ¾" headboard base with a scroll, coping or jig saw.

It is necessary to seal all the edges of the plywood or Novoply and then apply an attractive finish. If you wish, you can use hardwood boards, glued edge-to-edge, for the headboard. This produces a most striking result by combining an attractive grain with the scroll cutouts.

Header

A brick placed with its end toward the face of the wall is called a header.

Header Joist

Frequently, the header joist is referred to as a header. Usually consisting of two 2x4's or two 2x3's, a header is used as the top of a window or door opening. When this is made of metal or masonry, it is called a lintel.

It is also used to describe the joist into which the common joists are framed around openings for stairs, chimneys, etc.

Heat Lamp

The heat lamp has many uses in the home. In addition to providing heat for therapeutic purposes, you can use a heat lamp to:

• heat wood surfaces when being glued and to keep them warm while the glue is setting.

• thaw frozen pipes.

• remove small surface dents in furniture; see *Furniture Finishing*.

• cure retouch job on white sidewall tires, preventing dust from marring the finish.

• dry out portions of a leaky roof for repair.

• heat putty to make it easier to spread.

• hasten the drying of wood fillers and Plastic Wood when making repairs before finishing a surface.

• heat soft clay to make it easier to mold.

• force indoor blooming of plants.

Photograph courtesy of Eff's Post

While a heat lamp can be screwed into any socket, it is best to use the bulb in a special wire cage to prevent accidental burning. This cage comes with an adjustable base.

• thaw icy steps and surfaces.

• thaw frozen locks.

• dry spark plugs, ignition coils and wiring in a car.

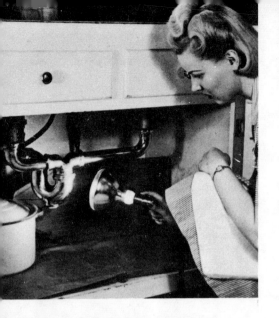

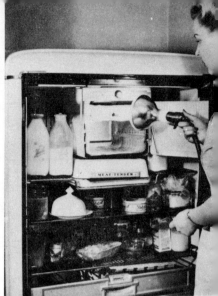

If the drain trap in the kitchen or any other pipes freeze in cold weather, a heat—lamp will help you to thaw it quickly.

Quick defrosting of a refrigerator is possible if you use a heat lamp.

Photographs courtesy of Sylvania Electric Company

• heat varnish and other surfaces on wood to make it easier to remove the old finish.

• warm linoleum and tiles to make them easier to lay.

• remove asphalt and rubber tiles from a floor.

• dry damp fireplaces and firewood.

• dry mold and dampness out of books and magazines.

• shrink cabinet or furniture drawers that have swelled from dampness.

• defrost frozen windshields and windows of a car.

• warm the motor, radiator, etc. before starting a car in cold weather.

• dry plant bulbs thoroughly before storing indoors.

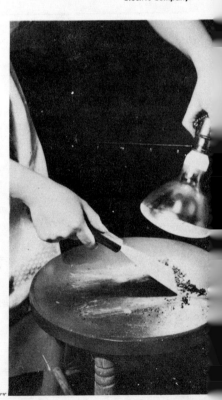

Heat lamp used to soften the old finish on furniture so that it can be removed with a putty knife.

Heating a Hard-to-Heat Room

If you have a room in your home that is difficult to heat, you can try several ways to make it more comfortable.

1. Insulate the walls. Either you can have loose insulation blown into the walls or you can add insulation yourself. Adding furring strips on the existing exterior walls, setting insulation between the strips and then adding a new wall, should help make the room a more comfortable place in which to live in cold weather.

2. Cold floors, in rooms on the street level, can be made warmer by adding insulation underneath. If there is a crawl space or basement (unheated), add insulation between the floor joists below. You can also add insulating board over the floor joists to prevent drafts from coming through.

3. If the room is located upstairs, check the insulation in the attic over the room. You might have to add additional insulation to that already there.

4. Stop air leaks around the windows and doors and through them as well. Make certain that all the panes of glass in the windows are securely held in place with putty. Add storm windows, if you don't already have them. If the room has an exterior door, weatherstrip the door and add a storm door. Also calk around window and door frames.

5. If it's possible, add additional radiators or air ducts in the room. This is often difficult for it involves ripping open the walls to run the pipes or ducts.

6. Add a space heater in the room. While you can use portable electric and gas heaters, a better technique is to use a radiant glass or ceramic heater which is attached to the wall. There is less danger of the heater being thrown over, of anyone stumbling over wires or being burned acidentally.

7. For localized heating, a heat lamp is very effective. This is particularly useful in a bathroom to warm the area around the baby's bath or dressing table.

8. Let an air conditioner heat the room. Some models have supplementary heat added to the cooling action. The fan helps to move the heat and you get filtered, fresh, warm air.

An electric ceramic heater which has a built-in thermostat and is attached to the wall.

Heating Cable

If you ever touched the electric cable that connects a toaster or a broiler to the wall outlet, after the appliance has been used for any protracted period, you undoubtedly found that the wire was warm. Specially prepared cable, that heats when connected, is used as heating cable.

This cable was designed primarily for use on farms, but it can also be used in homes. On the farm it can be used to keep the drinking water for animals from freezing in cold weather; in the home it can be used to melt snow and ice from the roof, in gutters or on outdoor stairs.

The amount of heat generated by the cable depends upon the diameter of the wire and the length of the cable. Most cables are made to give off from 2½ to 5 watts per foot. Thus, a cable that is 12' will be rated at 30 to 60 watts. These cables are well-insulated in a waterproof covering and can be used with specially-designed thermostats.

Heating cable comes with either plastic or rubber-covered exterior and can be immersed in water without danger. The plug, however, should be protected and used with a waterproof outlet.

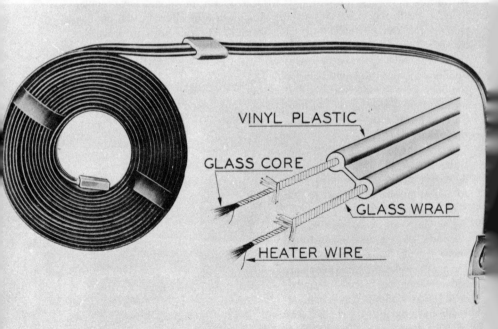

VINYL PLASTIC

GLASS CORE

GLASS WRAP

HEATER WIRE

Heating System . . . A, B, C's

Many types of heating equipment, both hand-fired and automatic, are used in homes today. The source of heat can be coal, oil, gas, electricity, sunlight, outside air, or even the earth, although the great majority of houses today use one of the first three. Which you choose for your new home, or convert to in an older house, will depend largely upon which is most easily and economically available and on the design of the house. For example, gravity systems and steam systems are not generally suited to houses with no basements. The room heating units which go with different systems vary greatly, and you may have a decided preference in that respect.

In general, the heating system will give satisfactory service if the capacity is adequate for the heating requirements of the house, and if it is properly installed, operated and maintained. The question of cost must consider not only initial purchase cost and installation, but the comparative costs of different fuels, as well as maintenance. All heating equipment should meet the standards of safety and performance set up by trade associations and technical societies, such as the American Gas Association.

Central heating systems which use coal, oil or gas consist of a burner, furnace or boiler, ducts or pipes, room heating units and usually controls.

Gravity Warm Air

Two of the basic systems used for gravity warm air heating are the central furnace system and the floor or wall furnace system.

In the central system a single furnace is used to heat a number of rooms. The furnace usually is located in the basement. However, some furnaces are designed for use on the main floor. The heat is piped to the various sections of the house where it is needed. As the air is warmed in the furnace it rises and flows through ducts and risers to the rooms. It enters the rooms through registers located in the floor or at the baseboards. In installations with the furnace on the main floor, the registers are usually located high on the walls or in the ceiling of the rooms since the furnace must be below the registers. Return air ducts at the floor allow the cool air from the rooms to return to the furnace for recirculation.

In the floor furnace and space heater systems a number of smaller furnaces are used. These furnaces are located either under the floor or at the wall of the rooms to be heated. Each furnace serves the room or rooms in its immediate vicinity. Heated air from the furnace rises and circulates into the room space. The cool air at the floor is drawn back to the furnace for reheating. Automatic controls are used with gravity warm air systems to regulate the heating.

This system is economical to in-

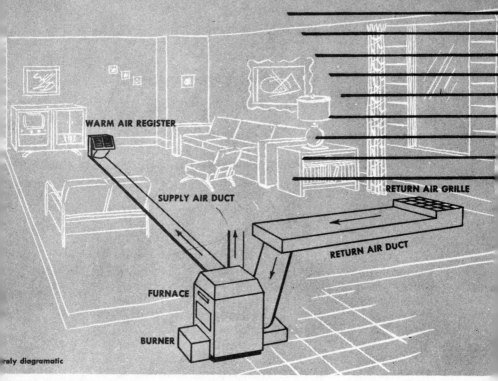

WARM AIR REGISTER

SUPPLY AIR DUCT

RETURN AIR GRILLE

RETURN AIR DUCT

FURNACE

BURNER

rely diagramatic

Sketches courtesy of Minneapolis-Honeywell
Rengular Co.

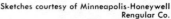

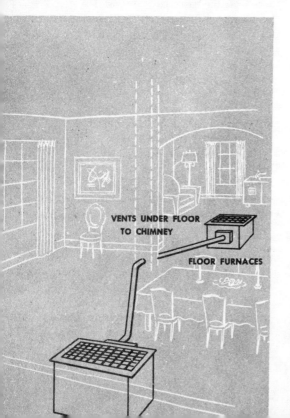

**VENTS UNDER FLOOR
TO CHIMNEY**

FLOOR FURNACES

stall, simple to operate and it responds to sudden changes in outside temperature. The air can be humidified by an evaporating pan inside the furnace casing. However, this system is best used in small, compact houses since the ducts should be as short as possible. The furnace and duct are comparatively large and reduce the amount of usable basement room.

The capacity of a gravity warm air system can sometimes be increased by installing a blower.

Forced Warm Air

Forced air heating systems may be used in both large and small homes. The furnace may be located at any convenient place in the basement or in a untility room. Heat for

the furnace is supplied by the burner. A blower located inside the furnace casing forces air through the heating chambers of the furnace. The warm air from the furnace is directed to the rooms through supply air ducts. The cool air from the rooms is returned to the furnace through return air ducts and grilles. Most forced warm air systems provide filters for cleaning the air and humidifiers for adding moisture.

In summer, the system may be used for air circulation. If the basement is cool, basement air can be distributed through the house. Proper selection of registers for the room outlets is very important. If plain registers are used, the air often does not spread out properly as it enters the rooms. The resulting air streams often produce undesirable drafts. This condition can be avoided by using diffusion registers; these have small metal blades which distribute the air softly and evenly.

Like the gravity system, forced warm air heating responds rapidly to changes in outside temperatures. It costs more to install but takes less space than the gravity system.

Gravity Hot Water

Gravity hot water heating sys-

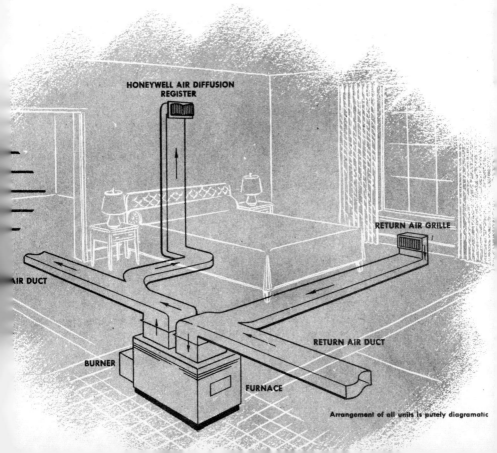

HONEYWELL AIR DIFFUSION REGISTER

RETURN AIR GRILLE

AIR DUCT

RETURN AIR DUCT

BURNER

FURNACE

Arrangement of all units is purely diagramatic

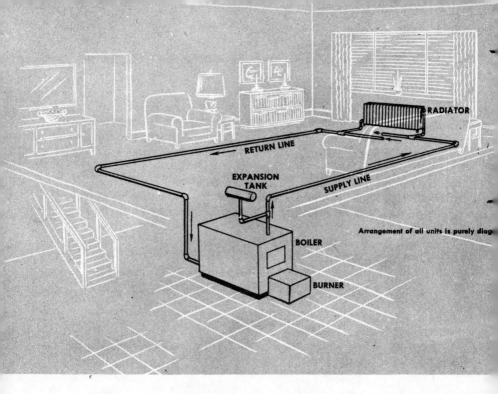

RETURN LINE

EXPANSION TANK

SUPPLY LINE

RADIATOR

Arrangement of all units is purely diag

BOILER

BURNER

tems may be used successfully in most types of homes. A basement is required as the boiler must be located below the radiators. The hot water supply line from the boilers to the radiators requires sufficient rise or pitch to induce circulation.

Heat is supplied to the boiler by the burner. The combustion chamber of the boiler is surrounded by a water jacket. As the water in the boiler is heated it tends to rise. Gravity effect causes the heated water to circulate through the supply line to the radiators (or convectors) in the rooms. Here the water gives off its heat and the rooms are warmed. The cooler water in the radiators returns to the boiler through a separate return pipe line. An expansion tank in the hot water system allows the water in the system to expand or contract with the changes in temperature.

In a closed system, higher water temperatures can be maintained and smaller room heating units can be used than in an open system. Since the water in the closed system is under pressure, the boiling point is raised and no steam is formed as it would be in an open system at the same temperature.

In a closed system, the expansion tank is usually near the boiler. In an open system it is located above the highest radiator and the water is exposed to air.

Both systems are economical to install but requires large supply and return mains. Response to temperature changes is comparatively slow because of the large amount of water retained in the pipes.

The capacity of some systems can be increased by installing a pump.

Forced Hot Water

Forced hot water heating sys-

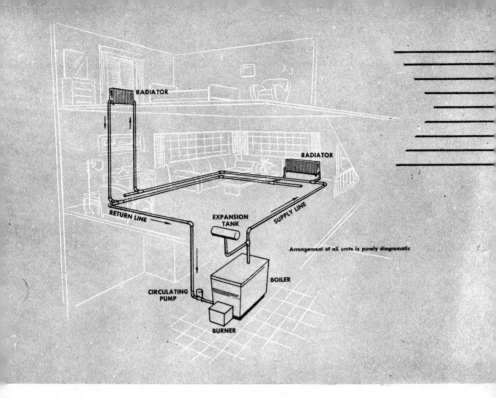

RADIATOR

RADIATOR

RETURN LINE

EXPANSION TANK

SUPPLY LINE

Arrangement of all units is purely diagramatic

BOILER

CIRCULATING PUMP

BURNER

tems may be used in homes of any size or shape. The boiler can be located either in the basement or the utility room. The heat for the system is produced by the burner which heats the water in the boiler. Two pipe lines, a supply and a return, connect the boiler with the radiators or convectors in the rooms. An alternate method permits the use of one pipe line for both supply and return by means of special pipe fittings.

A circulating pump, usually in the return water line, controls the flow of water through the system. It operates whenever heat is required in the rooms.

The function of the circulating pump in a hot water system is similar to that of the fan in forced warm air heating. It helps to get the heat quickly to where it is needed. An expansion tank allows the water in the system to expand or contract with changes in temperature. It also keeps the boiler and radiators filled with water at all times. Forced hot water systems are often used for radiant panel heating as well as for standard installations with radiators or convectors. Automatic controls regulate the heating for comfort, convenience, and safety.

This system responds rapidly to temperature changes. It costs more to install than the gravity hot water but the reduction in the size of the pipes used leaves a larger amount of basement space for other purposes.

One-Pipe System

A one-pipe steam system may be used in most types of homes. With this system the boiler must be located below the level of the rooms to be heated. Heat is supplid to the boiler by the burner. Steam for heating is generated in the boiler and rises through a large supply line.

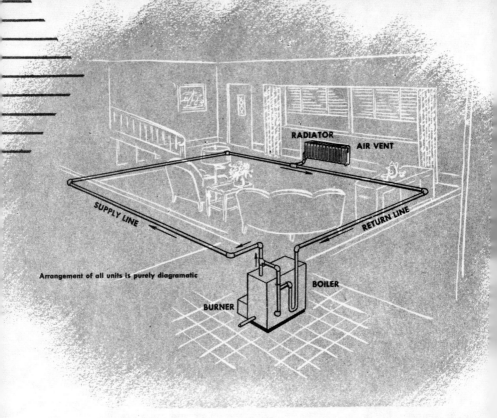

RADIATOR

AIR VENT

SUPPLY LINE

RETURN LINE

Arrangement of all units is purely diagramatic

BOILER

BURNER

Sketches courtesy of Minneapolis-Honeywell
Regulator Co.

Single pipes from this supply carry the steam to the radiators where it gives off heat and condenses to water. The water or condensate drains to the return line through the same pipe through which the steam was supplied. The return line carries the water back to the boiler. Air that may be in the radiators or steam lines is eliminated through air vents on the radiators. These vents emit the air but close upon contact with steam.

Two-Pipe System

A two-pipe steam heating system may be used in almost any type of home. The boiler may be located in the basement or in a utility room.

Heat for generating steam in the boiler is produced by the burner. The steam from the boiler rises through a supply line to the radiators or convectors in the rooms. Here it gives off heat and condenses to water. A separate pipe line from the lower end of each radiator drains the water to the return line. The return line carries it back to the boiler.

A special trap at each radiator prevents steam from returning with the water. Usually the piping is arranged so that gravity will cause the water from condensed steam to return to the boiler. However, if sufficient drop cannot be provided (as in a basementless house) then, a condensation pump must be used. It pumps the water from the return line to the boiler.

Radiant Floor Panel

Radiant floor panel heating usually is used in houses without base-

ments. In this, as in other radiant panel systems, no heating units are visible. When hot water is used, a network of pipes is laid on an area which has been prepared as the base for the panel. A layer of concrete is poured over the pipes to form the floor of the house.

In floor panel operation, hot water is circulated through the pipes by means of a circulating pump. The panel acts as a giant low-temperature radiator. The amount of heat delivered is controlled by regu-

lating the temperature of the hot water being circulated through the panel.

As heavy concrete panels do not change temperature very quickly, lowered night temperature is not recommended for radiant floor panel systems. The heating controls should be designed to anticipate heat requirements far in advance. Best results can be obtained with a system that measures both indoor and outdoor temperatures so that it can gage heating requirements quickly and accurately.

Arrangement of all units is purely diagramatic

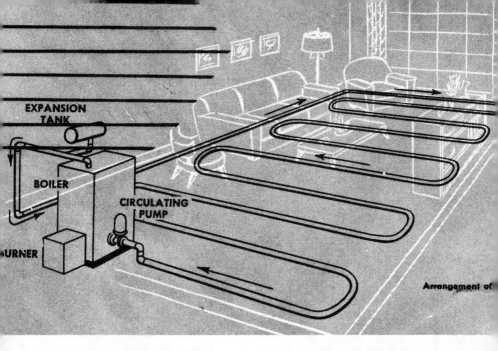

Arrangement of

Radiant Ceiling Panels

Ceiling-type radiant heating panels are used frequently for both single story and for multi-story dwellings. Their construction and operation is similar to that of floor

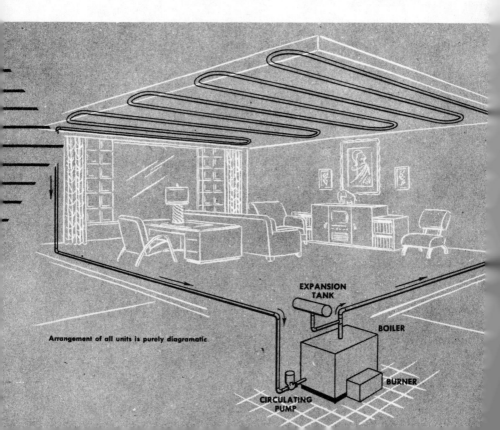

Arrangement of all units is purely diagramatic

panels. The heating coils are usually embedded in the plaster.

Radiant ceiling panels have considerably less weight or mass than concrete floor panels. For this reason, they can change temperature reasonably quickly. Automatically lowered night temperatures can be provided with excellent results.

In the hot water method, water from the boiler is circulated through the panels. The warm panel acts as a large radiator and supplies heat to the room.

Warm air or electricity may be used in place of water to heat the panels. In the warm air systems, the air is channeled through ducts in the ceiling. Sometimes a part of the air is distributed into the room. In electric panel heating, special rubber, glass or other heating units are used. They are installed either in the ceiling or in the wall where they radiate heat to keep the rooms warm.

Solar Heating

In true solar heating, the heat from the sun is absorbed and stored for later use. This heat is gathered by means of special heat collectors which are exposed to the sun. The collectors usually consist of a black metal plate behind a double panel of glass. Water or air is used to transfer the heat from the collectors

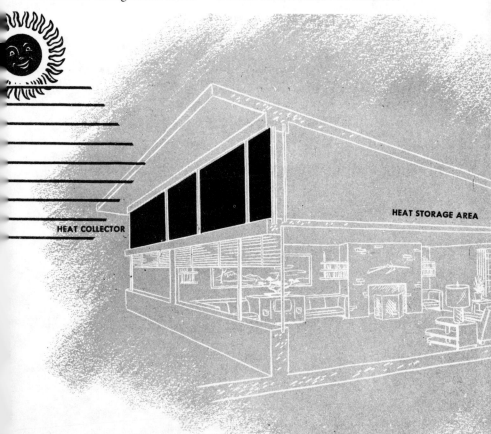

HEAT COLLECTOR

HEAT STORAGE AREA

to the heat storage areas.

The collected heat may be stored in various materials. Water works well and is easily available but requires a very large insulated storage tank. Chemicals, which provide for more compact heat storage, have been used successfully. Heat is released from the storage space as required to heat the home. Usually, the stored heat is converted into warm air and then circulated through the rooms by one or more fans. Solar heating systems must be able to store enough heat to keep the home warm at night and during cloudy weather.

Solar heat also may be used to supplement the conventional home heating system. Often large glass windows on the south are used to catch heat from the sun's rays. An extended roof provides for shading the solar windows in summer as the sun moves directly overhead. Many people, however, prefer to locate their picture windows on the north. This makes it easier to maintain even, comfortable room temperatures. The heat from the sun is absorbed by the larger wall area on the south.

Heat from a Pump

The latest development in home heating is the heat pump. It burns

Sketches courtesy of Minneapolis-Honeywell Regulator Co.

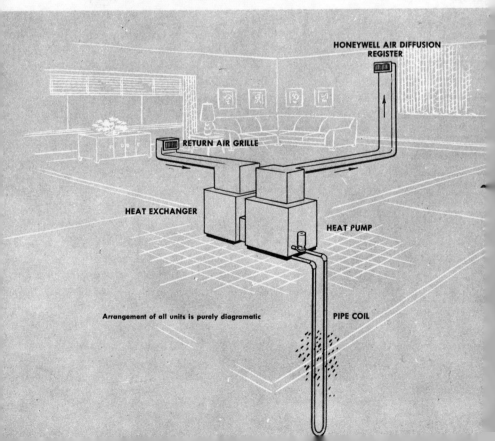

HONEYWELL AIR DIFFUSION REGISTER

RETURN AIR GRILLE

HEAT EXCHANGER

HEAT PUMP

Arrangement of all units is purely diagramatic

PIPE COIL

BASEBOARD GRAVITY REGISTER

BASEBOARD FORCED AIR REGISTER

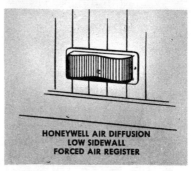

**HONEYWELL AIR DIFFUSION
LOW SIDEWALL
FORCED AIR REGISTER**

BASEBOARD RETURN AIR GRILLE

no fuel and therefore requires no furnace or chimney. Usually, its source of power is electricity. The heat pump utilizes the natural heat of the outside air or earth. It obtains this heat by means of a simple process of reverse refrigeration. If water is used, it is pumped from a deep well or through a coil of pipes buried in the earth. Heat for the home is extracted from the water. The process is similar to that used by your mechanical refrigerator in absorbing heat to keep the storage compartment cold. The water comes from the earth at its usual temperature. In the heat pump unit the water temperature is reduced a number of degrees as heat is removed. The chilled water is returned to the earth. The heat taken from the water is concentrated for heating the home.

Either a hot water or warm air heating system may be used to distribute the heat. In some heat pump applications the heat is taken from the outside air rather than from water. This method often is used in warmer climates where the air temperature stays above 30° F. In summer the heat pump process can be reversed and the unit can be used to cool the home.

Radiators and Registers

Usually the only parts of a heating system visible in the rooms are the registers or radiators which deliver the heat. Registers are used in homes with warm air heating while radiators are used in those with hot water or steam. Both registers and radiators are available in a number of different styles to meet your heat-

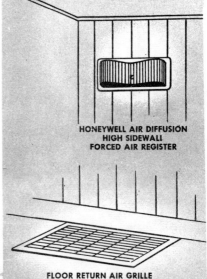

**HONEYWELL AIR DIFFUSION
HIGH SIDEWALL
FORCED AIR REGISTER**

FLOOR RETURN AIR GRILLE

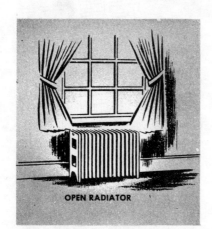

OPEN RADIATOR

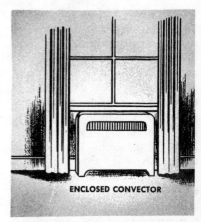

ENCLOSED CONVECTOR

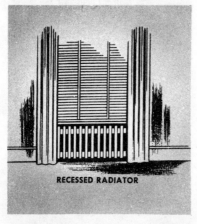

RECESSED RADIATOR

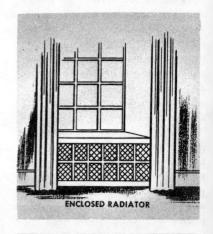

ENCLOSED RADIATOR

RECESSED CONVECTOR

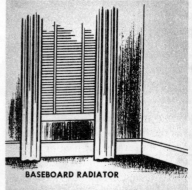

BASEBOARD RADIATOR

Sketches courtesy of Minneapolis-Honeywell Regulator Co.

ing and decorating requirements.

Register are designed for two types of warm air heating—gravity and forced air. In a gravity system baseboard registers are used to deliver the heat. Floor grilles provide for the return. In forced warm air heating, diffusion type registers are recommended as they distribute the air evenly and without drafts. These registers may be located either high or low on the walls or in the baseboard. The cold air return grilles are usually installed at the baseboard or in the floor.

Radiators of many types are used for hot water and steam heating systems. The familiar cast iron radiator is available in a number of designs and sizes. It may be installed as open radiation, enclosed within a grille, or may be recessed in the wall.

Another type of radiation unit used with hot water or steam heating is the convector. In a convector the hot water or steam is circulated through a finned metal tube. The fins heat the air which passes between them. Usually, the convector unit is enclosed in a cabinet which is designed to induce air circulation. If desired, the cabinet may be re-cessed into a wall.

A recent development in hot water and steam heating is the baseboard radiator. It looks like a regular baseboard but operates like a radiator.

Controls

Automatic controls are available for all types of heating systems and can be included in the original installation or added to existing systems. They are designed to save you time by running the heating system for you. They also add to your comfort by maintaining an even temperature in the house and save you money by preventing overheating. The temperature is maintained at a desired level by a thermostat, and if a clock mechanism is added, it permits you to lower the temperature for the night and have it raised early in the morning so that the house is again warm when you get up. Other controls include combustion controls, such as the damper controls on a coal furnace, operating controls for forced circulating systems, and safety controls such as the relief and reducing valves which regulate the pressure in a closed hot water system.

Heating Systems— Repair and Maintenance

To be sure that a heating sys-em will work successfully, you should use fuel suitable for the particular equipment and be familiar with its mechanical operation. Do not tamper unnecessarily with the controls or mechanism of the installation but, if competent, make small repairs. Major repairs, replacements or seasonal overhauling should be done by reliable and qualified heating mechanics.

A heating system should be maintained in good condition not only for operating economy but also to prolong the life of the equipment. Even during the heating season, the interior of the furnace should be inspected occasionally and cleaned if enough soot and dust have accumulated to lower materially the efficiency of the furnace. If the amount of soot collected seems excessive, it may be that the wrong kind of fuel is being used, that the furnace is not adjusted properly or that the dampers are not set to produce complete combustion.

At the end of the heating season, all heating surfaces of a furnace should be cleaned thoroughly of soot, ash and other residue. The smoke pipe should also be cleaned and the chimney, if necessary. In most localities, heating and plumbing concerns clean furnaces with vacuum systems which do not spread dust to other parts of the house. Professional chimney sweeps may be employed to inspect, clean and repair chimneys.

The smoke pipe of a furnace should be assembled with sheet-metal screws and held in place, if necessary, by wire or other incombustible supports. At the end of the heating season it should be inspected for holes or perforations caused by the corrosive action of flue gases. It should then be cleaned, dried and reassembled. Unless properly cared for, it may be necessary to replace the smoke pipe frequently.

All working parts of the heating system should be lubricated. Broken or defective parts should be replaced and all loose joints tightened.

Most cities require masonry chimneys with 4″ walls to be lined with a fire-clay flue lining, but unlined chimneys may be used if the walls are 8″ thick or more. The chimney should be examined to determine the soundness of the mortar joints. Sometimes mortar crumbles leaving openings in the joints and, unless these openings are repaired, they become a dangerous fire hazard, especially in cold weather when drafts are strong and the furnace is being fired to capacity. Joints in which mortar has crumbled, should be raked out to solid mortar before repointing. If the mortar has deteriorated too much, the chimney should be taken down and rebuilt. (See *Chimney Repairs*.)

Only flue openings that are in use should be left open. It is common practice, however, to connect gas and oil hot water heaters to the same flue that serves the house-heating equipment. Hot water heaters should be connected to the flue from 18″ to 24″ above the connection for the heating plant. If the smoke pipe extends into the flue space, it should be cut back flush with the flue wall. If the smoke pipe enters the chimney

on a descending slope, its position should be changed to enter at an ascending slope.

Soot Removers

Soot removers are intended to free heating surfaces of the furnace or boiler, the smoke pipe and the chimney from soot. Certain metallic chlorides, which can be vaporized by a hot fire and deposited on the surface of soot to lower its ignition temperature, may be used for this purpose. These chlorides are copper chloride, lead chloride, tin chloride, chloride of lime, zinc chloride and sodium chloride (table salt), of which copper chloride is the most effective and sodium chloride the least.

Some commercial soot removers contain a percentage of the metallic chlorides mentioned, but are more effective in reducing soot in the heating plant than in the smoke pipe or chimney. For information on cleaning chimneys see *Chimney Repairs*.

Get the Most out of Your Heating Dollar

The following list of suggestions will help you get more heat in your home for less money. Most of them require no mechanical know-how at all, the rest only the slightest.

1. Close doors promptly to keep all the heat inside.

2. Keep temperature moderate enough so windows won't have to be opened.

3. Turn off heat in rooms being ventilated.

4. Turn off heat and close doors of rooms not in use.

5. Close fireplace dampers when not in use. If dampers are missing and fireplace is not in use, close chimney opening.

6. Lower thermostat at night. (Setting it back 10° for 8 hours will save 10% or more.)

7. Lower thermostat to 55° when going away for a day or longer.

8. Check radiator valves for proper functioning. Replace non-adjustable steam radiator valves with valves of adjustable type. Drain air or water, if present, from radiators to allow them to heat up fully.

9. Check radiator enclosures to be sure they are not trapping heat.

10. Remove rugs and furniture from places where they block radiators or registers.

11. If your garage is heated, keep doors closed and temperature low.

12. Keep water in heating boiler clean for faster, more efficient operation.

13. Watch steam boiler water level. A boiler usually operates best if level is at center of gage.

14. Avoid overheating furnace. It wastes fuel.

15. Drain a pail of water from the bottom of domestic hot water tank monthly to insure efficiency.

16. Check and repair leaky hot water faucets. (A leak of only one drop a second means a loss of 700 gallons a year.)

17. Clean soot out of boiler. A mere 1/8″ soot deposit increases oil consumption as much as 10%. (Soot may be removed with stiff

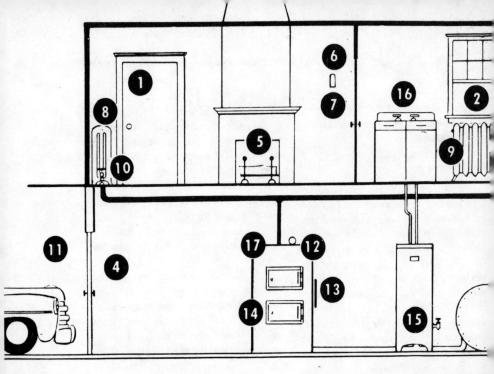

Sketches courtesy of American
Petroleum Institute

brush or special vacuum cleaner.)

The following changes cost you some money but pay big dividends in fuel savings.

1. Insulate your home.

2. Check your home for air leaks. See that hot water or steam pipes or warm air ducts are well insulated if they are located near outside walls.

3. Install storm doors, storm windows and weatherstripping. Put calking compound in all cracks.

4. Stop all air leaks around furnace.

5. Have furnace draft control checked to keep too much heat from going up the chimney.

6. The efficiency of a furnace may sometimes be increased by rebuilding the fire box.

7. Baffles in the fire box of some boilers and furnaces can give you more heat from less fuel.

8. Be sure your radiators are of proper size and are correctly placed.

9. Be sure the size of your heating plant is adequate.

10. Make certain that your radiators or heating ducts are "in balance." Avoid to much heat here, too little there.

11. Check the pitch of all steam pipes. Pipes of incorrect slope may block heat.

12. Be sure your thermostat is located so that rooms are evenly heated.

13. If you have a hot water tank, have a heat trap installed to stop heat loss caused by excessive water circulation.

14. Insulate hot water tanks.

15. Raise humidity by attaching water pans behind radiators or inside registers—or if your warm air furnace is equipped with humidifiers, make sure it is functioning properly—to increase comfort at lower temperatures.

Hot Water System

Ordinarily, it is desirable to leave the water in a hot water system from one year to the next to minimize corrosion, to prevent the introduction of air, and to minimize the accumulation of salts or sediment in the system. Air may accumulate in some radiators or convectors during normal operation. If the accumulation is too great, circulation is retarded and inadequate heating of the room or house will result. The room heating units should be vented regularly unless automatic air vents are used.

If it should be necessary to refill the boiler of a hot water heating system, it is easier if two people work together, one to control the flow of water into the boiler and the other to operate the radiator relief valves.

All radiator shut-off valves should be opened and the air valves on each radiator or convector closed. The draw-off cock at the lowest point in the system should be closed, and the valve in the supply line which feeds the boiler opened. As soon as the water in the pipes begins to rise, the air valve on each radiator should be opened, beginning with the one nearest the boiler, in order to release the air and permit the radiators to fill with water. When water begins to flow from an air valve, it should be shut and the operation repeated until all radiators are free of air and full of water.

When adding water to a boiler with fire under it, the fire should be low and the water should be allowed to flow in gradually. A large volume of cold water suddenly injected into a hot boiler may cause it to crack.

In an open hot water system, the water supply valve should be shut off when the water has risen to such a height that the expansion tank at the top of the system is about one-third full. The height of the water in the tank is usually indicated on a water gage glass attached to it. The water should be kept at the indicated level to insure complete circulation throughout the system. An overflow pipe attached to the expansion tank and leading to the outside of the

house or to a drain should be provided to carry off excess water.

In a closed system, the reducing valve will stop the intake of water at the required level.

Automatic Valves—Two automatic valves are usually provided to control the pressure in a closed hot water system. A reducing valve is used to admit water when the pressure in the heating system falls below the normal level and a relief valve is used to discharge water automatically when the pressure rises to a danger point. Occasionally, these valves become slightly corroded and fail to work properly. Under such conditions, they should be dismantled and the moving parts polished with fine emery cloth; they should then be cleaned and reassembled.

In an open system, which is not controlled by automatic valves, there is an altitude gage on the boiler to indicate the level of the water in the system. On the first filling, the water level is raised to the proper height in the expansion tank and this is checked by inspection. The red hand on the dial gage is then set in the same position as the black hand. Thereafter, proximity of the black hand to the red hand will indicate proper filling of the system.

Steam Heat and Hot Water Boilers

During operation, steam boilers should be kept filled with water at least to the center of the water-gage glass or to the level indicated by the manufacturer.

All accessories of the boiler should be in good working order and regulator parts oiled. A coat of paint applied to the external parts after the boiler is thoroughly cleaned will improve the appearance and promote durability of the metal. Silicone-aluminum and other suitable paints are available for this purpose.

If the water level is allowed to become low in a steam or hot water boiler, the heating surface of the boiler directly over the fire may be burned or warped, causing a serious leak.

Boilers should be kept filled with water when not in use. In fact, it is best to fill the entire system since rusting or corrosion is most severe at the water surface. However, attach a blue caution tag to a conspicuous part of the boiler so that there is no danger that the unit will be started without checking the water level.

Boiler Water Treatment—In localities where the water supply is unusually hard or where water is repeatedly added to the system, boiler water may require treatment. Commercial compounds are available for this purpose and should be used according to manufacturers' directions.

Fresh water is frequently treated with lime and soda ash (sodium carbonate) to precipitate scale-forming salts, and disodium phosphate or trisodium phosphate may be added to boiler water to produce non-scale-forming precipitates. Commercial water-treating compounds often contain some of these chemicals.

Blowing Down a Boiler—Sometimes an excessive amount of dis-

solved salts or the presence of oil or organic matter in the boiler water causes foaming or priming of the water, that is, the carrying of small drops of water out of the boiler with the steam. Trouble thus caused can usually be relieved by replacing part of the boiler water with fresh water. Foaming may also be eliminated by blowing the surface water along with the foam from the water while it is steaming. This is done through a special pipe or hose that has been connected to a threaded opening in the boiler at or near the level of the water line until no visible foam is discharged from the boiler. This work should be done by an experienced heating mechanic.

Repairing Boiler Sections—Occasionally, sections of a cast-iron boiler crack from sudden heating or other causes. If this occurs, it is sometimes possible to mend a crack by brazing or welding, particularly if it does not pass through a machined surface. Brazing is more often used since the welding of cast iron is comparatively difficult. It is usually desirable to employ experienced workmen to repair a cracked boiler.

For sealing leaks in boilers, there are many effective compounds on the market similar to those used in automobile radiators, but they should be regarded as temporary expedients.

Repacking a Leaky Radiator Valve

If a radiator valve leaks around the stem, it should be promptly attended to, to avoid damaging the floor and the ceiling below. Worn or

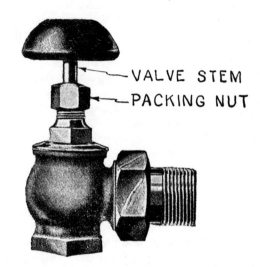

VALVE STEM
PACKING NUT

insufficient packing inside the nut, or a loose packing nut at the base of the stem may cause a leak. First try tightening the nut. If the valve continues to leak it is necessary to repack the valve.

Radiator valves are so constructed that the packing nut can be raised without lowering the pressure in the radiator. However, because you might loosen the valve accidentally, or the washer of the valve might be defective, this procedure is not rcommended for a steam system. For this system, it is advisable to let the fire go out, or at least to have a low head of steam, before starting work on the valve. For a hot water system, it may be possible to work without lowering the water level if the valve itself is in perfect operating condition. Close the valve and loosen the nut slightly; if there is no increase in the rate of water leakage you may proceed with the packing. If there is more leakage, lower the level of the water until it is below the radiator being worked on by opening the drain cock of the system.

To repack the valve:

1. Be sure the valve is closed.

2. Lower the steam pressure or the water level if necessary, as indicated above.

3. Remove handle by loosening the screw that holds it in place.

4. Remove packing nut by slipping it off the stem.

5. Clean out existing packing and any dirt which has accumulated.

6. Wind graphite-impregnated packing thread around the stem in a clockwise direction. Use a sufficient amount to fill the packing space in the nut. It should form a seal tight enough to prevent water and steam from escaping, but not so tight as to produce excessive friction on the stem when the valve is turned. (Metallic-coated cords are available for this purpose but are not recommended for the average handyman.)

7. If fiber or metallic washers have been used, replace them with identical units. If these are not available, use cord as in step 6.

8. Replace the packing nut; the packing cord can be pushed into the space between the nut and stem with a small screwdriver or other blunt-edged instrument. Tighten the nut.

9. Replace the handle and refill the system.

Radiator—More Heat

Want more heat from the radiator? Place a sheet of aluminum foil between the radiator and the wall; it will reflect the heat into the room.

If it is against an outside wall, this is a fine heat-saver.

Paint the radiator with interior wall paint. It may be more attractive to use gold, bronze, or silver paint; however, they are poor conductors of heat and you will not get the full value from your radiator.

Don't put damp clothes on the radiator to dry. This keeps some of the heat from the room.

Warm Air Systems

Filters are often used in forced warm air heating systems to insure cleaner air in the living space. They require occasional cleaning, however, or replacement if they are the throw-away type. If the filters become overloaded with dust and dirt, the amount of air circulation will be diminished, the air overheated and the efficiency of the heating plant reduced.

The frequency of cleaning or replacement of filters will depend upon the amount of dust which accumulates. Permanent-type filters may be cleaned by tapping the filter frame to shake the dust out or by washing the filter medium with soap and water or cleaning fluid. Throw-away type filters are not intended to be cleaned and are made of inexpensive materials so that they may be replaced at nominal cost.

In gravity warm-air heating systems where air filters cannot be used or in forced warm-air systems that have no filters, dust may accumulate on the heating surfaces of the furnace, and in the warm-air supply ducts. In such cases, the accumulated dust on the heating surfaces may give off an unpleasant odor when the furnace is being fired to capacity. If this odor becomes objectionable, the furnace and piping should be cleaned by commercial vacuum cleaning methods. If such services are not available, it may be necessary to dismantle the furnace and piping, in order to properly clean them. Where possible, an air filter should be installed to avoid recurrence of this trouble.

Humidifier Pans—Manually and automatically supplied humidifier pans are used in warm-air heating systems. In the automatic type, the mechanism for regulating the water flow to the pan sometimes fails to work properly because of the continuous evaporation of water. Precipitates, scale, or solids may form on parts of the mechanism, eventually preventing free movement of the levers and pins. Thorough cleaning of all parts should restore normal operation. The valve that controls the flow of water into the pan may also become

Automatic bleed valve for a closed hot water heating system.

warm after long use and require replacement. If excessive dust, dirt, or scale has accumulated in a humidifier pan it should be cleaned to avoid unpleasant odors.

Grilles—Floor grilles or registers may require frequent cleaning, since dust and small objects can easily fall in. This cleaning can usually be done from above the floor with a vacuum cleaner. If large objects have become lodged in the warm-air supply pipe, however, it may be necessary to dismantle the pipe in order to remove the objects.

Wall grilles or registers are not directly subjected to dust or other accumulation as are floor grilles, but may require dismantling for cleaning if they become clogged.

Coal Furnace

The inside of a coal burning furnace should be cleaned through the clean-out door with a wire brush and scraper. Furnace door hinges should be inspected, and warped or broken grates replaced. The grates and ashpit should be cleaned.

The fire should be shaken down at least twice a day to remove the ashes and to afford a better draft through the grates, if the furnace is hand fired. The ashpit should be cleaned daily, because if it is permitted to fill to a level where ashes touch the grate bars, there is danger of warping or burning out the grates.

In a stoker burning bituminous coal, the ashes are fused into clinkers which can be removed through the furnace door. In an anthracite stoker, clinkers are not formed, but the ashes are pushed aside and fall into an ashpit.

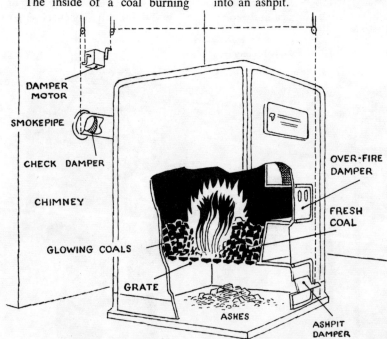

For a hand-fired furnace use egg, nut, or stove size coal. For a stoker use the kind of coal specified by the manufacturer. The coal should be treated to eliminate dust, but if necessary it may be sprayed lightly with water.

Automatic Coal Stoker—Stokers are intended to feed coal automatically into a furnace or boiler. The most common residential stoker is the underfeed type where a coal-feed screw, driven by an electric motor, supplies fresh coal from either a hopper or a storage bin into the firepot of the furnace. Air necessary for combustion is forced by a motor-driven fan through openings in the firepot.

A shear pin is usually provided in the shaft of the coal screw to protect the other parts of the mechanism in case the feed screw becomes jammed with large pieces of coal or other solid material which may be in the coal. If this occurs, the obstruction should be removed and the shear pin replaced.

Sometimes the "hold-fire" control, the purpose of which is to maintain the fire in the firepot, whether or not heat is required, feeds too little coal allowing the fire to go out, or feeds too much coal causing the house to be overheated in mild weather. Adjustments to correct this condition should be made by someone experienced in such matters.

Water pipe—When the heating

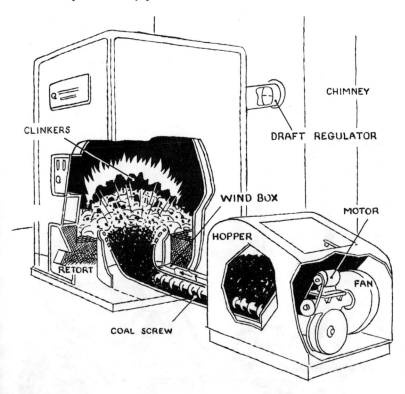

CLINKERS

CHIMNEY

DRAFT REGULATOR

WIND BOX

MOTOR

HOPPER

RETORT

FAN

COAL SCREW

season is over, coal, ash and clinkers should be removed and the stoker cleaned. The coal-feed screw and inside surfaces of the hopper should be coated with oil to prevent rust. Before the system is again put in operation, the stoker should be inspected, repaired if necessary, and adjusted by a competent service man.

The water pipe found frequently in the combustion chamber of coal furnaces for heating domestic hot-water may need replacement at intervals of a few years. These pipes may become burned on the outside from overheating or clogged on the inside with scale precipitated from the water as it is being heated. They may be renewed by draining the hot water system and replacing the original coil with lengths of standard pipe, bent or coiled to fit.

Automatic Oil-Burning Equipment

For mechanical service during the heating season, firms that supply oil for domestic burners have a yearly basis plan for repair and replacement of defective burner parts. This service generally includes emergency service calls as well as general maintenance.

1. Be sure your dealer sends a man to clean, adjust and repair your heating plant at least once a year.

2. Have this expert check size and angle of nozzle in your burner and clean filters, check blower, controls, ignition, etc.

3. Also have him make "stack temperature" and "CO_2" (carbon dioxide) tests on your furnace to determine its combustion efficiency.

4. Stop air leaks around the furnace. This is done with asbestos cement.

5. Stop all oil leaks, no matter how small.

Gun- and Rotary-Type Oil Burner—If the yearly maintenance is not available, the homeowner will find that the usual sources of trouble with gun- and rotary-type burners are clogged strainers, nozzles and fuel lines, and improperly located

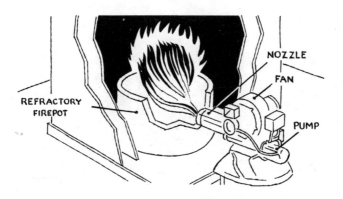

ignition electrodes. Most oil burners have a strainer or filter attachment in the oil line at the outlet to the tank or at the inlet to the burner. The filter or strainer is readily removed by taking off the housing or cover plate after the oil supply line has been closed. Use of a wire brush or jet of compressed air often proves the most effective means of removing the foreign matter from the strainer. Filters are not easily cleanable and should be replaced if they cannot be cleaned.

The nozzle and electrodes in most gun-type burners can be removed as one assembly through the rear of the burner. The nozzle should be removed by the use of an open-end wrench and should be carefully cleaned and reassembled. The electrode spacing is often about ¼ ", but is not the same for all burners and the manufacturer's literature should be consulted for exact information. The electrodes should be near the oil spray, but far enough forward and above or below the nozzle so that the spray will not strike them.

Pot-Type Oil Burners—To avoid a smoky, sooty flame in a vaporizing pot-type oil burner, the proportion of fuel and air should be properly adjusted. In the case of improper draft or wrong adjustment of

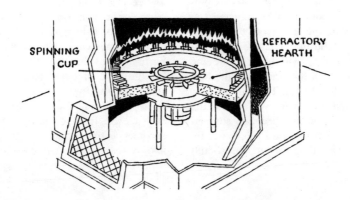

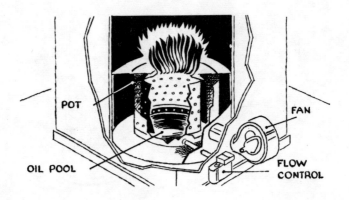

POT

FAN

OIL POOL

FLOW CONTROL

the combustion air, the burner may need cleaning more frequently than once a season, and sometimes as often as every few weeks.

A chimney of at least 15′ or 20′ in height is usually required to produce enough natural draft to operate at pot-type burner. An automatic draft regulator, placed between the oil burner and the chimney, is often used to maintain a steady draft at the proper level. Draft regulators will not function, however, if the chimney is not of sufficient height, in which case a small forced-draft fan can be used. The pot-type burner is usually cleaned by hand through the inspection door of the heater.

Soot in Oil Burners—Commercial soot removers may assist in removing the soot from the burner and combustion chamber, but ordinarily they will not remove the hard carbon that forms on the bottom of the firepot. The oil-feed pipe between the float valve and the burner sometimes becomes stopped with carbon and must be cleaned by forcing a rod through it. This should be done by a professional.

In any case, where a soot remover is used to burn the soot from a heater that has a smoke pipe, the chimney should be carefully watched for an hour or so because a soot fire may develop in the chimney which might ignite combustible material adjacent to the chimney.

Gas Burners

The most frequent difficulties with gas burners are the sticking of the plunger of the main gas valve, the accumulation of gum or other foreign matter in the pressure regulator, and the extinguishing of the pilot light. Repairs to the gas valve and regulator should be made only by the utility company's representative. A pilot light may be relighted by the homeowner after ample opportunity has been given for the combustion chamber to be aired out and after making certain that the main gas valve of the appliance has been closed. In case the pilot light becomes extinguished for an unknown reason, the furnace opera-

tion should be watched carefully for a time after relighting it to determine whether further maintenance or repair may be necessary.

Another source of trouble is improper adjustment of the primary air nozzle. If too much air is supplied, the flame will burn above the burner ports and not be in contact with the burner ports as it should be. If, on the other hand, too little air is supplied, the flame tips may become yellowish. Adjustments of the primary air shutters should be made by a representative of the utility company.

Pilot lights on gas-fired furnaces are sometimes left lighted during the summer to prevent condensation and rusting inside the furnace.

Photograph courtesy of Cleveland Heater Co.

Gas heating for closed hot water heating system.

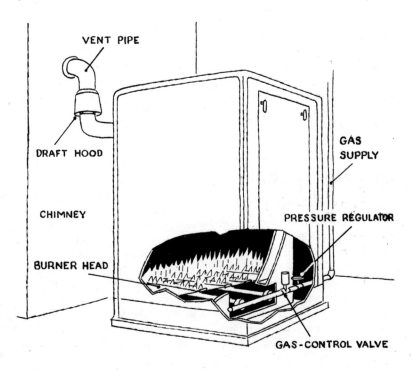

Coal Stoves

Where there is no central heating, and the coal stove is used for that purpose, it must be maintained in most efficient condition.

Cracks—A crack in the iron casing of a stove can be repaired by filling with stove putty or commercial iron-repair cement made of iron filings and water glass (silicate of soda). Enough of the filings should be used to form a thick paste. The paste should be forced well into the crack with the aid of a small trowel or putty knife, and the surface of the crack plastered over with the same material. Heat from the stove will harden the cement and make a tight joint.

Summer Storage—Stoves for heating are usually stored during the summer months. Before being placed in storage, however, they should be cleaned and polished and, if possible, wrapped with newspaper, burlap, or old carpet to protect them from dust and rust. They should then be stored in a dry place.

It is well to examine the grates and lining as soon as the stove is taken down and to have any needed repairs made at that time. If parts are found to be defective, an order should be placed promptly for replacements. The make and number of the stove should be given to the hardware or heating-equipment dealer when the order for the new parts is placed.

Stovepipe—Stovepipes need frequent cleaning, especially if the draft is poor. Soot collects in the pipe, particularly if soft coal is burned. Before taking down the pipe, it is well to cover the floor beneath and around the stove with newspapers or a drop cloth to protect the floor covering. The pipe should then be taken out of doors and away from the house before cleaning it of soot. When handling the pipe, be careful not to pound, dent, or bend the ends so as to make it difficult to fit them together again.

Stovepipe is usually made of sheet iron and should be kept polished to prevent rusting. When being put away for the summer, each length should be wrapped in paper and stored in a dry place.

Heating Systems— Insulation

Insulation on the boiler and pipes of a heating system will increase the efficiency of the system and reduce the cost of operation. Heat loss from a furnace or piping that is not properly insulated is not entirely lost as it warms the basement and first floor. However, in summer, if a boiler is operated to provide hot water, such heat losses serve no useful purpose and are, in fact, undesirable and uneconomical.

The small amount of heat that escapes through the insulating materials on hot water pipes, combined with radiation from doors or other exposed parts of the boiler, will warm the basement slightly, if it is well constructed and weather-

proofed; but ordinarily is not enough to provide a comfortable temperature in cold weather.

The extent of insulation is usually governed by the type of heating system and the results desired. The boiler and pipes through which water or steam is distributed to radiators should be covered, but the advisability of covering the return pipes depends upon the type of system and the amount of heat desired in the basement.

In hot water heating systems, covering the return pipes is recommended in order that water may be returned to the boiler with a minimum heat loss. In steam heating systems, it is advisable to leave return pipes bare, to aid in the condensation of any steam which might escape into the returns through defective thermostatic traps.

Boiler or Furnace Insulation

The tools and materials needed to insulate a boiler are included in the following list. Select the particular ones you need according to the method you will use to insulate.
TOOLS:

    Steel tape measure
    Heavy shears or sharp knife
    Marking pencil
    Trowel
    Wire-cutting pliers
    Container for mixing asbestos cement
MATERIALS:

    Corrugated asbestos pipe covering
    Galvanized wire
    Asbestos cement
    Wire netting

Applying chicken wire netting reinforcement.

Asbestos Cement—This method is best used on boilers that are not cylindrical. Apply a coat of asbestos cement over boiler using a trowel; this first coat should be ¼″ to ½″ thick. When the first coat is fairly dry and before applying the second coat, the wire netting should be stretched and fastened over the surface to hold the first coat. This might cause some cracking but the wire will serve as a reinforcement for both coats. Apply a third coat. Both the second and third coats should be about as thick as the first.

When the insulation is thoroughly dry, paint it. Aluminum paint is generally used but other colors are available as well.

Corrugated Asbestos Paper—A furnace which is cylindrical in shape may be covered with corrugated asbestos paper, although some asbestos cement will be needed as well. The quantity of asbestos paper would be sufficient to provide a three-layer covering for the cylindri-

Covering a cylindrical furnace.

To cover the vertical surface of the furnace, wrap three layers of corrugated asbestos paper around it and fasten with wire bands. The ends of the wires may be attached to bolts or other projections at or near the furnace doors. Obviously, holes for doors and other attachments should be cut in the covering.

The furnace top can also be insulated by laying three or four layers of corrugated asbestos paper over it. These pieces may be held in place by extending the asbestos-cement shoulder coating up over the edges of the covering.

The sloping shoulder of the furnace from which the ducts lead can be insulated with a covering of asbestos cement to a thickness of ½″ to 1″. The cement, which comes in powdered form, should be mixed with just enough water to make it workable, applied to the furnace, and troweled smooth.

Fiberglas—In newer systems, the boiler is generally protected with Fiberglas batts and may require no further insulation. If more insulation is necessary add Fiberglas batts.

Heating Pipes

For information on materials

cal surface of the furnace. The material is sold in rolls about 37″ wide that contain about 250 sq. ft. For the average 7-room house two rolls are sufficient. The galvanized wire should be #16 or #18. One small roll is required. A 100 lb. bag of asbestos cement should be sufficient to cover the sloping shoulder of the furnace, about 20 to 25 sq. ft. of surface, to a thickness of ½″–1″.

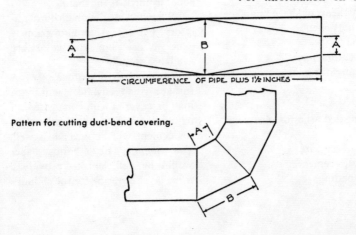

Pattern for cutting duct-bend covering.

SPLIT PIPE COVERING

META BAND

and methods for insulating heating pipes see *Frozen Pipes*.

Ducts

The ducts in a warm air heating system may be insulated to prevent the basement or utility room from getting too warm. If a warm basement is desirable, the supply ducts may be left uninsulated. In any case, it is not necessary to cover the return ducts.

Straight Ducts—Before ducts are covered, they should be clean and in good condition. To get the measurement of the covering, add an extra 1½″ to the distance around the duct to allow for thickness of the material and cut a strip of that length from the roll. Wrap it around the duct and tie it in place with a cord or wire in the middle and at each end. After this, measure around the outside of the covered duct and add 1½″ to get the length of the second piece. Tie this piece around the duct over the first piece, staggering the end and longitudinal joints, and proceed in the same way to apply the third or top layer. Finally, the three layers should be bound together by fastening bands of wire around the covering at intervals of about 18″.

Bends in Ducts—It is not absolutely necessary to cover the bends in ducts because they form but a small part of the system, but it is not a difficult job and will add to the efficiency and appearance of the covering. A 90° bend will require two or three pieces cut especially to fit, depending upon the number of separate sections in the bend. These

pieces should be diamond-shaped to conform to the surface to be covered. The dimensions may be obtained by measuring the widest and the narrowest parts of the bend, as shown in diagram. When all of the ducts and bends have been covered, a smooth, finished appearance can be gotten by pasting strips of asbestos covering over the joints.

Hot Water Tank

Hot water tanks heated by pipe coils in a coal furnace should not be insulated because such tanks are more likely to become overheated than uninsulated tanks.

Domestic hot water heaters are usually insulated. If a hot water tank is not well insulated, a cover can be bought ready-made to fit tanks of standard sizes. They are made of incombustible thermal insulators, similar to those used for pipe and boiler coverings. Some look like a large section of pipe covering, split lengthwise on one side so that they may be readily wrapped around the tank. If connection pipes are in the way, openings for them can easily be cut in the covering at the joint edge. Metal bands, laces, or other forms of fastenings are furnished to hold the covering together. The top of the tank may be covered with asbestos insulating cement.

Hedges

The selection of hedges to be used in landscaping is given in the section on *Landscaping*, according to the different varieties and sizes.

Hexagon Nut

The ordinary nut used with a bolt and which has six sides is called a hexagon nut. To tighten this type of a nut use an open-end or adjustable wrench, a nutdriver, a monkey wrench or, if the edges of the nut are protected, a parrot-head pliers. Hexagon nuts are the most commonly used type on machines or in cars.

Hexagon nuts come in many different sizes to fit the threads of bolts and hanger bolts.

Hickey

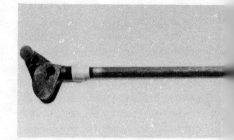

A hickey, encountered when doing electrical work, can be either a fixture or a tool. The fixture hickey is a small threaded brass or iron fitting placed in a fixture assembly be-

A conduit hickey is used to bend conduit or other pipe to the desired shape.

tween the support and stem to provide an outlet for the wires coming out of the fixture stem. It is used primarily in fixture boxes where the electrical ceiling light is fastened to a stem in the center of the box.

The tool hickey is known as a conduit hickey and is used to bend electrical conduit or other pipe to shape.

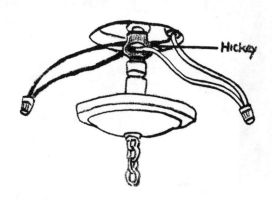

A fixture hickey provides the means of running the electrical wires to a ceiling fixture where the fixture is attached to a stem in the ceiling fixture box.

Hidden Surface Line

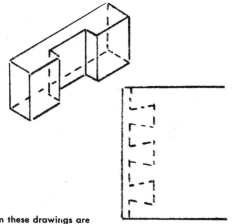

To designate a hidden surface, draftsmen and architects use a series of small dashes. This technique is used when illustrating perspective drawings of plans for furniture or other handicraft projects. A series of small dashed lines always indicates the surface of the hidden part.

Hidden surface lines in these drawings are shown in a series of small dashes.

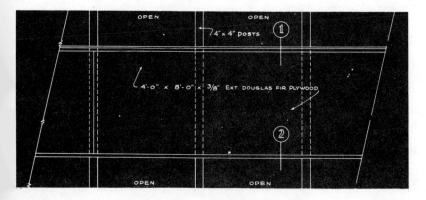

High Fidelity

What is high fidelity? As we apply it to home music systems, it is just about what the two words would imply: the reproduction of speech and music with as much realism and faithfulness to the original performance as is technically possible. There is no such thing as perfection in the reproduction of sound, but during the past few years improvements have been made which can best be described as startling.

How do we achieve this prodigious thing we call high fidelity? It comes of applying new and rigorous standards of performance to objects which are in appearance very similar to those commonplace items in the American home—the radio and the phonograph. There are also high-fidelity television sets and the tape recorder.

For almost three decades, the consumer bought radios with his eyes. Cabinets were fancy, dials were impressive, and the sound they produced, considered as an afterthought if at all, was barely intelligible. A few individuals, mainly engineers and musical hobbyists, knew what good reproduction can be, and constructed systems for their homes which astonished those who heard them. But until a few short years ago, when the long-playing microgroove record appeared on the market, the total of high-fidelity home radio-phonograph systems in the country was negligible. True, the number was growing every year. But there is no doubt that these wonderful discs sparked an amazing revival in the public's interest in listening to music at home. In the face of the competition of television, which monopolized the publicity until recently, a number of small manufacturers have been quietly building home reproduction equipment which has such intrinsic superiority to the conventional products it resembles that it has caused many to sit up and take note. Suddenly, high fidelity has been discovered by the entire electronics industry.

The incentive to develop a concert atmosphere at home is stronger than ever. The long-playing record has made a new source of uninterrupted diversion available to all. Tape recordings have long been used in making records and by broadcast stations for repeating programs. Now, several companies are introducing to the consumer market pre-recorded musical programs on tape. New developments in the technology of manufacturing tape recordings would indicate that this new medium of home entertainment may someday rival the long-playing record.

The Nature of Musical Sounds

For those willing to make the journey through the technical side of "Understanding High Fidelity" by Louis Biancolli, music critic, and Lester H. Bogen, member of the Audio Engineering Society, what follows is offered as a helpful guide.

Where necessary, analogies will be made that may seem over-simple and perhaps not completely parallel. Sound is a phenomenon of nature that does not always yield to ready-made definition or facile illustration. We take its presence for granted, but we seldom consider what it is.

Sound is largely a matter of vibrations moving through the air. It is important to stress "air," rather than space, because sound needs an "elastic" medium such as air to be able to travel at all. Sound cannot exist in a vacuum. Put another way, sound is a disturbance of molecules along its route of progression.

Now, it is the function of the ear to receive these vibrations and convert them into messages which the brain interprets as sound. The ear is so constructed that such vibrations, to be heard at all, must be of a certain minimum intensity. They must also be heard at a certain rate of repetition. The number of such cycles of repetition that occur in one second is known as the frequency of the sound. This accounts for the phrase "cycles per second." It is these frequencies that account for the pitch of a musical note.

Low frequencies (slow rates of repetition) determine a low note and high frequencies a high one. The highest frequency audible to humans is perhaps 20,000 cycles per second, and the lowest around 20. The majority of people, however, cannot hear well over the entire range, especially in the upper registers (over 15,000 cps).

Suppose we examine some of the advantages of high fidelity over other music systems by a comparison of their merits in reproducing the tone of brass instruments. These produce a characteristic sound in addition to the fundamental note played on them. This whirring sound results from a turbulent rush of air out of the bell or horn of an instrument like the trombone. It is located in the higher frequencies, not very loud, but very definite. The sound—or noise, if you will—is audible to the concert-goer. It is another mark of identification, one might say, of the brass instrument. It is lost in ordinary reproduction, but conveyed through high fidelity as another lifelike detail of realism.

The measure of the ability of a system to transmit all frequencies is known as frequency response.

Wide range frequency response is the most dramatic and widely publicized feature of the high-fidelity system, but equally important is the reduction of distortion. It is necessary to understand this clearly because, as much as anything else, it demonstrates the superiority of high fidelity over any other mechanical medium.

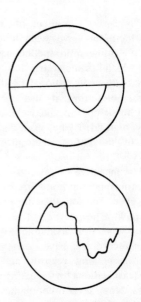

Distortion—Top: typical undistorted waveform. Bottom: typical distorted waveform.

Sketch courtesy of David Bogen Co., Inc.

Let us recall what we said before that a musical tone is a combination of the basic note and a web of surrounding sounds called harmonics. If the proportion between these is altered, the shape and quality of the tone resulting alters too. This means that the reproduced tone is not quite what was played on the instrument or uttered by the human voice. Distortion manifests itself usually by the generation of spurious harmonics which cause a slurred effect on what would otherwise be described as a sharply defined tone. High fidelity has reduced this harmonic distortion (as it is called) to an absolute minimum. Tests have shown that nerves grow fatigued from over-exposure to distorted sound reproduction.

How high fidelity adds realism

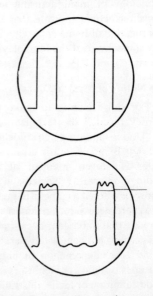

Transient Response—Top: good response to transients. Bottom: poor response to transients.

may also be seen in a study of certain percussion effects. Drums and other instruments of the percussion family produce sharp, staccato sounds. The picture of these sounds can be caught by an instrument called the oscilloscope. This is a device used by engineers to measure and examine electrical currents and percussion instruments appear on the oscilloscope as a succession of sheer walled plateaus, separated by flat plains. The effects take this form because the energy which produces them is enclosed in a very short interval of time. Both the sounds and the electrical impulses they give rise to are called transients. When properly reproduced, these effects are part of the realistc picture of "live" music. When they are not reproduced, the critical listener misses them. Sensitive response to these quick bursts of energy—or transients—is another achievement of the high fidelity system. It is one more clean, sharp, natural detail in the truthful picture of sound.

Distortions in Sound

Here, through the use of photographs, it is possible to show what is meant by distortion in sound. Your eye can see the differences easily, whereas, in sound, the untrained ear cannot detect the difference unless it is pronounced.

1. This print is good reproduction—it is similar to listening to recorded or broadcast music that sounds as if you were there with the orchestra.

2. This photograph is the visual equivalent of distorted narrow

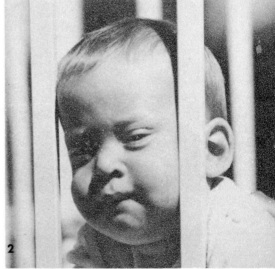

Speaker Enclosure

Photograph courtesy of Karlson Associates, Inc.

These are the components of a typical Hi-Fi system: the AM-FM tuner, record player and tape recorder feed their electrical impulses to the amplifier, which feeds electrical impulses to the speaker (inside of an enclosure) which converts them into sound waves.

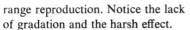

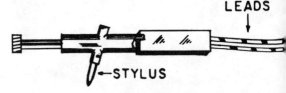

range reproduction. Notice the lack of gradation and the harsh effect.

3. This print represents the effect of poor transient response.

Elements of a High-Fidelity System

The word "system" is chosen advisedly to describe the high-fidelity hook-up. It is a system in which everything functions towards the one goal of absolute tonal naturalness; in which every component plays an equal and indispensable part. It is a system, in short, which has strength and quality only to the degree that each unit does its work in close technical harmony with the others. Before examining these separate units in detail, let us take a quick view of the complete system and notice how it differs from the conventional radio or phonograph-radio combination. A typical high-fidelity system begins, of course, with a phonograph player or tape recorder-player and a radio tuner. The electrical impulses put out by these units are fed into an amplifier. This, in turn, operates a loudspeaker unit in a suitable acoustical enclosure.

Cartridges

How does the cartridge work? Let us recall that the phonograph record is a storehouse of musical reproduction. When the original recording is made, the impulses which constitute the performance inscribe —or "graph"—on the disc a mechanical picture of the sounds produced by the performers. The record we play is a reproduction of the

Sketch courtesy of David Bogen Co., Inc.

The cartridge converts the signals engraved in the phonograph record into electrical energy and transmits them to the amplifier. The crystal cartridge is one of the methods of accomplishing this.

original disc. It contains the same "graph" made by the original impulses. When the record rotates on the turn-table, the phonograph needle—or stylus—is drawn through the grooves. As it moves from side to side, it is guided by the pressure exerted by the walls of the grooves.

To make use of the signals engraved in the phonograph record it

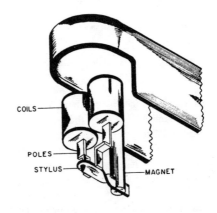

The magnetic cartridge, despite its added cost and the extra amplification required, is frequently preferred because the added compliance of the stylus means less wear on the records and a more nearly exact reproduction.

Today, many radio tuners and amplifiers are attractively designed in individual cases so that they need not be hidden in large cabinets with the other components or built into a wall unit. All you need is a convenient bench, shelf or table top on which to rest the tuner and amplifier. A single pair of wires to the speaker in its enclosure from the amplifier is all the wiring necessary.

Photograph courtesy of David Bogen Co., Inc.

is necessary to convert them to electrical energy, so that they may be amplified to operate the loudspeaker. The phonograph cartridge is the device which does this. The two most popular are known as the crystal and the magnetic. The crystal cartridge operates on a principle many hi-fi owners will recall from their high school physics, known as piezo electric effect. Certain materials, among them crystals of Rochelle salts, will produce tiny electrical currents if pressure is prop-

erly applied to the crystal. Connect a phonograph needle to a piece of this material and you have the phonograph cartridge. The magnetic cartridge performs the same function, but in a different way. Here the change from mechanical to electrical energy is made on the same principle that gives us the electrical generator.

A crystal cartridge is generally less costly, and some, using man-made crystals known as ceramics often give surprisingly good performance. But neither, it is felt, approaches the quality of the magnetic cartridge. It is therefore to be preferred, despite the added cost and the 'extra amplification needed by the signals produced by the magnetic type.

Another important factor to be considered in the choice of a cartridge is the compliance of the stylus assembly. This is the measure of the ease with which it responds to the sideways pressure exerted by the groove walls in order to produce the sounds we hear. The better cartridges are so constructed as to exhibit high compliance and, consequently, their use results in less wear on the records, as well as a more nearly exact reproduction.

This brings us to the subject of the needle or stylus. While this would seem to be contradictory, it has been found that the harder the needle the less damage it does to the record. Ordinary steel needles tend to wear out of shape after relatively short use. Once this happens, the needle may act as a chisel and cut into the sides of the record

Photograph courtesy of Flooring Division of the Rubber Manufacturers' Association

While a speaker can be mounted in an enclosure, located in a section of the room away from the tuner, amplifier and changer, you can mount the speaker on a baffle board, which is attached to the book shelves. In this way, you can add a Hi-Fi system—speaker in the book shelves and tuner and amplifier on a bench or table top—without adding another priece of furniture in the room.

groove. Two or three playings with the needle in this condition may suffice to spoil the disc. On the other hand, a hard needle, one made of precious stones such as sapphire or diamond, will retain its shape over a longer period and thus spare the record early wear. A diamond stylus naturally costs considerably more than either a sapphire or steel-pointed needle. However, it lasts many times longer, and because it does, it is actually cheaper in the long run. One has only to remember that each record represents an investment of several dollars. The rest is simple arithmetic.

Record Players

To some extent, the type of rec-ords you now own. or plan to own will dictate the type of reproducing device your high-fidelity system will feature. If you prefer to play all speeds and find changing records by hand a nuisance, the answer to your needs is an automatic record changer. If you plan to play only LP records you may choose a manual transcription turntable.

Manufacturers have for years made available automatic changers requiring a minimum of effort for the playing of all-speed records. Not all record changers are of the same quality, however. A perfect record player would revolve the turntable in complete silence without any fluctuation in speed. Its turntable would be level at all times. The arm

Corner Music Wall

All the comforts and quiet of home are in this handsome den. There is a Hi-Fi music wall with a TV set built into the corner and random hole acoustical tile is used on the ceiling. This is one way to build a folded horn into a room.

Photograph courtesy of Armstrong Cork Co.

which supports the needle should be light, but rigid, and mounted on bearings which cut friction to a minimum. Unfortunately, the conventional record changer is not capable of such perfection.

A slight fluctuation in speed, referred to by engineers as wow, is known to affect the pitch to some degree, and accordingly the quality of the music being reproduced. A noisy motor or set of gears will pass unwanted sounds through the amplifier and loudspeaker. Record changers found on conventional equipment usually have inferior car-

tridges and needles as well. The result is a clouding or blurring of the music, especially in low-register passages.

In order to minimize these defects, more care must be given to both the design and manufacture of the unit. Recognizing this, several manufacturers have introduced high-fidelity record changers which are available with a selection of high quality cartridges. These cost slightly more, but pay for themselves by increasing the life of the records played on them. There are also manual players which, in point of tech-

A pull-out drawer mounted with phonograph slides is used to house the turntable in the bottom of this corner music wall. See **Built-ins** and **Furniture** for how-to details. The tuner and amplifier are mounted on a shelf behind a drop door just over the turntable and the TV set slides into an opening left for it in the wall. This makes it easy to remove the set for servicing. The folded horn is attached to the wall and fits above the TV set.

nical performance, can meet all features of a record changer at considerable economy. There is often no loss in convenience because most single records are meant to be played on both sides. This is particularly true of LP recordings.

A good transcription turntable, because it is larger, heavier, and more precisely tooled to sensitive responses, will be used by the perfectionist. Driven by a sturdier motor, such a turntable eliminates noise and reduces speed fluctuations (wow) to an almost inaudible minimum. The tone-form is longer than the one usually seen on a changer, has an easier side movement, and leaves next to no trace of wear on either the record or the stylus. Excellent turntables have been designed to operate at all three speeds. They will handle records of any type or size.

Tape Recorders

To understand how a tape recording is made, we must apply the theory of the magnetic cartridge to the old high school physics experiment involving a permanent magnet and a quantity of iron filings. If we lay a sheet of paper over the two ends of a permanent magnet and sprinkle iron filings on top of the paper, the filings will orient themselves so as to produce a graphic reproduction of the magnetic field between the poles.

Magnetic recording tape is made by coating a base of either plastic or paper with millions of very fine particle of iron oxide. When the tape is passed through a magnetic field the particles tend to become magnetized themselves in proportion to the strength of the field. The recording head of the tape recorder is an electro-magnet, i.e., one whose magnetism varies both in strength and polarity with that of the electric current which energizes it. If the energizing current is a reproduction of a sound wave, we can see then that the magnetizing of the particles will follow a pattern which is a magnetic reproduction of the same sound. That, reduced to essentials, is tape recording.

Playback is achieved by passing the now magnetized tape over another head which, as it happens, is constructed in the same manner as the recording head. The variations in the magnetic field of the tape—which were caused by the recording head—produce an electrical current in the playback head. This current, amplified and properly equalized, is used to produce sounds in the same manner as the electrical current produced in the magnetic phonograph cartridge described earlier.

All that is necessary to re-use a tape that has been previously re-corded is to erase the magnetic image which it carries, and this is done by an erase head which re-aligns the iron oxide particles into an approximation of their original (prior to recording) condition. Most modern tape recorders are so designed that recording and play-back are accomplished automatically with the erasing feature only in use during recording.

Because of the limitations of the recording and playback head, re-corded tapes also require equalization, as do phonograph records. While the amount and type of equalization are not the same, the same general techniques are used to achieve it.

Radio Tuners and Receivers

Broadcasting in this country uses two systems—AM and FM. These initials stand for "Amplitude Modulation" and "Frequency Modulation." The latter offers infinitely wider frequency response, besides a superior filtering out of static and noise. Development in FM was proceeding apace when World War II

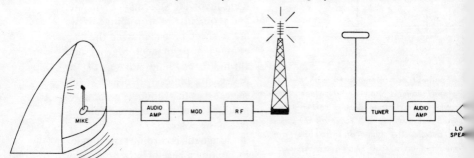

Schematic diagram of AM or FM radio broadcasting and reception. Those who insist upon getting the most out of a broadcast, frequently use a separate tuner to pick up the signals and convert them to audio frequency, and a separate amplifier which strengthens the signals so that they can drive the loudspeaker.

broke out and slowed it down. The number of FM stations is still small as compared to AM outlets. However, keener practical interest in FM has developed recently in radio circles because of growing public awareness of its superiority over AM. Many stations now broadcast simultaneously on AM and FM, and of course the sound portion of TV broadcasting is conveyed through Frequency Modulation. But most of the advantages of FM sound for TV are lost because the audio section of most TV sets is no better than that of a conventional radio.

Both types of radio broadcasting may be picked up by relatively simple, though different, receivers. However, those who insist on getting the most out of a broadcast must go one step further. To be able to pick up and hear the station in satisfactory clarity is one thing. The ordinary receiver will do that. But to respond to the finer subtleties and sensitivities of broadcast music, the receiver must contain special mechanical and electronic refinements. That, in turn, means more components to the system and added circuits, necessarily increasing the size of the unit. The receiver in many deluxe systems is therefore divided into 3 units to make installation easier. One is the tuner which actually picks up the signals and converts them to audio frequency. Another is the amplifier which increases the strength of the signals so that they can drive the loudspeaker, and the third, often combined with either of the first two, is the preamplifier.

Performance Characteristics of Radio Tuners			
Characteristic	Excellent	Good	Comments
Sensitivity	FM—5-10 microvolts, 30 db quieting AM—10 microvolts	10-25 microvolts 25-30 microvolts	This is usually expressed as a ratio of signal strength in microvolts to the amount of quieting or reduction in noise.
FM Drift	±25 KC, after a minute warm-up period	±50 KC, after a minute warm-up period	This is a measure of the ability of a tuner to keep tuned-in on the program.
Distortion	0.5% harmonic	1% harmonic	This is a measure of the fidelity of the tuner. It is expressed in terms of the output signal which the tuner feeds to the amplifier.
Hum level	60 db, below standard signal output	50 db, below standard signal output	This is a measure of the ability of the tuner to eliminate interference from its own power supply.

Data courtesy of David Bogen Co., Inc.

Like every other component in a typical high-fidelity system, the tuner is engineered to the finest precision. It is manufactured to feed into the amplifier signals that are almost the exact facsimile of those broadcast by the station. The distinctive features of high-fidelity radio reception may be summarized as follows:

1. *High sensitivity*—This is essential when amplifying a weak signal in order to provide the same strength and clarity that can be achieved with a strong signal.

2. *High selectivity*—A good tuner will be capable of separating two closely spaced stations so as to eliminate interference between them.

3. *Fidelity*—With a good tuner this may be achieved in two ways: a) by amplifying the handling signals without distortion; b) by accommodating the full range of frequencies transmitted by the broadcasting station.

Further considerations to bear in mind about tuners are these: The tuning should "stay put," that is, the tuner must be free from drift after tuning. Such drift is virtually impossible on a high quality tuner. A safeguard against it is known as automatic frequency control (AFC), a feature of many popular tuners. This consists of electronic circuits which prevent wavering and at the same time correct inaccurate tuning by the operator; thus tuning to stations is much easier.

Reduction of noise is another accomplishment of the high-fidelity tuner. To begin with, the tuner must have a noise limiting device as part of its design. Further, the tuner must be sensitive enough to amplify the signal to a point where this noise limiting mechanism will operate. A tuner which lacks sufficient sensitivity may bring in weak stations but fail to eliminate noise and static. Sensitivity is particularly important in suburban and fringe areas. If the FM tuner does not eliminate background interference, this will be much more conspicuous in a wide-range system than in a conventional narrow-range radio receiver.

A low hum level is still another feature of the high-fidelity tuner. Hum is a term used to describe the effect which household electric current can have when it interferes with the program. It would be particularly troublesome on a high-fidelity system for a very simple reason. Hum occurs at the frequency of the alternating current in the power line (60 cycles and its first harmonic, 120 cycles). Even with loudspeakers reproducing the lowest frequencies, a good tuner will keep the hum so low as to be negligible as a source of distraction.

It might be asked how ordinary radio sets function at all in view of their severely limited design. The answer, of course, is that the conventional receiver picks up only a small portion of the wide range of frequencies contained in the orignial program. Most of the hum, noise, and static is outside this band. So a radio set of the ordinary kind is spared a good deal of unpleasant distortion. There is a very simple way of showing the inferiority of the conventional product and, by the same token, the superiority of the high-fidelity technic. That is to play the conventional radio through a high-fidelity amplifier and loudspeaker. The inadequacies of the radio will be as clear as day.

Amplifiers

To understand the role of the amplifier, we start with the fact that electrical impulses are generated by the radio tuner, phonograph, or tape recorder. These impulses, as a rule, are too weak to be of any practical use. Vibrations must be produced in the loudspeaker which can be heard. To achieve this, tremendous amplification is required.

Here we see the difference in the range of tone correction provided by the high-fidelity tone controls (bass and treble) as contrasted with the limited action afforded by the single knob (tone control) used on conventional equipment. The solid lines show maximum deviation possible from the mid-position or zero correction setting. Top: control range with two controls, usually used with high-fidelity equipment. Bottom: single control knob range.

Sketch courtesy of David Bogen Co., Inc.

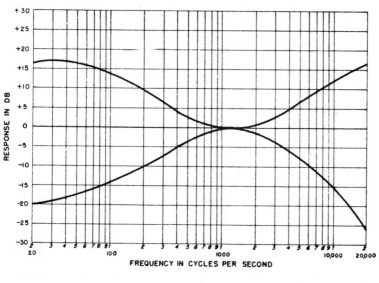

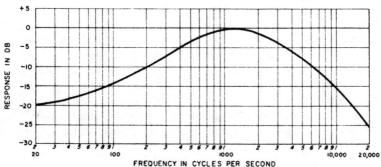

To explain in detail how the audio amplifier works is much too ambitious an undertaking for this exposition. Perhaps the easiest way of grasping the idea is to remember that the British call vacuum tubes (which make up the heart of the amplifier circuit) "valves." The use of the tube as an electronic valve gives the engineer the ability to magnify small currents. Consider the action of your foot upon the gas pedal of your car. A very slight pressure causes the motor to exert a large amount of power upon the wheels. This happens because the pedal is connected to a valve which controls the flow of gasoline to the engine. The engine does the work of moving a 3 to 4 thousand pound vehicle, but the movements of your foot do the regulating.

In the electronic amplifier, the current to be amplified, known as the signal, is applied to the circuit in such a manner that it controls the flow of a much larger current through the tube. In this case, with proper design and construction, the response of the large current to control can be so sensitive that it becomes an enlarged replica of the signal.

A power amplifier, moreover, must do its job of amplification without in any way marring or altering the electrical reproduction of the performance. Music, it will be remembered, covers a frequency range from 40 to 15,000 cycles. An adequate amplifier must achieve this range without serious distortion or omission of sound values. In the amplifier of a high-fidelity system

the extended frequency response insures in the performance an abundance of minute detail and shading unavailable to the set containing a conventional amplifier.

Amplifiers are usually rated according to the power they deliver to the loudspeaker with a specified amount of harmonic distortion. The lower the amount of such distortion, the better the output of the amplifier. Ordinary radios are rated at 10% distortion. This is the standard figure used by the radio and television industry in assessing vacuum tubes. Compare that figure with high-fidelity rating. Distortion in an amplifier delivering ten watts to the loudspeaker, measured according to the same standards, is held within a negligible range of less than ½% to a maximum of 3%. Ten watts is merely the nominal power rating of a high-fidelity amplifier. Many have reserves of power that can accomodate loud passages in a symphony requiring as high as 15 and 20 watts of electrical power, although at average levels less than one watt may be required. It has been shown that the human ear tolerates such quantities of power more easily when there is a minimum of distortion. This is why a radio set with a high degree of distortion sounds uncomfortably loud when compared to a hi-fi system which may be playing at the same or a higher intensity level.

Amplifying the electrical signals produced by a tuner or phonograph is only one of several functions performed by the amplifier. Ordinary volume control is of course found

Corner Music Center

Here is a corner music center that houses all the necessary components in a striking cabinet. It is easy to decorate and becomes the focal point of this handsome room setting.

Look at what you can get into a cabinet that takes about 4' of space along each of the two walls: the TV set is mounted in the center and directly below it between two hinged doors are the tuner and amplifier. In the cabinets on either side are space for record storage on the open shelf in the center and a speaker enclosure at the bottom. In the drawer of one side cabinet is a record changer and in the drawer of the other cabinet is a tape recorder. See **Built-ins** and **Furniture** for the how-to details.

Photograph courtesy of Armstrong Cork Co.

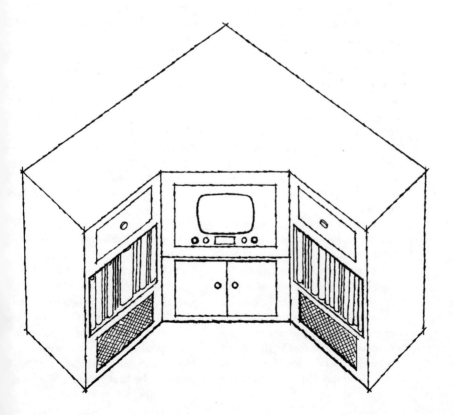

on every radio and phonograph. Besides this, however, high-fidelity systems incorporate more flexible controls that provide satisfaction over a much wider range of listening conditions. A high quality music system includes ways of providing record equalization through specially designed networks, tone controls, or both.

Record equalization, we will recall is a method of restoring the tonal balance of a recording to a close facsimile of the original performance. Such equalization, however, is valid at only one particular listening level. To enhance the beauty of the performance it is necessary to compensate for the special characteristics of both the room in which the system is located and the speaker and enclosure that are being used. This added flexibility is made possible in high-fidelity equipment through a set of controls that individually raise or lower the relative strength of high and low notes being reproduced by the system. Conventional equipments, if they have tone control at all, usually achieve it by means of a single knob, which, when turned, cuts either high or low frequencies.

Everyone knows that the acoustics of a room produces an effect on sound reproduction, just as the acoustics of a concert hall partly determines the effectiveness of a performance. Therefore, it is easy to understand the need for flexible tone controls. There is still another factor, however, and that is the actual level of intensity, what is ordinarily called "loudness," at which we listen

to music. This too has a decided effect on the fidelity of sound reproduction. It is a peculiarity of the human ear that, when exposed to sounds at various levels of intensity, it does not hear them all equally well. When listening to loud sounds, the ear registers well over its entire range. Listen to these same sounds at much lower levels. What happens? A considerable amount of the bass register, and to a lesser extent the treble, is lost to us. Now, since hearing and loudness are really subjective matters, we have a problem here.

The difficulty is introduced by the fact that the ear is not a good judge of "loudness." Assume that you're driving along on a summer's day and you have the volume of your car radio adjusted so that you can hear comfortably while you are doing 40 or 50 miles an hour. Have you ever noticed what happens when you stop for a red light, or if you happen to close the windows? The radio suddenly seems to be playing louder. That is because under the original conditions it had to overcome a considerable amount of background noise to attract your attention.

When you go to a concert in a large hall the orchestra is generating a large amount of acoustical energy. But, because even the best behaved audience makes some noise, you are much less conscious of the actual loudness at the live performance than you are when you listen to a reproduction in your home. Unless your home conditions are very unusual, the background noise level

will be considerably lower. This seems to be one of the reasons why people often listen to music at home at lower than concert hall level. When you adjust the volume control of your home music system to a setting which you consider to be a satisfactory equivalent to the loudness of the original performance, you are usually playing it at a much lower intensity level.

This explains, incidentally, why some early high-fidelity addicts insisted on playing their equipment at very high volume levels which made other wince. Luckily, this is one situation in which you can now have your cake and eat most of it too. That is, it is possible to play recordings at comfortable levels of intensity and at the same time to compensate for the deficiencies of the ear. A good set of tone controls can be used for this purpose simply by advancing the bass control as you diminish the volume and by adding a lesser amount of treble boost at the same time. Some manufacturers also feature what is known as compensated volume controls. These automatically increase the bass content of the audio signal as the volume level is turned down.

To achieve the same effect with a greater degree of precision, there has been developed a new device known as the "Loudness Contour Selector." Depending upon the level desired, the selector is set at one of the positions corresponding to the compensation required. More precise adjustments are then made through the volume and tone controls also provided in the high quality units which incorporate this device.

Loudspeakers

The loudspeaker is to radio what the receiver is to the telephone. The principle involved is pretty much the same. Just as the same electrical impulses enter both systems, so the same vibrations, translated into

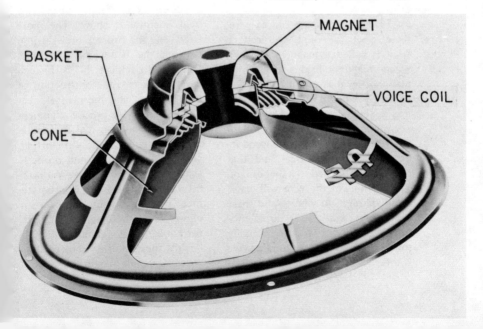

MAGNET

BASKET

VOICE COIL

CONE

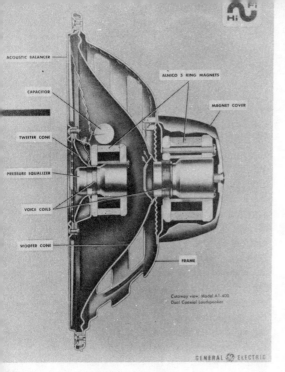

ACOUSTIC BALANCER

CAPACITOR

TWEETER CONE

PRESSURE EQUALIZER

VOICE COILS

WOOFER CONE

ALNICO 5 RING MAGNETS

MAGNET COVER

FRAME

Cutaway view: Model A1-400
Dual Coaxial Loudspeaker

GENERAL ELECTRIC

Cutaway view of a coaxial speaker showing tweeter and woofer.

music or words, pass through the radio loudspeaker on the one hand and the telephone receiver on the other..

Flowing through a coil of wire, these electrical impulses produce what is called a magnetic field. A second magnetic field is caused by a magnet. Because of the interaction of these fields the wire will move, if it is flexibly suspended. Let us now assume the current flowing through the wire is the electrical reproduction of a musical note and that the wire is attached to a diaphragm. The motions of the wire will cause the diaphragm to vibrate and these movements will set the air in motion, thus producing corresponding sound waves. Thus, the loudspeaker is a device for converting electrical

energy into mechanical energy. This, in turn, reaches us as sound.

The wire which is connected to the amplifier and receives from it the electrical impulses to be converted to sound waves is known as the voice coil. The magnetic field which interacts with that of the voice coil is produced by a permanent magnet. This is made of a special steel alloy containing aluminum, nickel, and cobalt, known as Alnico. The diaphragm operated by the voice coil is usually constructed on a cone of specially-treated paper and is designed to be light, but strong and tough.

Quality, again, is of paramount importance in the selection of a loudspeaker for a high-fidelity installation. The nominal size of the cone is alone no guarantee of quality. Often a well designed 8″ loudspeaker will produce better results than a 10″ or 12″ speaker of inferior design. For example, the performance of the loudspeaker depends on the interaction of the two fields mentioned above. The more effectively the two are brought into contact, the better the operation. One way to achieve this is through careful design and construction of both the coil and the magnet. Another factor is the precise alignment of the two units so that the coil is properly centered. It is important, also, to have a large and properly shaped magnet to achieve the powerful magneic field that is a requirement of high fidelity. Comparison of weight of the magnetic material used in conventional units and high-fidelity speaker often shows differences of pounds to ounces.

To capture the low notes of the organ or contrabass, otherwise known as the "bull fiddle," a powerful loudspeaker is needed to generate large movements of surrounding air. The voice coil must be capable of moving back and forth over a much longer path than that required for musical notes in the middle registers. To set these large masses of air in motion for the proper reproduction of rich low notes two things are essential—a large cone, or driving surface, and a a large and powerful magnet.

A note of caution must be injected at this point. This heavier equipment, while ideal for the reproduction of low notes, is less effective for high notes. Large cones tend to respond sluggishly to the short staccato pulses which generate the upper tones of the scale. To capture these high frequencies best a light and rigid diaphragm and a delicate and quick-acting voice coil are required. For the fastidious music-lover no one loudspeaker unit will meet both tests to perfection. Hence the recent trend towards divided units, with two or more separately handling the low and high frequencies.

It is not suggested that this multiple system has replaced the single unit. Far from it. And it should be stressed that a well-designed single unit will prove a better investment than a poorly-designed double unit. For one thing, it can later be utilized in a more extensive multiple speaker system, should the owner decide the time has come to improve his equipment. Actually, the very first step in improvement—that is,

from any mass-produced "set" loudspeaker to the most modest priced high-fidelity speaker—can be far more dramatic and breathtaking than any later one.

One method of splitting the frequencies without a complete double unit is to employ two driving surfaces, one a metal diaphragm and the other a paper cone, connected to one voice coil. These are so mechanically designed that the diaphragm reacts to the high notes and the cone to the low.

In the multiple speaker system each unit can be separately mounted or two or three can be mounted coaxially, and systems are now sold in which the audio spectrum is divided into two, three, or four bands. There are many ways of designing a speaker system even after the number of bands to be handled has been decided. On the low frequency end, for example, several methods are possible for achieving the large

A 12″ loudspeaker for high fidelity reproduction.

A dual coaxial speaker for full range sound reproduction.

Photographs courtesy of General Electric

notes a special speaker designed for reproducing only the higher frequencies. Equally picturesque is the designation for a loudspeaker designed to operate only at the lower frequencies: woofer.) Improvements at both ends of the frequency spectrum can later be made without discarding the initial equipment.

Enclosures

In selecting the loudspeaker or loudspeakers for a high-fidelity system, it is essential to have in mind exactly where it is to be housed. The nature and location of the enclosures cannot be separated from an intelligent choice of speaker. Here again the superior virtues of a high-

The "1221" speaker has a wide range of sound coverage.

cone area required. Loudspeakers as large as 18″ in diameter are commercially available. Electrically connecting a number of loudspeakers is also a possible method. Common arrangements for the more ambitious systems involve two 15″ speakers, two or more 12″ speakers, or a whole array of smaller units. For the middle and upper regions both cone speakers and small horns are used. Since upper notes are highly directional, it is necessary to incorporate a device for dispersing them, so that a broad area may be covered.

In the choice of a loudspeaker one or two other considerations should be weighed. If a moderate initial investment is intended, with hopes of future improvement, it is advisable to select a 12″ co-axial unit, or a 12″ single radiator speaker with separate tweeter. (Among audiophiles the word tweeter de-

fidelity installation become apparent.

Let us recall that the loudspeaker produces its effect by virtue of the back-and-forth movement of the diaphragm setting the air in motion. This motion, in the case of low notes, radiates out in the same way that ripples do from the splash of a pebble in a calm pond. Now, if the wave produced by one inward movement of the cone should reach the front of the loudspeaker just as the cone was moving to the front in the act of generating another sound wave, there would be the risk of impeding the formation of this second wave. To prevent this, a barrier must be set up around the loudspeaker to lengthen the path of the low notes. In that way, the opposite movements of air generated by the rear of the cone will not reach the front and cancel out the sounds. Enclosures which are designed merely

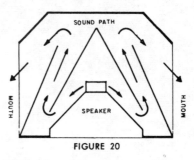

FIGURE 20

A folded horn is a complex speaker enclosure which helps to produce and emphasize the base tonal qualities and enriches the higher tones as well. See **Folded Horn.**

to separate front and back radiation of the loudspeaker are referred to as baffles. Such devices are known as infinite baffles when the above mentioned path is long enough to prevent any cancellation of low notes. This is achieved by mounting the speaker on a very large board or in the wall of a room, or if the baffle is completely enclosed.

These are the simplest forms of loudspeaker enclosure, and are quite effective if properly designed and constructed. However, the diameter of a baffle large enough to prevent loss of low notes must be several

A bass reflex speaker enclosure. The center sketch shows the opening made for the speaker itself and the port below. The sketch on the right shows how the enclosure operates to enhance the bass response.

Photograph and sketches courtesy of
Jensen Mfg. Co.

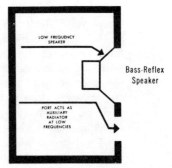

Bass-Reflex
Speaker

Photograph courtesy of Permoflux Corp.

The speaker enclosure aids materially in the truthful reproduction of sound. The enclosure is usually designed for use with specific types or makes of speakers. This unit, 24" wide, 23" high and 14" deep is used to house an 8" speaker and tweeter, assuring undistorted reproduction from 36 to 16,000 cps.

yards. This makes apparent the defects of the type of commercial radio console cabinet in which the loudspeaker is contained in an open-backed enclosure barely large enough to accommodate it.

It is not generally realized that air confined in a small, rigid container is not readily compressed. Thus, if we try to solve the baffle problem by enclosing the rear of the loudspeaker in a small box, without providing any means of relief for the pressure which builds up within it, the speaker diaphragm encounters a resistance to its largest movements. This resistance overcomes the force exerted by the voice coil and physically distorts the cone. The effect on reproduction can be very objectionable.

To improve speaker performance, several enclosures have been

designed to meet this need for venting in a small cabinet. The oldest and most commonly used of these is the bass reflex or phase inverter cabinet.

An 8" speaker can be housed in a bass reflex cabinet of only 1½ to 2 cubic feet. Satisfactory results can be achieved with a 12" speaker by enclosing it in a minimum volume of 6 cubic feet. For a 15" speaker 7½ to 8 cubic feet of volume will achieve the best results. This volume, proportional to the size of the loudspeaker is required to prevent the compression effect described above.

Man's ingenuity being what it is, loudspeaker enclosures of smaller size have lately been designed which produce startlingly good results. Most of these are similar to the bass reflex and employ the principle of the Helmholtz resonator developed in the 19th century—which goes to prove that there is nothing really new under the sun. But for perfectionists there is nothing to compare with the results achieved by a true infinite baffle, which to the engineer means housing the speaker in a structure of formidable proportions or in a wall separating two rooms. Nothing, that is, except the use of an exponential horn—a device even more cumbersome and complicated, which does for the low notes what nothing else can.

To see why this is so, consider that to produce low notes we have to generate large movements of the surrounding air. For a simple loudspeaker to achieve such results is almost impossible because it is so

Where space is limited, it is still possible to obtain faithful reproduction of sound and quality bass and treble reception through the use of specially designed small speaker enclosures. This small unit, contains two speakers and a tweeter with a range of 45 to 16,000 cps.

small compared to the volume of air which it is attempting to set in motion. But if in front of the loudspeaker we place a tube which flares out in a certain manner, the tube, known as a horn, acts as a coupling between the loudspeaker and the air, and more than doubles its efficiency. The performance of horns is determined by the rate at which their cross section increases, known as the rate of flare, and the area of the aperture from which the sound finally emanates. Horns designed for tweeters are short and small, but to reproduce a 60 cycle note, the horn must have an aperture of 10

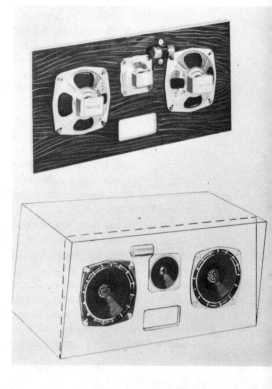

Here is a view of the actual unit without the decorative grille front, showing the two 6" speakers and the tweeter mounted in the center.

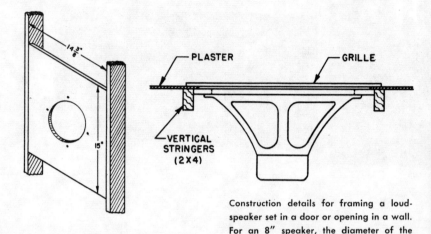

Construction details for framing a loudspeaker set in a door or opening in a wall. For an 8" speaker, the diameter of the opening should be 6¾"—for a 12" speaker, 10½"—for a 15" speaker, 13½".

square feet and a length of 4' to 8'. Obviously not many people are so interested in high fidelity as to desire an object of this size in their homes. But again, the engineers have been able to improve matters somewhat. Taking advantage of the fact that low notes tend to ooze around corners with ease, they have designed what are known as folded horn cabinets of reasonable size. If you happen to have a spare corner in your listening room, a horn type cabinet can produce extremely rewarding sounds. The trick is that the walls of the room act as extensions of the horn, and take over where the cabinet leaves off.

Whatever the size, shape, and type of enclosures you use, high fidelity can only be achieved by good construction. This means, for one thing, that cabinets should be firmly built, braced and padded to prevent internal reflections. The walls of the speaker cabinet should be made of wood not less than ⅝" in thickness.

One inch or more is preferred for large enclosures. This will prevent the sides of the enclosure from competing with the loudspeaker cone as a source of sound.

How To Conduct a Listening Test

It may seem presumptuous to offer suggestions on how to go about listening to equipment immediately after telling you that the subjective factor plays such a large part in selection of components for a high-fidelity home music system. But the human ear is fallible—and notorious for its bad memory. It is very difficult to compare sounds unless there is a good deal of difference between them, or unless you hear them almost simultaneously. This would indicate the necessity for making choices on the basis of direct comparisons, known in engineering circles as A-B listening tests.

Fortunately, it is not necessary to trundle your old radio console down to the hi-fi dealer's showroom

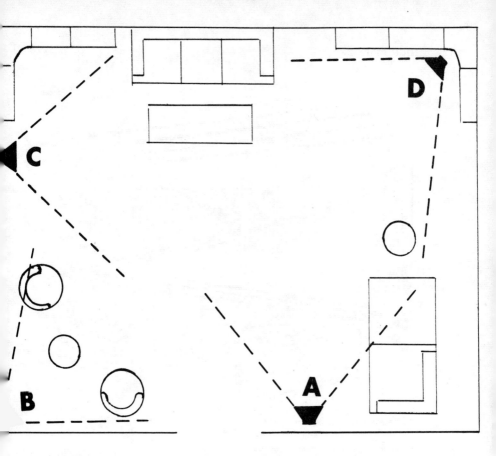

This sketch shows the effect of speaker placement on performance. Low frequency response has to be separated from high frequency because each imposes its own requirements, but obviously the best location is one which satisfies the needs of both. High notes, because they are directional, should not be blocked off from the listener. Upholstered furniture, in particular, will absorb a good deal of the high frequency energy radiated by the loudspeaker, so the arrangement of a room should not be such that furniture obtrudes between your ear and loudspeaker. Otherwise the speaker should be shifted to a different location.

• A speaker situated at point A will produce blind listening spots in the room. If you sit in the corner chair next to the speaker, you will not be able to hear the high frequency notes. Nor will you be able to hear them if you sit in either of the two round chairs in the other corner of the room.

• A speaker located at point B will be ineffective because the upholstered pieces and the round lamp table between the chairs will block the high frequency notes.

• A speaker situated at point C has limitations similar to those of a speaker placed at A. The listener in either of the two round chairs in the corner will be unable to hear the high frequency notes.

• A speaker located at D, possibly built into the corner book case, will produce the best results in a room of this type. The high frequency notes go forth unblocked throughout the room.

The angles speakers disperse sound evenly throughout the room. The three speakers are mounted at a 7° angle from the perpendicular. This lengthens the reflected sound path by directing it around the cabinet and breaks up direct back-wave reflections between the back of the cabinet and the speakers. It also tilts the sound waves up toward the ears of the listener.

Sketch courtesy of Permoflux Corp.

in order to hear the difference between it and a high-fidelity system. The impact of hearing high-fidelity sound for the first time is so startling that the differences will be obvious. It is in the selection of individual components, and in the comparison of one high-fidelity system with another that the actual listening tests become profitable.

In order to best evaluate the equipment which you audition, you should proceed in a logical manner. The best method is to start from

your own ears and work backwards; that is, decide on a loudspeaker first. If you have an idea of how much you want to spend for your entire system, use as a rule of thumb that the cost of the loudspeaker and its enclosure should be at least equal to the cost of the amplifier. If you plan to buy a separate speaker enclosure be sure that you listen to the speaker in that enclosure or in one which closely approximates it. If you are planning to use a console cabinet be sure that the loudspeaker you are evaluating is housed in a cabinet which approximates the dimensions of the enclosure of your console.

Ask that the speakers you wish to consider be connected to a high quality amplifier and program source (tuner, tape recorder or record player). For your first test listen at a level somewhat higher than that at which you ever expect to operate the system in your home, and note which of the speakers sounds best to you. Then repeat the tests at a lower loudness level. If the speaker you preferred on the first test does not sound as well to you the second time, ask that the various controls of the amplifier be adjusted to see if they will compensate for the difference. When you have made your selection, this loudspeaker should be used for listening tests of the other components you plan to purchase.

This is how critical listening to high fidelity should proceed. First select a phonograph or tape recording of a musical selection which has a wide range of frequencies. High-fidelity salons usually have a number of such records on hand for demonstrating the equipment. When listening at high levels try to detect such things as distortion, overhang, and acoustic feedback. We have already described distortion, and it manifests itself in sounds which are distinctly muddy and unpleasant to the ear. Overhang is a name we give to lack of crispness as the result of poor transient response. It is particularly noticeable on percussion instruments when, for example, you cannot separate the sound produced by the impact of stick against drumhead from the rumble which accompanies it.

Play a good recording containing high frequency sounds such as triangles, flutes, etc. and turn up the treble control so that you can hear the scratch in the record (or back-

ground hiss if you are listening to FM). Check the dispersion of your loudspeaker by walking back and forth in front of it and notice where the efficiency of reproduction of these high frequencies begins to drop off. A good high-fidelity loudspeaker should be able to disperse high frequency sounds so that you can get satisfactory results when you are so much as 45° off the axis of the speaker. This is important, because normally you may not be able to place your loudspeaker so that you will always have it facing directly at you, and the greater the angle of dispersion of the high frequency portion of the speaker, the more flexible can be your installation in the home.

The first comparison of amplifiers should be conducted at high level. But it is at moderate and low levels that the action of the individual controls for tone, loudness, equalization, etc. meet the real test. If the amplifier you are considering incorporates refinements which appear to be of doubtful value, you have the opportunity to assess them under conditions which are close to those under which you will actually listen at home. Notice particularly the effect of the various controls at all three levels. When your system is installed you will probably operate it at varying levels, depending upon the number of people in the room at any one time, the acoustics of the room, and the program material. Even though you may normally lean toward reproduction on the quiet side there may be times when you feel like turning it up.

Note what happens to low notes

A built-in across the end wall of this room has space between the cabinets for a TV console set. On either side, behind the hinged doors, is space for a record changer, tuner, amplifier, and if you like, a tape recorder plus record storage space. The TV speaker is used for the tuner, changer and tape recorder.

Photograph courtesy of The Upson Co.

Music Centers with TV

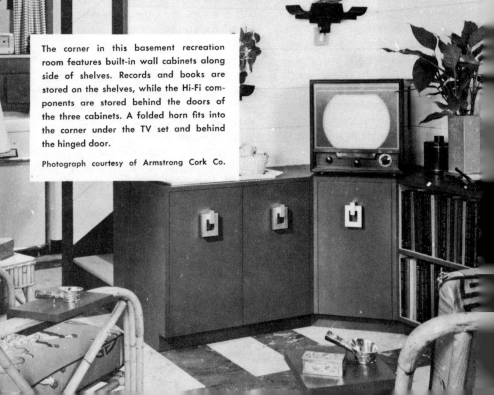

The corner in this basement recreation room features built-in wall cabinets along side of shelves. Records and books are stored on the shelves, while the Hi-Fi components are stored behind the doors of the three cabinets. A folded horn fits into the corner under the TV set and behind the hinged door.

Photograph courtesy of Armstrong Cork Co.

when you advance the bass tone control. Be certain, of course, that the record you are using contains passages which employ the bass instruments such as the string bass or the bass drum. The organ is also excellent as a test of bass response at high level. Are the real low notes being increased or is the tone control merely raising the lower middle frequencies? The tympani and the string bass in an orchestra usually play a tune. If after listening to several records, the bass always seems to strike the same note the chances are your loudspeaker is at fault.

Notice the way the record equalizer operates, if one is incorporated in the amplifier, and try it on several records of different manufacturers. Do not be perturbed if simply setting the equalizer does not provide complete satisfaction. Tone controls are meant to be used.

Next try listening to a record or an FM program (live) featuring a male voice. Naturalness in speech reproduction is a critical test for high-fidelity systems. A man's voice is to be preferred because it gives a better test of the smoothness with which the loudspeaker and amplifier reproduce the bass passages. Notice also whether or not the sibilance in speech is reproduced. When we talk, certain sounds, notably those making use of the letter S, are accompanied by a hissing sound known as sibilance. Insufficient loudness compensation results in a tone which has a "thin" sound. The full tonal range of the performance at high level is missing. You can dramatize this simply by turning from high level to low level without

The closet door installation has much to recommend it, particularly in rented quarters. The original door can be removed and stored, and replaced by an inexpensive door on which the complete music system is mounted. Only a hole for the speaker is cut for the door. The tuner-amplifier and changer are mounted on shelves attached to the inside of the door. With the door closed, the clothes give excellent acoustic absorption.

Sketch courtesy of Federal Purchaser

Audible Frequency Range For Music, Speech and Noise

frequency in cycles per second

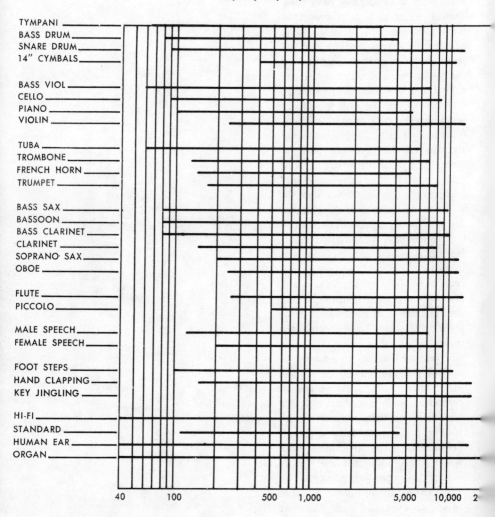

TYMPANI
BASS DRUM
SNARE DRUM
14" CYMBALS

BASS VIOL
CELLO
PIANO
VIOLIN

TUBA
TROMBONE
FRENCH HORN
TRUMPET

BASS SAX
BASSOON
BASS CLARINET
CLARINET
SOPRANO SAX
OBOE

FLUTE
PICCOLO

MALE SPEECH
FEMALE SPEECH

FOOT STEPS
HAND CLAPPING
KEY JINGLING

HI-FI
STANDARD
HUMAN EAR
ORGAN

40   100   500   1,000   5,000   10,000   2

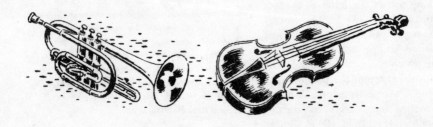

introducing any compensation at all, and then attempting to add compensation as required.

When checking built-in loudness controls be sure to try several records of different manufacture. Aside from the normal manufacturing variations in the production of records, different manufacturers record at different sound levels. The continuous-acting "compensated" loudness control used on some equipment is difficult to adjust for this variation because it is designed on the assumption that the signal fed into the amplifier is constant. Often it can be proved, by listening to phonograph records, that this is not the case. On AM radio reception, the variation in signal level of different stations is even greater. One solution to the problem is the Loudness Contour Selector described earlier. This device provides separate control of input signal and compensation, so that a wide range of variation in recording or radio program level can be accommodated.

With the choice of loudspeaker and amplifier out of the way, it becomes a simple matter to evaluate tape recorders and record players. Performance requirements imposed upon them are determined by the equipment through which they are played, as discussed previously.

The conditions for radio reception at your location must be taken into account when selecting a tuner. However, assuming that these do not dictate the purchase of an ultra-sensitive tuner, you should consider primarily convenience of operation

and listening quality when the unit is played through the rest of the system. Notice particularly the ease with which you can tune in on various stations. If you live in a metropolitan area check to see whether or not it is possible to hear separately stations which are close together on the dial. If the tuner includes a built-in preamplifier, the audio features should be tested in the same manner as suggested for amplifiers.

Demountable Music Wall

Here's an inexpensive fir plywood built-in that makes sense for music lovers. Instead of letting the components—radio tuner and amplifier, TV, record changer, record storage cabinets—clutter up the room, all are grouped together in one compact and efficient music wall.

Simple, interchangeable fir plywood "boxes" hold the radio tuner and amplifier, changer, TV, records and even have space for books. The speaker for the entire system is housed in a large "box" placed at the end of the music wall.

Materials Needed:		

FIR PLYWOOD

Number	Size and Grade	Where Used
2 panels	4'x8'x¾"— Interior A-A	Movable tops and sides, when these are visible from both sides
1 piece	4'x4'x¾"— Interior A-A	
3 panels	4'x8'x¾"— PlyPanel A-D	Bottoms, sides and backs where only one side is visible; TV front, speaker front, etc.

LUMBER

Size	Quantity	Where Used
1x2	12'	Speaker unit, radio, TV
2x4	30'	Legs, frame

HARDWARE AND MISCELLANEOUS

Item	Quantity	Where Used
Extension arms	3 pairs	Hold lid of radio, record player and speaker
12"x12" acoustical tile	1	Underside of record player lid
Fabric	as needed	For speaker cover and TV air vent
28½"x16½" asbestos sheet		Radio lid
Semi-concealed cabinet hinges	3 pairs	Lid tops

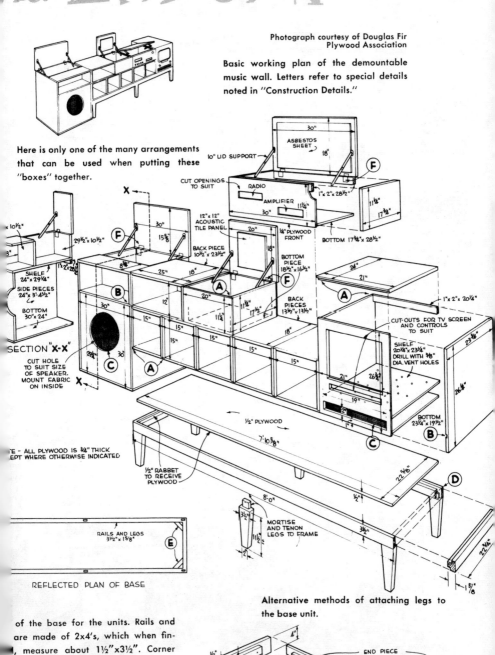

Photograph courtesy of Douglas Fir Plywood Association

Basic working plan of the demountable music wall. Letters refer to special details noted in "Construction Details."

Here is only one of the many arrangements that can be used when putting these "boxes" together.

30"
ASBESTOS SHEET
18"
10" LID SUPPORT
F
CUT OPENINGS TO SUIT
RADIO
AMPLIFIER
1"x 2"x 28½"
11¾"
11½"
17¾"
30"
BOTTOM 17¾" x 28½"

12"x 12" ACOUSTIC TILE PANEL
20"
¼" PLYWOOD FRONT
BACK PIECE 10½" x 23½"
15⅝"
18"
BOTTOM PIECE 18½" x 16½"
F

x 10½"
F
29½" x 10½"
30"
8½"
25"
18"
B
12"
20"
11½"
11¼"
17½"
BACK PIECES 13½" x 13½"

24"
21"
A

SHELF 24" x 29¼"
SIDE PIECES 24" x 3'-4½"
1½" x 28½"
BOTTOM 30" x 24"

SECTION "X-X"
CUT HOLE TO SUIT SIZE OF SPEAKER. MOUNT FABRIC ON INSIDE

30"
C
A
15"
15"
15"
15"
15"
24½"
30"

1"x 2"x 20¼"
CUT-OUTS FOR TV SCREEN AND CONTROLS TO SUIT
23⅜"
SHELF 20¼"x 23¾" DRILL WITH ⅜" DIA. VENT HOLES
26¼"
21"
26⅝"
19"
BOTTOM 23¼" x 19½"
B
C

NOTE - ALL PLYWOOD IS ¾" THICK EXCEPT WHERE OTHERWISE INDICATED

½" PLYWOOD
7'-10⅜"
22⅝"
½"
½"
½" RABBET TO RECEIVE PLYWOOD
D

8'-0"
3½"
11½"
2"
MORTISE AND TENON LEGS TO FRAME
3½"
22⅝"
1⅝"

RAILS AND LEGS 3½" x 1⅝"
E

REFLECTED PLAN OF BASE

... of the base for the units. Rails and ... are made of 2x4's, which when fin-... , measure about 1½"x3½". Corner ...es, 3" long with beveled corners, are ... to strengthen the base.

Sketch courtesy of Douglas Fir Plywood Association

Alternative methods of attaching legs to the base unit.

4"
½"
2"
3½"
2"
VIEW FROM INSIDE

END PIECE
ALTERNATIVE METHOD OF CONSTRUCTING CABINET BASE OF 1"x 4's AND 1"x 2's. ½" PLYWOOD TOP SHOULD BE CUT 22¼"x 7'-10¼" FOR THIS METHOD
4"
15"
1⅞"
VIEW FROM OUTSIDE

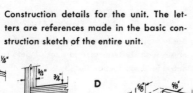

Construction details for the unit. The letters are references made in the basic construction sketch of the entire unit.

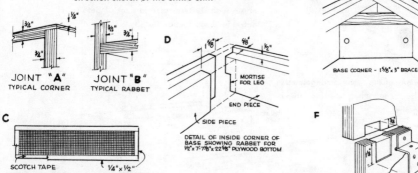

JOINT "A"
TYPICAL CORNER

JOINT "B"
TYPICAL RABBET

C

SCOTCH TAPE   ¼" x ½"

STRETCH OPEN-WEAVE FABRIC OVER INSIDE
OF SPEAKER AND VENT-OPENINGS WITH
SCOTCH TAPE OVER WHICH NAIL ¼"x ½"
WOOD STRIPPING WITH ½" BRADS

D

MORTISE
FOR LEG

END PIECE

SIDE PIECE

DETAIL OF INSIDE CORNER OF
BASE SHOWING RABBET FOR
½" x 7-7⅞" x 22⅝" PLYWOOD BOTTOM

BASE CORNER - 1⅝" x 3" BRACE

F

SEMI-CONCEALED
CABINET HINGE

Music and TV Center

With this compactly planned high fidelity music and TV center, you can have the best in listening enjoyment without clutter or inconvenience. Record storage is planned for 12″, 10″ and 6″ records plus record albums. The controls for the various components fit nicely into the design and are handy to get at.

The TV set has been placed on

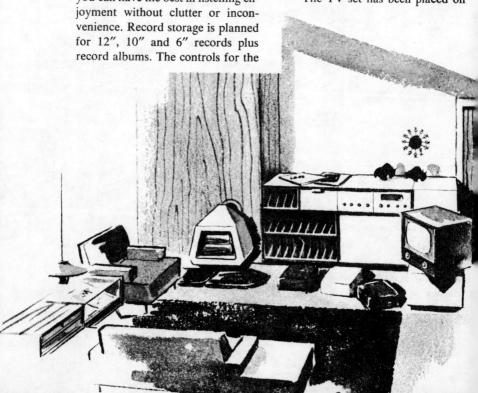

an easy-to-make turn-table mounted on window rollers so that the set can be revolved around 180°, providing a clear, head-on view of the screen through a full half circle.

The entire cabinet fits against a wall or it can be incorporated in a storage wall, either ceiling height or free standing. The speaker construction is the result of exhaustive research by General Electric sound engineers. The fabric for the speaker enclosure is mounted on a frame that is held in place simply by four spring catches for easy access to the speaker.

The unit can be stained or painted (see *Finishing—Plywood*) or it can be covered in laminated plastic, such as Formica or Micarta, or in vinyl plastic, like Boltaflex or Naugahyde.

Materials Needed:		
Number	**Size and Grade**	**Where Used**
4 panels	4'x8'x¾"— Interior A-A	Top, sides, bottom, partitions and shelves
2 panels	4'x8'x¼"— Interior A-A	Back, record partitions, mountings
LUMBER Size	**Quantity**	**Where Used**
1x1	26'	Speaker frame, separators for mountings, stringers, nailing pieces
1x2	2'8"	Changer slide mountings
1x3	11'	Speaker cover frame
2x3	25'	Base support
¼"x⅝"	33'	Edging strip for face of cabinet
¼"x½"	13'8"	Edging for shelves and dividers
¼"x¼"	10'6"	Beading for outside of frame for speaker covering
HARDWARE Item	**Quantity**	**Where Used**
Door pulls	4	Drop door, cabinet door and changer drawer
1'5" Piano hinge	1	Drop leaf door on changer
Semi-concealed hinges	2½ pair	Doors and drop leaves
Spring catches	4	Speaker covering enclosure
Lid supports	1 pair	Record changer drop leaf
"C" type slides	2	Changer drawer
Window rollers	3	TV turntable
Copper tubing, 1⅝" diameter with flange attached	3'	Axis for turntable and lead for wiring
Fabric	6 sq. ft.	Speaker enclosure face

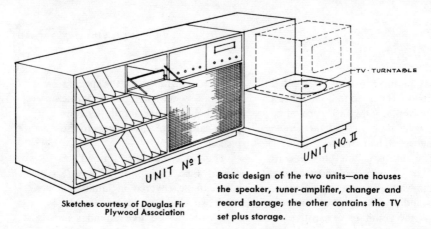

UNIT № 1

UNIT NO. II

TV · TURNTABLE

Sketches courtesy of Douglas Fir
Plywood Association

Basic design of the two units—one houses
the speaker, tuner-amplifier, changer and
record storage; the other contains the TV
set plus storage.

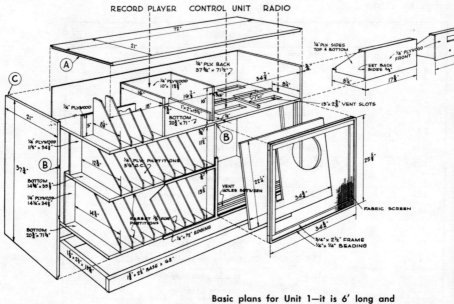

RECORD PLAYER   CONTROL UNIT   RADIO

Basic plans for Unit 1—it is 6' long and
21" deep with ample storage for a good-
sized record collection.

Detail plans for the changer drawer and
drop leaf door.

MOUNTINGS
CONTROL UNIT AND RADIO

DRAWER
RECORD PLAYER

LID
SUPPORT

3/8" x 1/2"
RABBET

PIANO
HINGE

DROP DOOR
RECORD PLAYER

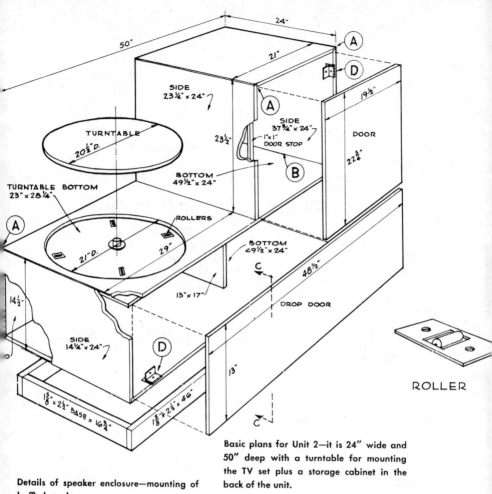

24"

A

50"

21"

D

SIDE
23¼" x 24"

A

SIDE
37¾" x 24"

19½"

DOOR

23½"

1" x 1"
DOOR STOP

22¾"

TURNTABLE
20½" D.

BOTTOM
49½" x 24"

B

TURNTABLE BOTTOM
23" x 28¼"

ROLLERS

A

29"

BOTTOM
49½" x 24"

21" D.

13" x 17"

C

48½"

DROP DOOR

14½"

SIDE
14¼" x 24"

D

13"

1⅝ x 2½" BASE x 16¾"

⅛" x 2½" x 46"

C

ROLLER

Basic plans for Unit 2—it is 24" wide and
50" deep with a turntable for mounting
the TV set plus a storage cabinet in the
back of the unit.

Details of speaker enclosure—mounting of
baffle board or screen.

¼" PLYWOOD TOP
14¾" x 34¾"

6"

1" x 3"

3"

1" x 1"

1" x 1"

1"

10½" D.

¼" x ½" EDGING

BULLET
CATCH

1" x 1"

¼" x ¼"
BEADING

1" x 3"

FABRIC
SCREEN

13"

14"

8⅝"

11¾"

SECT. ·A·

12¼"

2⅝"

SPEAKER
PANEL

A

1" x 1"

BULLET
CATCH

4½"

1" x 1"

1" x 1"

B

¾" ⌀ VENT HOLES
FACE OF BASE

DRILL ¾" ⌀ VENT HOLES
BEHIND - SEE SECT. B.

SECT. ·B·
4"

SPEAKER PANEL

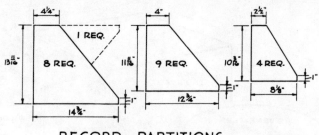

RECORD PARTITIONS
¼" PLYWOOD
Patterns for dividers for record storage.

DETAILS CONSTRUCTION

Construction details of basic parts. Letters
are details referred to in basic plans for
units 1 and 2

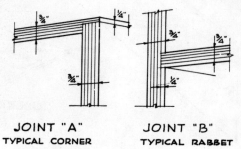

JOINT "A"
TYPICAL CORNER

JOINT "B"
TYPICAL RABBET

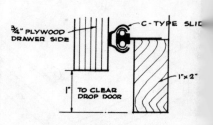

DETAIL - RECORD PLAYER DRA

Sketches courtesy of Douglas Fir
Plywood Association

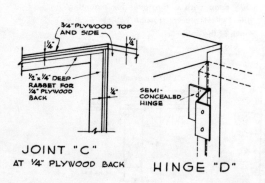

JOINT "C"
AT ¼" PLYWOOD BACK

HINGE "D"

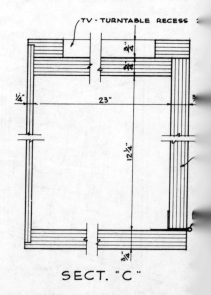

SECT. "C"

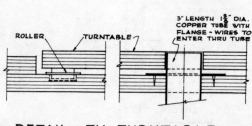

DETAIL - TV - TURNTABLE

Recess Your TV Set

If you want to recess your TV instead of building out from the wall to accomodate it, choose a spot against an unused deep space, such as a stairwell, or a closet, utility room or pantry where the small amount of space the set will need can be spared. The opening for the set can then be combined with space for a record player, cabinet or bookcases, depending on what you need and how much space you want to use.

The framing for the wall opening isn't hard to make. If you are making the bookcases, use 1"x12" pine boards for the sidepieces, nailed to the wall. Nailed to these is a front frame made of 1x3 strips,

TV set, viewed from living room at left, protrudes through wall into stairway, saving space. Exposing back also provides good ventilation, easy access.

doweled and glued at the corners, with a crosspiece at the point that divides the lower cabinet from the shelves above. The top and bottom of the bookcase are trimmed with molding to match that in the rest of the room. For details on joints and attaching shelves, see *Furniture*.

Finished off with one coat of flat and two coats of enamel, the result is a fine home entertainment center that takes up little space, yet houses everything needed for hours of leisure enjoyment.

Sides of bookcase (right, above) make use of stock, inexpensive 1"x12" boards, but dimensions can be varied as desired. Jig for gluing front frame can be made with 2x4's and wedges (lower left, above). Doors can be ¼" plywood panels set into grooved frames (top left) or simply plywood panels with decorative molding nailed at edges.

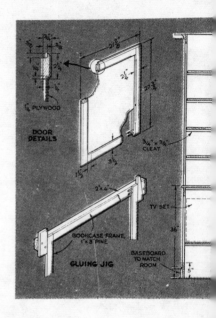

How To Cut and Frame Wall Opening

1. Drill starting hole at corner, insert keyhole saw and cut through stud (you may hit two) and both wall faces at the same time. Ends of cut stud are then trimmed back 1⅝" (the thickness of a 2x4) to take frame.

2. 2x4 spacer is nailed to adjacent stud on one side of opening, and header is shoehorned in to rest on top of spacer. Second spacer is nailed to stud on opposite side of opening to hold other end of header.

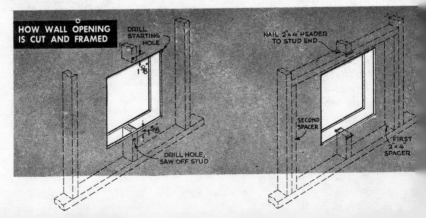

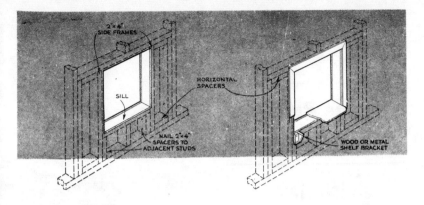

3. Side frames are nailed against horizontal spacers nailed to floor and underside of header on both sides of opening. Two short vertical spacers are then nailed to side frames at bottom and 2x4 sill nailed on top.

4. Opening is trimmed with decorative molding, wide enough to cover saw holes made in wall. Short shelf, deep enough to take set's overhang, is nailed to sill and brackets. Opening on bookcase side is also trimmed.

Sketch from "Tool Guide" courtesy of Stanley Tools

High Spots

This term is used in machine shop and woodworking shop practice to describe excess areas or surfaces. It designates spots to be taken down by grinding, scraping or planing in order to obtain an absolutely plane or flat surface.

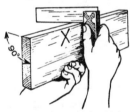

A square is used to test for high spots on a board. A plane is generally used to remove these high spots.

Hinge Nails

These oval-head nails are sometimes used in place of screws to fasten hinges to doors and trim and occasionally used with cabinet door hinges. The light hinge nails are $\frac{3}{16}''$ in diameter, while the heavy type are $\frac{1}{4}''$ in diameter. Available in sizes from $1\frac{1}{2}''$ to 3", the heavy type comes up to 4" long.

A hinge nail has an oval head and is $\frac{3}{16}''$ or $\frac{1}{4}''$ in diameter.

Hinge Repairs

See *Doors*.

Hinges

A hinge is a mechanical device consisting primarily of two plates and a pin. One plate is attached to the door and the other plate is attached to a fixed surface, either a cabinet side or a door jamb.

There are many types of hinges used about the home. Some are merely functional—bare essentials to do the job—while others are also decorative in design. Still others are invisible and cannot be seen from either side of the door when it is closed.

Hinges can be mounted in one of three ways. Many hinges can be

Special thin butt hinges are made which require no mortising. These No-Mortise hinges can be mounted without any special cutting. The space between the door and jamb is a minute fraction of an inch larger than when a butt hinge is mortised in place.

Folding screens require special hinges so that the individual panels can be moved or folded in either direction. Here is a special leaf hinge which opens in either direction. Available in different sizes, it should be set into a mortise.

A piano hinge is a special type of butt hinge. It is made in one continuous piece and comes in sizes ranging from about 6″ to several feet in length.

mounted in only one way, but the ubiquitous butt hinge can be mounted in all three ways, depending upon your requirements.

The Butt Hinge

Let's use the butt hinge as an example to show the three different ways in which a hinge can be mounted.

1. The hinge can be attached to the edge of the door and the cabinet with both pieces mortised or cut out, called a "gain," to receive the hinge. The edge of the door and the cabinet practically touch each other; a minimum of clearance is needed.

2. The hinge can be attached to the edge of both the door and the cabinet without any cutting. This leaves a gap between the door and cabinet, the thickness of the hinge.

3. The hinge can be surface mounted on the face of the door and the cabinet. The space between the door and cabinet is practically the same as if the two are mortised, but here the hinge is exposed.

Cabinet Hinges

In many kitchens built within the past several years, two major types of cabinet hinges have been used. The decorative surface hinge is widely used on natural-finished knotty pine cabinets while the semiconcealed hinges are used with the painted cabinets.

There are many types of semiconcealed hinges. Only a portion of the hinge is visible when the door is closed, just like a butt hinge when mortised, but the semi-concealed hinges do not have to be mortised.

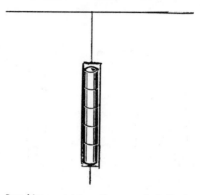

Butt hinge set in mortise or gain in both door and cabinet.

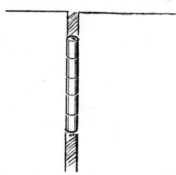

Butt hinge flush mounted to edge of door and cabinet. Shaded section is gap between door and cabinet frame—its width is the thickness of the butt hinge.

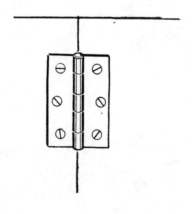

Butt hinge mounted on the surface.

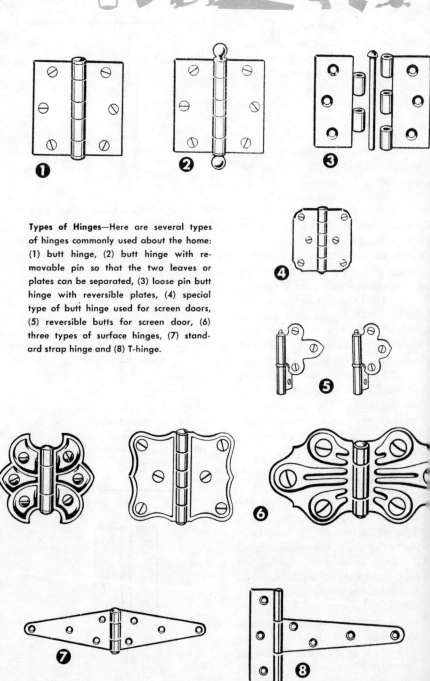

Types of Hinges—Here are several types of hinges commonly used about the home: (1) butt hinge, (2) butt hinge with removable pin so that the two leaves or plates can be separated, (3) loose pin butt hinge with reversible plates, (4) special type of butt hinge used for screen doors, (5) reversible butts for screen door, (6) three types of surface hinges, (7) standard strap hinge and (8) T-hinge.

Therefore, they are quicker and easier to install.

Semi-concealed hinges are made for mounting with doors that have rabetted edges as well as for flush doors. In the accompanying sketch, you will see 6 different hinges used for these two types of installations. The hinges are mounted either on the edge or the face of the cabinet side and along the edge or rear face of the door. No matter which is used, only as small portion of the hinge itself is visible when the door is closed.

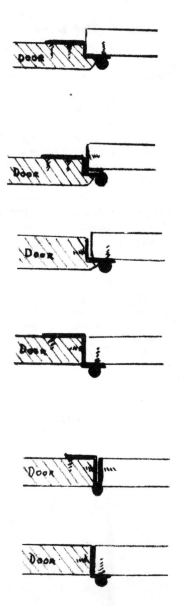

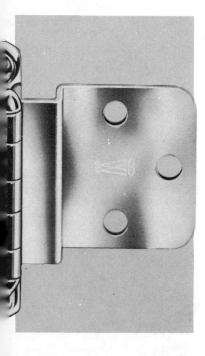

A semi-concealed hinge used with a lipped or rabbeted door. This smartly de-signed hinge shows only a thin decorative section when installed.

Photograph courtesy of Washington Steel Products, Inc.

Top cross-section view of semi-concealed hinges mounted on doors and cabinet face. The upper three show different types of hinges used with lipped or rabbetted doors. The lower three show hinge mountings for flush doors.

Pin Hinges for Flush Doors

Pin hinges are ideally suited for modern flush-face cabinet doors. When the door is closed, you see only ⅛″ of the pivot tip; the rest of the hinge is not visible.

Pin hinges are made in two types, depending upon the technique of mounting. One type is made for doors which are hinged to the cabinet side or partition that runs vertically. Another type is made for mounting doors to horizontal members of the cabinet case, usually the top and bottom (see accompanying sketches).

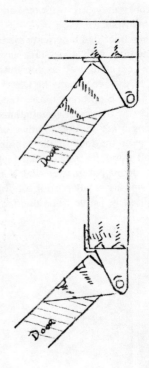

Mounting of pin hinges—top shows hinge mounted to door and to cabinet case which is parallel to the door when closed. Bottom shows pin hinge attached to door and cabinet side, which is at right angles to the door when it is closed.

How To Attach Pin Hinges

1. **Preparing the door**—Lay hinge on corner and flush with door edge. Mark angle cut and mortise in ⅛″ for hinge to fit flush.

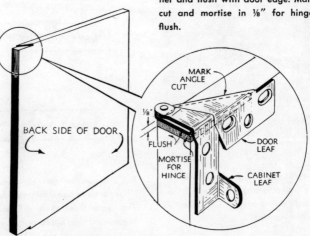

BACK SIDE OF DOOR

MARK ANGLE CUT

⅛″

FLUSH

MORTISE FOR HINGE

DOOR LEAF

CABINET LEAF

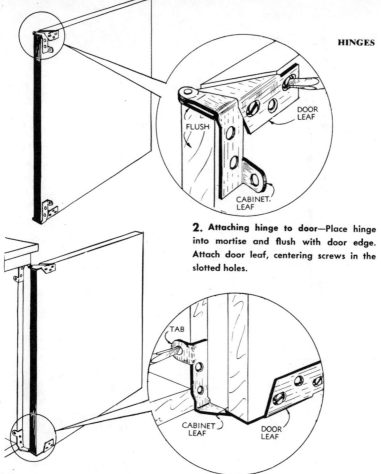

2. **Attaching hinge to door**—Place hinge into mortise and flush with door edge. Attach door leaf, centering screws in the slotted holes.

3. **Hanging the door**—Open the hinges up and set the door in place against the side of the cabinet. Attach tabs to cabinet first by setting screws into holes in hinge.

4. **Final step in hanging**—Swing the door open as wide as possible and drive in the remaining two screws into each hinge, top and bottom.

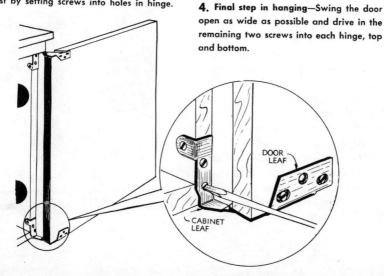

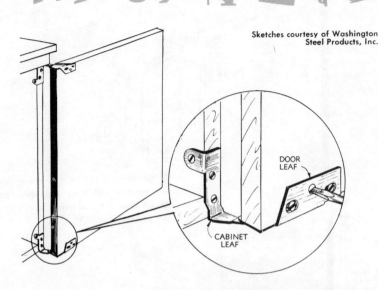

Sketches courtesy of Washington
Steel Products, Inc.

DOOR
LEAF

CABINET
LEAF

5. Adjusting the hinges—If door installation is not perfect, the slotted screw
holes in the door leaf allow for adjusting. Loosen the screws in these slotted
holes and tap the door to correct the fit.
When correct fit is obtained, tighten the
screws in the slotted holes and then drive
in the remaining screw in the anchor hole.

Invisible Hinges

The Soss invisible hinge can be
used in many places within the
home—for room doors, cabinet
doors or secret panels. No portion
of the hinge is visible when the door
is closed, thereby leaving the entire
outer surface of the door and frame
free from any projections and for
any desired treatment or decoration.
These hinges are made for all types
of doors no matter what their size
or weight.

The invisible hinge allows the
door to open fully, 180° and since
it is not visible, it can be used without concern about its matching
other hardware.

The invisible hinge has laminated link
construction which reduces friction and permits the hinge to operate freely and
smoothly.

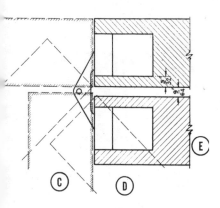

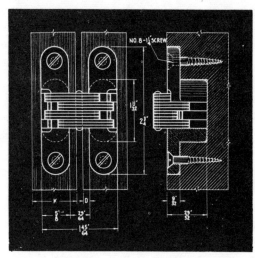

Top view showing position of hinge. Position A shows door closed; B shows door partially opened; C shows door at right angles to the face of the cabinet; D shows door opened further and E shows door fully opened and parallel to face of cabinet.

Plan view of a Soss invisible hinge made for 7/8" or 1" wood or metal doors. On left is open view of hinge attached to both door and edge of cabinet. On right is cross-section view of hinge inserted into edge of door or cabinet side.

How To Install Invisible Hinges

1. Select the proper size invisible hinge for the door and set the template or pattern that comes with the hinge at the proper location on the door. For a standard room door, the top hinge should be 5" from the top of the door, the bottom hinge 10" from the floor and a third hinge should be centered between them.

2. With a punch, mark the exact locations indicated on the template. There are dots with circles around each. These dots indicate where you start to drill. Use a punch to position each of the dots; a nail or other pointed tool will do.

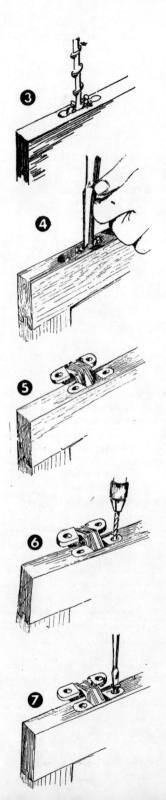

3. Using the proper size drill (as specified on the template), bore holes into the edge of the door into which the hinge will fit. It is a good idea to use a depth gage with the bit so that you drill the holes to the required depth.

4. With a chisel, you should recess the sides smooth by removing the excess wood between the drilled holes.

5. One half of the hinge (it doesn't matter which half) is forced into the drilled section or mortise.

6. Drill pilot holes for the screws that hold the hinge in place in the door.

7. Drive the screws that come with the hinge into position so that the head of the screw is flush with the surface of the hinge. Now repeat the same process in the edge of the cabinet side or door jamb for the rest of the hinges.

Hip Roof

A roof which makes equal angles with all four sides of the building is called a hip roof.

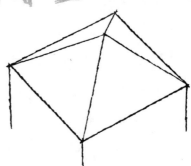

A hip roof.

Hole Saw, Metal

There are many methods of cutting round holes in metal. The circular-hole saw does the neatest job. This cup-shaped saw can be clamped in the chuck of the hand, electric or breast drill.

The hole saw comes in many diameters of whole inches, or inches and fractions of an inch. It has a centering adapter shaft to which the saw is clamped by a locking nut, which also clamps the pilot drill in place.

The pilot drill is allowed to extend about ⅛ʺ past the cutting teeth of the saw. Running the pilot through material in which the hole is to be cut tends to hold the saw steady. When completed, it leaves a perfectly round, clean hole.

If overheated, the saw becomes jammed and clogged with metal which, under pressure, often cracks the cup-shaped body. To prevent this, have a little soap or kerosene handy to apply to the cutting teeth.

See *Drill, Electric—Accessories.*

Hollow Chisel

A hollow chisel has four cutting edges which cut a square hole. The chisel is part of mortising equipment usually used with a drill press although there are mortising adaptors for a quarter-inch electric drill.

See *Mortising.*

Hollow Chisel Bit

This bit is somewhat similar to an ordinary wood bit but does not have a feed screw. It is used with the hollow chisel to make square holes in wood. The bit fits inside the chisel and in the mortising operation, it removes the bulk of the wood. The chisel merely squares the corners.

See *Mortising*.

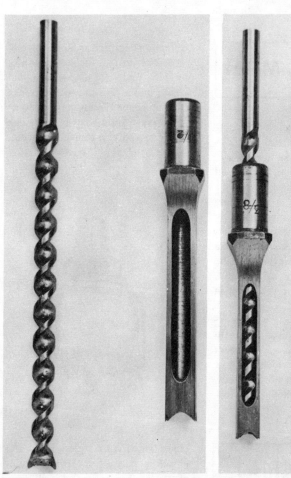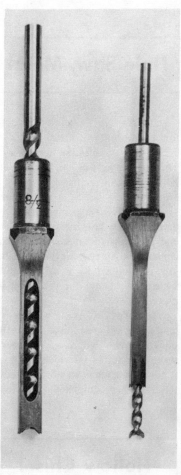

Hollow chisel bits come in various sizes to fit within hollow chisels.

Home Building
and
Buying Guide

With more American families than ever before moving to the suburbs, a great many questions arise regarding which suburb to choose. The family which is moving away from the city permanently wants to know that the location it selects offers advantages it cannot get in the city. A mistake in choosing a new home can be costly. Unless the prospective buyer inspects the lot, the house and the community carefully, the mistake is never obvious until it's too late. When in doubt, get expert advice; it will pay for itself.

Evaluating the Lot

If you are starting from scratch and buying land there are many factors to check.

1. Is the land accessible to all essential utilities including water, electricity, gas (if desired), storm drainage, sanitary drainage (although this can be provided for the individual house by septic tanks), telephone service, street lights, fire alarm boxes and hydrants?

2. If storm and sanitary drainage are provided, are they adequate?

Is the area subject to floods, or does the water back up into the basements because the sewers are too small or too shallow? If the area is expanding rapidly, will the drainage system be adequate to meet future needs?

3. Is the street and a sufficient area around it zoned for residential purposes only?

4. Are the homes in the neighborhood of approximately the same value as the one you want to build? Are they well maintained and fairly new? Good maintainance is more generally found in areas where the houses are mostly owner-occupied rather than rented.

5. Are there any unsightly areas nearby such as open lots used for dumping? Are there any smoke-producing industries?

6. Is the particular lot you are considering so situated as to permit you to orient your house in the direction you want? For example, can you have a southern exposure for your living room and still have privacy on the terrace which adjoins it?

7. Is the lot large enough to accommodate all the facilities you plan when building line restrictions are observed? Will you be able to include the size garage you want, the play area, terrace, etc.?

8. Are the streets paved?

9. Can you get a clear title and deed? Get legal advice on this.

10. Is it a heavy traffic street?

Don't expect to find all these advantages in one spot. You'll probably have to compromise or add some improvements yourself. While many can be added, you must take full account of them when figuring costs; some will be added immediately to construction costs while others will be added later in the form of assessments or higher taxes.

Evaluating the Neighborhood

It is wise to consider junior and adult requirements when choosing a community to move to.

1. Are schools available in the community or will the children have to travel each day to another community? Are there adequate school facilities to accommodate all the children without overcrowding or double-shifts? Are school buses provided if it's too far to walk?

Considering the increase in the number of children who will reach school age during the next decade, it is important that school boards plan now for the coming generation. Are there plans for increasing school facilities to meet the demands which be made upon them? This is particularly important in areas where there is a rapidly expanding population in addition to the normal increase in children of school age.

2. Has sufficient land in the community been set aside for parks, play areas around the houses and playgrounds? Do the schools have after-hours recreation programs?

Photograph courtesy of American Community Builders

The family moving to a new community should check the school situation very carefully. "The modern curriculum," say educators, "which goes beyond textbook teaching is important to the complete education of children. This is a scene in a home economics class.

3. Is there adequate police and fire protection?

4. Transportation facilities are very important. Measure transportation in time rather than in miles; 25 or 30 miles on a good highway may be covered in the same time as 10 or 15 miles in heavy city traffic. If you depend on trains or buses, be sure they run on a convenient schedule.

5. Check the tax rates in the area. Do not be satisfied with a "taxes are low" statement. Remember, unless streets, water and sewer systems are paid for, they will have to be paid for by residents in the form of assessments or tax increases. Also, new schools, while essential, are expensive.

6. How far and how complete are shopping facilities? These should include food stores, clothing stores, service stores, professional offices, drug stores and the basic service organizations such as a bank and post office.

7. How high are utility costs? This frequently includes water. Are there limitations on the use of water in the summer for gardens? How frequent are power failures?

8. Is the community organized for service and group activities. Look for churches of various denominations, scout groups, P.T.A., Little League, arts groups, amusements centers and libraries.

Well spent after-school hours are one of the vital factors in the successful educa- tion of children. Sufficient area should be left for playgrounds.

The lady of the house will be particularly interested in the availability of shopping facilities. This is an ultra-modern shopping area in a new community.

Building a House— Budgeting

First, decide upon how expensive a home you can afford. A safe, approximate figure to start with is 2½ to 3 times your annual income for the house and land. With the average down payment, this price range will take about one-fourth of your take-home pay to maintain.

The price of the house is paid in two parts, the cash down payment, which ordinarily comes out of savings, and the mortgage payments, which come out of current income, if, as most families, you finance your house with a loan.

Cash Investment

If you are building rather than buying a house, the bulk of the initial payment will go for land and preliminary extras. Land should come to approximately 15% of the total home cost; lending institutions do not prefer this figure to go over 20%. This is the figure for a fully developed site. If the lot is undeveloped, you must allow for clearing, grading, bringing in the utilities, sidewalks, etc. The extras include legal fees, survey costs, insurance premiums, fees for plans, etc. Allow about $300.00 for this. And, in deciding how much cash you'll need, don't forget extra furnishings for the new house, landscaping and appliances.

Monthly Payments

Your current income should determine how high your monthly payments can be. There is no one formula for determining what you can afford for housing, but for most families the figure runs between ⅙ and ⅛ of their income.

In addition to the monthly payments direct to the lending institution for repayment of the building loan and interest on the principal you must include the following costs in monthly charges:

1. Tax payments—these may include real estate or town tax, county tax, school tax, utilities tax, garbage collection tax.

2. Insurance costs—In addition to the insurance you carry on furnishings, the lending institution will require you to carry fire and perhaps other insurance on the building itself to protect their investment.

3. Heating—The builder can probably give you a reliable estimate of how much it will cost to heat your house.

4. Maintenance costs—Set aside a specific amound each month for repairs and maintenance. Approximately $20 to $25 a year per $1,000 value of the house should be a good starting point, although experience will probably alter it somewhat. A lot will depend on how much you do yourself and how much you have done for you.

House Plans

A good plan and working drawings are essential in home building. You can, of course, get these from an architect, but if you want a less expensive but reliable method, you

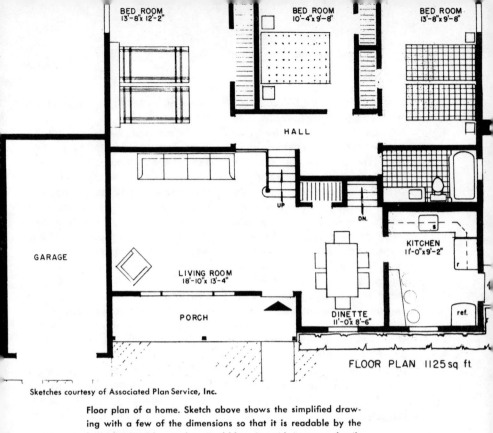

BED ROOM
13'-8"x 12'-2"

BED ROOM
10'-4"x 9'-8"

BED ROOM
13'-8"x 9'-8"

HALL

UP

DN.

GARAGE

KITCHEN
11'-0"x9'-2"

LIVING ROOM
18'-10"x 13'-4"

s

r

ref.

PORCH

DINETTE
11'-0"x 8'-6"

FLOOR PLAN 1125 sq ft.

Sketches courtesy of Associated Plan Service, Inc.

Floor plan of a home. Sketch above shows the simplified drawing with a few of the dimensions so that it is readable by the
home buyer. Below is the actual blueprint with its many details
for the builder.

get your plans from a recognized home plan service organization.

Standard working drawings, though a technical sounding designation, are actually the simplest pictorial method of portraying a structure. There are no complicated codes or practices, no involved computations necessary to translate working drawings into the house or other structural unit for which they stand. Working drawings attempt to record on a flat surface, much as a camera would, the three dimensional object envisioned by the designer or architect. Even the symbols used to indicate the location of mechanical and electrical elements such as switches, fuse box, etc. resemble those items diagramatically.

If a camera were used to make a visual record of a building, two sides of that building could be shown at one time by locating the camera opposite a corner. Professional working drawings can be compared to photos produced directly opposite one side, with the camera on center. Thus, four shots are required to show four sides. These are known as the four elevations: front, left, right, and rear.

Exterior Plan and Elevations

The front elevation is usually drawn to ¼″ scale; that is, one quarter of an inch equals one foot. Most of the information that applies to all four elevations is shown on the front elevation. For that reason you often find the other three elevations drawn to ⅛″ scale. The left elevation refers to the side of the house that is on your left when you stand

in the street facing the front of the house.

These four elevations are the main drawings devoted to the outside of the house, especially when the roof line is simple and when there are no overlapping wings. Several ridge lines on a roof can cause complicated valleys which only a roof diagram can properly explain; it can be compared to an aerial view. A U-shaped plan to be really complete would require two additional elevation drawings to show the inside faces of the left and right wings.

All of these exterior drawings are surprisingly simple and unencumbered with dimensioning and symbols that characterize the drawings for the interiors. They are devoted to depicting the shape of the house, its over-all design, the size and type of windows and the nature of the materials used.

In addition, a plot plan will be used to show the location of the house on the site. This is also in the nature of an aerial view taken from a higher altitude than the roof diagram, so that the outline of the property line can be seen. The architect uses the survey, converting the surveyor's feet and tenths of a foot into feet and inches to show the size of the site. The outline of the house is emphasized by cross-hatching. Driveways, walks and patios are usually shown by dotted lines fully dimensioned. Also dimensional are the distances which the house is set back from front and side property lines.

This plot plan is often used as the title page for a set of working

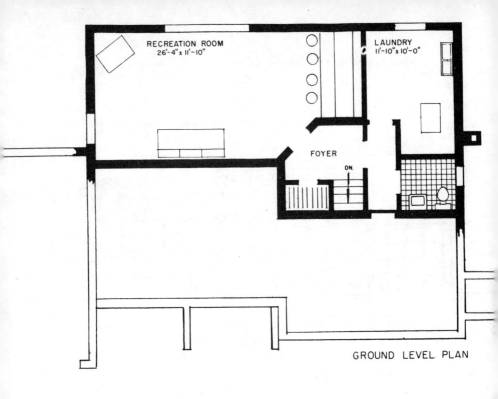

RECREATION ROOM
26'-4" x 11'-10"

LAUNDRY
11'-10" x 10'-0"

FOYER

DN.

GROUND LEVEL PLAN

Sketches courtesy of Associated Plan Service, Inc.

Floor plan showing the basement of the home. Top is a simplified
drawing of the basement of this home. Below is the detailed
foundation drawing showing footings and other details for the
builder.

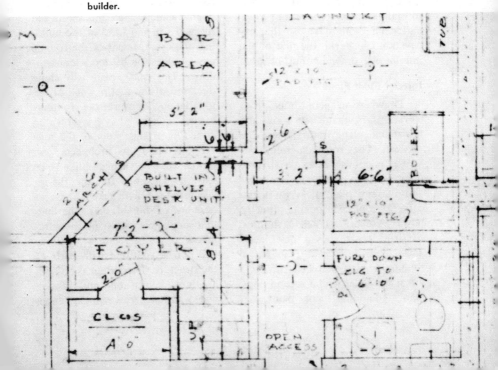

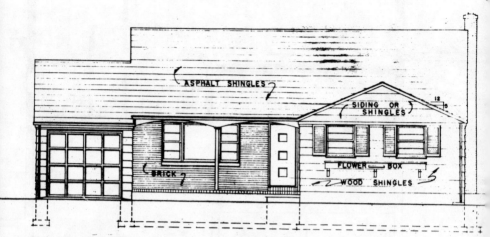

FRONT ELEVATION

Photograph and sketches courtesy of Associated Plan Service, Inc.

drawings. It is the first page that is used in the construction of a home, for its gives the location of the first stake driven into the ground. Now to outline properly the entire foundation line with stakes so that excavation can begin, the first of the interior plan drawings must be used.

Interior Floor Plans

Drawings in plan differ from elevations in that they show the horizontal plane rather than the vertical. The roof diagram, described previously as an aerial view, is a drawing in plan; so is the survey and the site plan. It is as if the camera is placed looking directly down. A shot is taken each time construction reaches a new level. Thus there is a cellar plan (or a foundation plan if no cellar exists), a first floor plan and a second floor plan. Additional floor plans are

drawn if the residence has more stories.

Each plan, starting with the foundation or cellar plan, is thoroughly dimensioned and shows the over-all size and form of the building, the arrangement of the rooms, and the location of doors and windows. The cellar plan will show thickness of the footings and of the foundation. Because the footings cannot be "seen" they are shown by dotted lines. This is one of the conventions used by architects and draftsmen. The visible outline is always shown with a full line, the invisible outlines with a medium thickness line of short dashes. The lines that show dimensions and measurements are also different so that they will not be confused with parts of the structure. These dimension lines are drawn lightly and tipped at each end with an arrow which defines

Here are three stages of a home. The first, on the page to the left is the architectural drawing of the front view showing some of the building details. Stage two, above, is an artist's rendering of the same house based on the architectural drawing. Stage three, below, is the finished home as shown in a photograph.

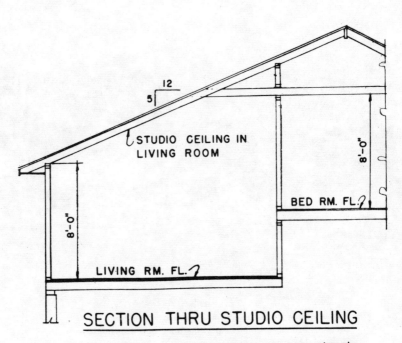

SECTION THRU STUDIO CEILING

Above: architectural drawing showing a cross section through the studio ceiling. Below: simplified drawing showing the different floors and their position in this split-level home.

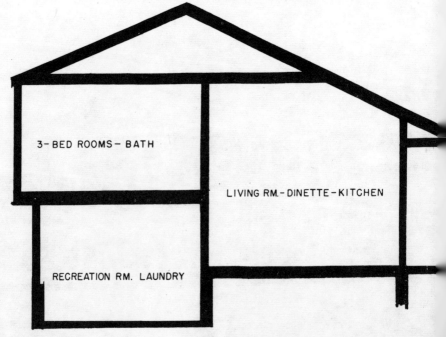

SECTION

precisely the distance that is being measured. The numbers denoting this distance are usually placed midway between these two arrows. This avoids confusion where several dimension lines of varying lengths run parallel and close to each other.

Floor plans tell the biggest story: window sizes are written in, door sizes are given together with an arc showing the direction the doors swing open, electric outlets and fixtures are spotted with dotted lines running to the switches, if any, that control them; posts, flues, ramps, etc, are dimensioned; bathroom fixtures are drawn in together with the location of cabinets and other built-ins.

Floor plans may also bear legends that give all the necessary framing information. However, separate framing details are often provided that show the location of every floor and ceiling. Thus the floor plan becomes the busiest sheet in a set of blueprints, complicated at first glance but simple as it becomes familiar and you become accustomed to locating the particulars you are looking for.

Although construction drawings are done to scale they should be fully dimensioned, making it necessary for the workman to measure the blueprints to determine a distance. "Scaling" blueprints, as this procedure is called, is inaccurate and time-consuming.

Additional Notes and Diagrams

Complete notes will also be supplied on a good set of working drawings. They permit you to work from the blueprints without constant reference to the specification. On the cellar plan, for instance, there will be printed reference to the matter of reinforcing in the concrete. The small slope usually provided in a basement floor will be spelled out. Necessary information about the heating plant, water service, sewer system, etc. will be set forth in written notes.

Most architects supply what is known as a section diagram as part of the working drawings. This is equivalent to a photograph taken as if half the house had been cut away. It shows details of interior construction to which an exterior elevation cannot penetrate. Used in conjunction with each of the plans, it sets forth visually all three dimensions of the structure's skeleton; e.g. the depth and cross-section of the footing and foundation wall are seen at a glance in the section diagram, while the horizontal linear course is defined in the plan.

Similarly, when you proceed to the first floor plan to erect partitions that divide the space of the home into rooms, the section diagram shows the structural elements that must be provided. For example, 4x12 joists 16" on center might be called for, with plywood sub-flooring and asphalt tile. While this information can be written in on the plan, when shown in cross-section on the section diagram, it gives a more helpful pictorial explanation. It also helps to keep the floor plan free for other necessary information that must be inserted.

With the plans and elevations forming the heart of the blueprints and with the plot plan, roof diagram

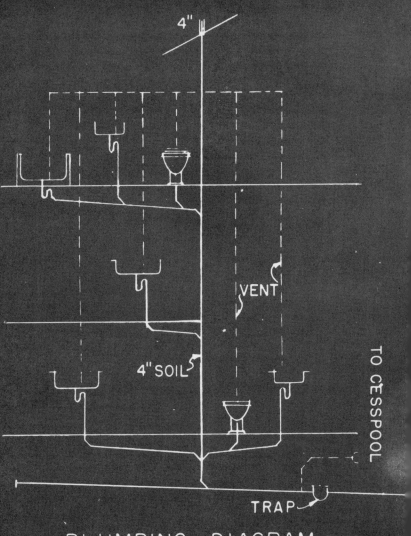

4"

VENT

TO CESSPOOL

4" SOIL

TRAP

PLUMBING DIAGRAM

and section diagram supplied to aid the visualization, capable workmen can construct a conventional home to duplicate exactly what the architect had in mind. A sound principle usually followed by good builders is that there should be no deviation from the working drawings. It is especially important that the foundation and basement be constructed in strict accordance with the blueprints; changes can weaken the structure and complicate the construction of related or adjoining elements of the building.

However, some homes have special structural members and most homes have special features to meet the living requirements of the family for whom it was designed. To portray these special features additional drawings are obviously needed. These are called detailed drawings. They might show a fireplace, kitchen cabinets, or a special trussed rafter to support the roof. These detailed drawings can be ½″ scale or even 1″ scale. This permits each shelf to be dimensioned or each bolt located.

The builder frequently needs working drawings for specific details of standard equipment and these are often supplied by the manufacturer of the equipment.

Sketches courtesy of Associated Plan Service, Inc.

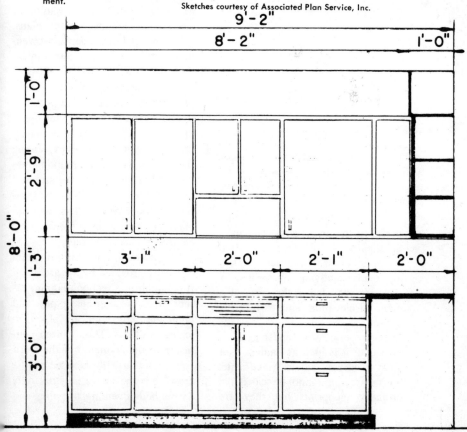

CABINET DETAILS

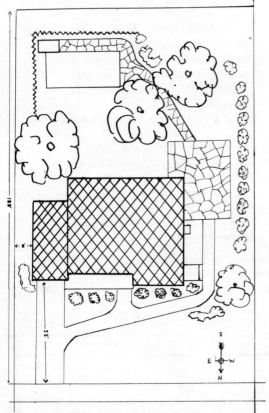

Although a site drawing comes with the house plans, you might like a landscape architect or gardening service to lay out your shrubs, trees, play areas and other outdoor living centers.

Detailed drawings are especially useful to the amateur as they spotlight parts of the structure which might otherwise be obscure. They are read exactly as blueprints, as they are provided in the form of a plan, an elevation, and/or a cross-section.

On rare occasions an isometric is provided; it is like the camera shot **from a corner,** but to exact scale. Such a drawing cannot be scaled like ordinary blueprints but they are usually clearly dimensioned.

Shop drawings can also be included among the details that make up the working drawings of a house. These are generally supplied to the architect by the manufacturer of some special equipment that is being incorporated into the structure, such as a sliding glass door or a wall-hung refrigerator.

A home is not just a solid structure. Running through its members are wires, pipes, ducts and conduits that provide water, heat, light, sanitation, ventilation and communication. These arteries are not installed at random, but, like the structural members, are clearly specified and precisely located. The location of electrical items appears on the plans. The same applies to telephones, ventilating fans, and inter-communication systems. However, heating plans are necessary and if not supplied by the architect, are provided in clear detail by most reliable heating contractors. These are usually drawn in plan with notes explaining the size, materials, and brand names involved. They specify the size and make of the furnace, show the location of room heat outlets, and explain the connection of thermostatic controls and zoning, if any.

A schematic plumbing diagram is usually provided by the architect. It is similar to a section diagram except that the various pipes and plumbing fixtures are not placed in scaled positions. This is often confusing to the layman, but the word "schematic" usually labelled on the drawing is the indication that only the method of venting, trapping, and

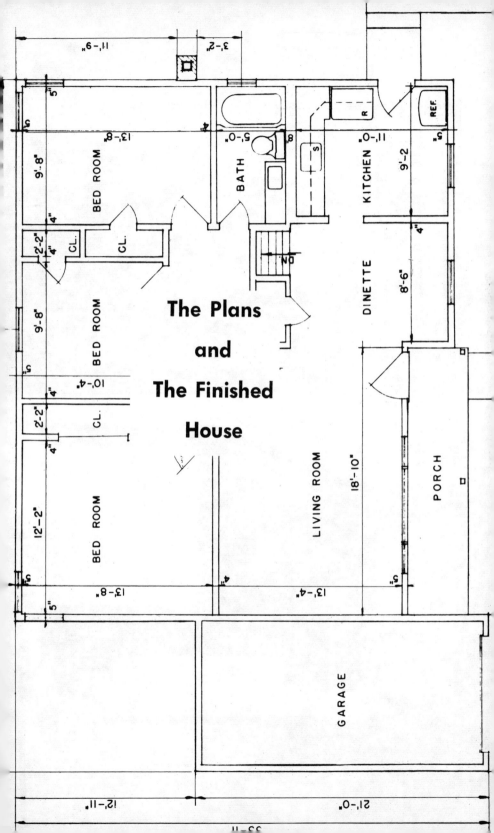

The Plans

and

The Finished

House

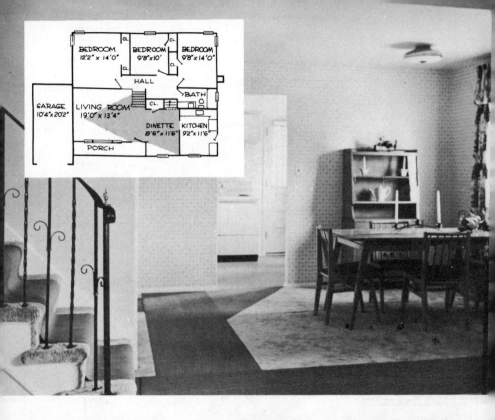

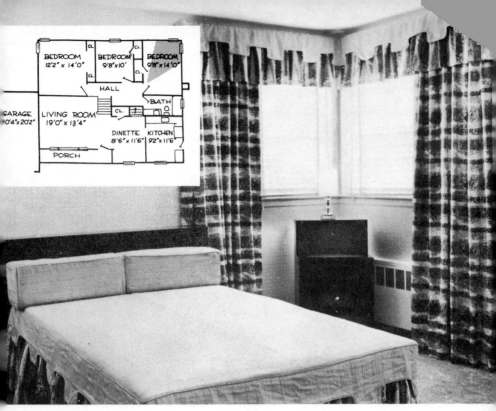

Sketches and photographs courtesy of Associated Plan Service, Inc.

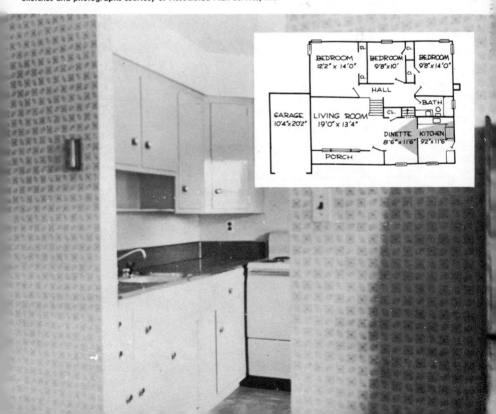

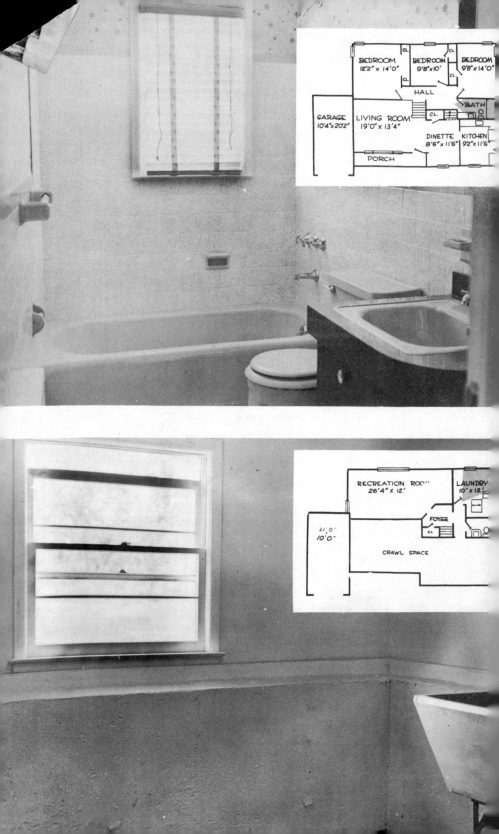

BEDROOM
12'2" x 14'0"

BEDROOM
9'8" x 10'

BEDROOM
9'8" x 14'0"

HALL

GARAGE
10'4" x 20'2"

LIVING ROOM
19'0" x 13'4"

BATH

CL.

DINETTE
8'6" x 11'6"

KITCHEN
9'2" x 11'6"

PORCH

RECREATION ROOM
26'4" x 12'

LAUNDRY
10' x 12'

FOYER

21'0"
10'0"

CRAWL SPACE

RECREATION ROOM
26'4" X 12'

LAUNDRY
10' X 12'

FOYER

CRAWL SPACE

21'0"
10'0"

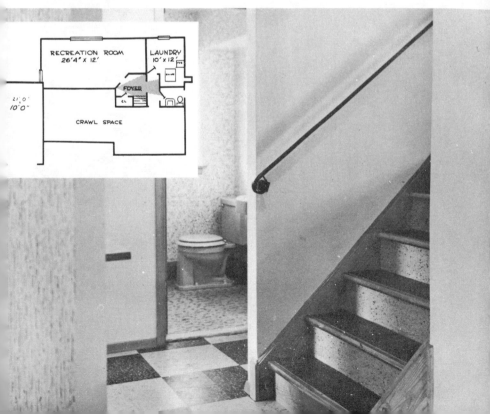

RECREATION ROOM
26'4" X 12'

LAUNDRY
10' X 12'

FOYER

CRAWL SPACE

21'0"
10'0"

BEDROOM
12'2" x 14'0"

BEDROOM
9'8" x 10'

BEDROOM
9'8" x 14'0"

CL

CL

CL

CL

HALL

BATH

GARAGE
10'4" x 20'2"

LIVING ROOM
19'0" x 13'4"

CL

DINETTE
8'6" x 11'6"

KITCHEN
9'2" x 11'6"

PORCH

Homes for America

Here are four model homes, each designed for its own geographical region: East, South, Midwest and West. A leading architect from each region created the plans for the home in his region. The development of homes within the budget of young couples of average income and the presentation of these homes was sponsored by the Hotpoint Co. which dramatized the role of major appliances.

The living-conditioned home for the East is a tri-level house designed for a flat lot. Through this arrangement, all activity areas, the rooms in which active family living takes place, are on one level, away from the quiet areas of the bedrooms.

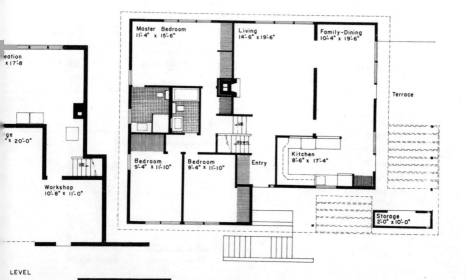

LEVEL

The model home for the South is built on one level with 3 bedrooms, living-dining rooms, family recreation room or all-purpose room, kitchen, two baths and a carport.

A 12′ wide utility strip, running through the middle of the house, splits the house into two sections. This places the activity areas on one side and the sleeping areas on the other. The utility strip houses an all-electric kitchen, laundry, two baths and the heater room. On one side is the living area, composed of a living-dining room and family recreation room. Both rooms open on the terrace. The other side is occupied by the three bedrooms, closets and linen storage space.

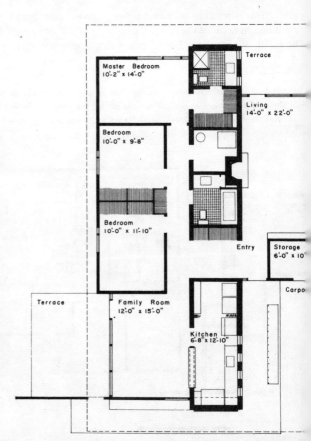

The one-story model home for the Midwest is built around a central utility core, housing the heater room, two baths and a kitchen. All rooms in this core are accommodated by natural light through a skylight in the center of the roof of this contemporary home.

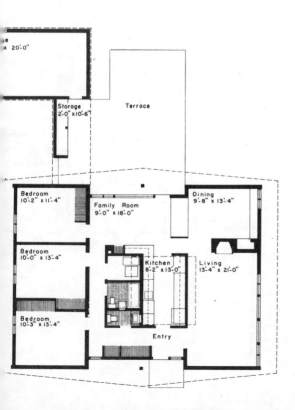

In this living-conditioned home for the Midwest, a fireplace only 4′ high separates the large living room from the dining room. Because of its low elevation, the fireplace separation permits the vision to travel through the upper levels of both rooms and provides the spaciousness of one enormous room, with the privacy of two. The family room provides an outdoor living atmosphere by opening through an almost completely glass wall on to a terrace, which leads into the play and recreation areas behind the house.

In typical California style, the living-conditioned home for the West utilizes the entire lot as a living area, some of which is enclosed and some open. The exterior walls are made of redwood with large areas covered with glass to bring the outdoors inside the home.

Every room is arranged with sliding doors, leading into outdoor living areas. Each bush, tree, shrub and flower has been blended into the overall plan of the house. The entire lot is enclosed by a fence, which is architecturally a part of the house. A central utility unit houses the kitchen, laundry and bathrooms. It separates a living room and bedroom on one side from a family recreation and two bedrooms on the other. Bedrooms are insulated from active living areas by corridor and closet space.

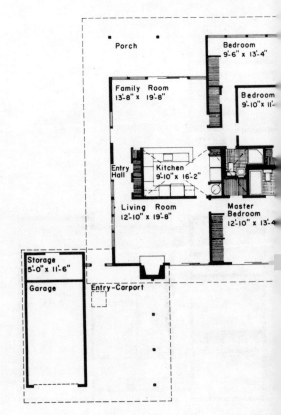

Porch

Bedroom
9'-6" x 13'-4"

Family Room
13'-8" x 19'-8"

Bedroom
9'-10" x 11'-

Entry
Hall

Kitchen
9'-10" x 16'-2"

Living Room
12'-10" x 19'-8"

Master
Bedroom
12'-10" x 13'-4

Storage
5'-0" x 11'-6"

Garage

Entry-Carport

connecting the pipes is intended to be shown by the drawing.

Using the Drawings

Individuals who plan to construct a home from blueprints for the first time are cautioned against expecting detailed do-it-yourself instructions in a set of professional drawings. True, they are simple to read; none of their vast store of information is obscure or uninterpretable. Yet they do assume that the individual knows how to pour a footing, how to join pieces of wood, how to secure one member to another, how to use the right number and size of nails, how to stiffen a joist. In short, blueprints give you the whole story of a structure but they do not give you the whole story of craftsmen's skills and know-how. For the beginner, they must be supplemented with other necessary how-to literature or with the help of an experienced supervisor.

Picking a Builder

When you have selected your plan, bought the land and found out how large a mortgage you can get, you are ready to pick a builder. This is a most important choice, because it is up to him to transform your plans into a well-constructed, livable house.

If you don't know any reliable builder, ask at your local bank, your Chamber of Commerce and your lumber dealer. You may have to go looking for him on the job; builders are out supervising rather than sitting in offices. Get estimates

from several builders, and get the names and addresses of people for whom they have built houses. Go to see the houses they have built and talk to the owners. If one bid is very much below the others, be wary of it; don't take it just because it's low.

When requesting a bid, give the builder:

1. The complete set of blueprints and the bill of materials that comes with the plans.

2. A survey of the property showing the terrain, so he can tell the problems he will encounter.

3. A list of special things you want in the house; the type of electrical fixtures, kitchen and laundry appliances, fans floor finishes, types of doors, built-ins, etc.

When the bids are in, check to see that all the things you wanted were included. If you have difficulty in evaluating the estimates, your lending institution can probably help you. If all the bids are too high, ask the lowest builder to suggest changes to bring down the cost, but if there are to be structural changes, have them checked professionally.

When you have selected a builder, you are ready to sign a contract. If you don't use the standard legal form, have the contract examined by an attorney.

Once the building has begun, work closely with the builder. Notify him in advance of any changes you wish to make in materials, finishes or equipment. Take your complaints to him as well. In no case should you deal with the sub-contractors.

Check periodically to see that the building is being done according to plans.

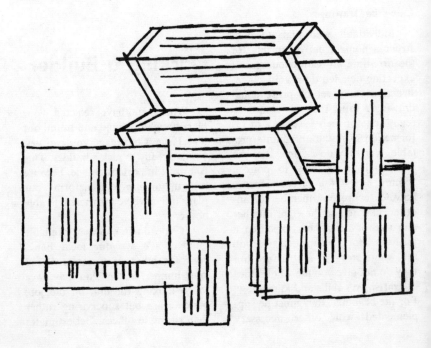

House—Structural Parts

Residents are often aware of the defects in a house, but sometimes it is necessary to have an inspection made by experienced workmen whose training enables them to discover defects not apparent to the average householder. Some homeowners wish to make their own inspection; the accompanying illustration and list of the essential parts of a house will be helpful when looking over the house in detail.

House—Structural Parts

1. Gable end.
2. Louver.
3. Interior trim.
4. Shingles.
5. Chimney cap.
6. Flue lining.
7. Flashing.
8. Roofing felt.
9. Roof sheathing.
10. Ridge board.
11. Rafters.
12. Roof valley.
13. Dormer window.
14. Interior walls.
15. Studs.
16. Insulation.
17. Diagonal sheathing.
18. Sheathing paper.
19. Window frame and sash.
20. Corner board.
21. Siding.
22. Shutters.
23. Exterior trim.
24. Waterproofing.
25. Foundation wall.
26. Column.
27. Joists.
28. Basement floor.
29. Gravel fill.
30. Heating plant.
31. Footing.
32. Drain tile.
33. Girder.
34. Stairway.
35. Subfloor.
36. Hearth.
37. Building paper.
38. Finish paper.
39. Fireplace.
40. Downspout.
41. Gutter.
42. Bridging.

BUYING A HOUSE

The following discussion indicates the factors to consider when buying a house. It is not intended to be complete in every detail; you can get additional ideas of what to look for by referring to many sections throughout these volumes such as *Foundations, Windows, Damp-proofing, Chimneys, Stairs, Termites,* etc. In any case, it is advisable to have competent professional advice before you actually buy; but by using the following guide, you can eliminate until you think you have found the right one. Legal advice is essential for the title and deed.

If the house you want is not perfect in every respect, and it is very unlikely that any one will be, get estimates on essential repairs from a contractor, so that you may add it to the cost of the house. Some repairs, of course, you can do yourself, but be sure that they are really handyman jobs before you undertake them. If there are many signs of neglect in small things, you will probably find major installations neglected as well.

Many of the items in the following list do not apply to new houses, but the basic cautions on layout and construction do apply.

Inside the house, check:

The basic plan—Is it adequate in size and does the layout meet the needs of your family? For example, can you arrange your furniture so that some members of the family will have a quiet place to read or talk while the younger ones watch TV? Do you have any oversize furniture that might not fit the available wall space? Is there adequate closet and storage space?

Floors—Are they smooth, level and not squeaky? Actually walk across all the floors of the house. Linoleum or other tile coverings should be even; bulges are a sign of trouble.

Walls—Check plaster walls for cracks; wallboard for dents. Are there any signs of wet spots, particularly around windows? If the walls are papered, check carefully for blistering or peeling. This is a pretty sure sign of dampness.

Doors—Do they swing easily, close tightly without sticking? Are the doorway openings of adequate size, or will you find when you move in that the washing machine can't get through the door to the basement? There should be screen doors for all exterior doors, and if it is in a cold climate, weatherstripping and storm doors as well.

Windows—Try sliding the windows up and down. Check for cracks around the frame. There may be small spaces as a result of settling, but these should be puttied. All the cords, if cords are used, should be in operating order. Screens are essential, and in colder climates storm sash is advisable.

Stairs—Rails and banisters should be firm. The stairs shouldn't squeak and there should be no cracks between the riser and step.

Plumbing—Is the water pressure

Look the house over from all sides. Is there an established lawn? How about the shrubs? Are there adequate shade trees to provide the needed shielding from the sun when you relax outdoors? Is the property line clearly defined, possibly by a fence?

Investigate the heating system of the house. What type of heating does the house have? Is there sufficient radiation? What is the condition of the heating unit itself? Is it old or new? Does it look so old that it will have to be replaced shortly or will it be necessary to keep a repairman on the premises? Meanwhile, check the extra appliances. Are laundry facilities adequate? Is there space for drying clothes indoors?

Adequate plumbing is often lacking in a really old house. Homes with iron pipe, which has rusted, have insufficient water pressure. Turn on several faucets to check the flow of water. Look the pipes over, if exposed along the attic ceiling, and check to see what material they are made of: galvanized iron, copper tubing, brass? Is there sufficient access to pipes in case you wish to add an extra outlet outdoors or if you wish to shift the laundry room?

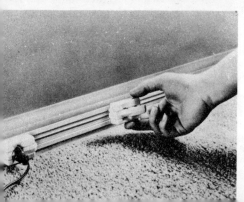

How about the house's electrical system? Many older homes were wired well below today's needs. Check the fuse box to determine the total amperage coming into the house. A 60-ampere unit is passable but a 100-ampere unit is preferred. Look over the individual rooms to determine if there are sufficient outlets or will you have to get to work and add more later? Do the room light fixtures have wall switches or pull chains? Is the fixture big enough to provide the necessary light for the room?

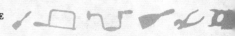

adequate? Turn on two or more faucets at one time; there should be no obvious slowing of the water flow. In a house with more than one story, check the pressure upstairs. If there is a pressure drop it may indicate corrosion of the pipes. If the water is not supplied through the community, check the well to see if it will give you an adequate water supply in the summer as well as in the winter. Flush the toilets and see how long it takes to refill the tank. What is the condition of the bathroom fixtures?

Kitchen—Is the cabinet space adequate or is there room to add more? Is the stove in good condition? Is the refrigerator large enough?

Electrical system—What is the capacity of the lines coming into the house? If you want to add a dryer, air conditioner, or other major electrical appliance, will you have to bring new lines into the house?

Heating system—If possible, run the heating system for a while and make sure all the room heating units heat uniformly. If the system requires modernization, such as the conversion from coal to oil or gas, check with a contractor to see whether the existing equipment can be used at all.

Insulation—Is there any and has it been properly applied?

Attic—Is there evidence of leaks; are there any sagging joists?

Basement—Check all exposed timbers for dry rot. Does the basement smell damp, or are there any wet spots on the walls? Are there any cracks in the concrete walls or floor? Is any of the concrete crum-

bling? Look for termite tubes; they are sometimes found inside the house.

If the house has no basement, check to see if the crawl space is properly ventilated.

In general, check all wood parts by rapping; if there is any suspicion of a hollow sound, pierce the wood. If it is even partly hollow, and particularly if sawdust comes through the opening, there are probably termites.

Outside the house, check:

Layout of house and grounds— Is there sufficient backyard for the activities you want? Is the house too close to the next one? Do the windows face in the proper direction to give you privacy where you want it, to make use of the sun's warmth in winter and avoid the heat in summer?

Landscaping and Grading—The land should slope away from the house. What is the condition of the grass, shrubs and trees? A poor lawn is often very difficult or expensive to correct, and if a large tree dies, it is not a simple matter to remove it.

Foundation—A concrete foundation is made of regular masonry units it can be checked to see if it's level. However, some settling may be expected in an older house.

Outside walls—Check for worn paint, cracks, warped or missing shingles, crumbling mortar in masonry, and bulges in the walls.

Windows and doors—Are there any cracks which require calking?

Gutters and Downspouts— These should be supported, straight, free of rust, and painted, if paint is

required. They should not drain directly into the earth, but should at least have splash blocks at the base. Check the drainage of the area by observing whether water remains standing on the surface of the earth after a heavy rain.

Roof—Check for loose or broken shingles. Closer checking requires going up on the roof.

Chimney—Check the masonry for loose mortar.

Hone

See *Sharpening* and *Whetstone*.

Hook Bolt

Instead of having a head, a hook bolt has an unthreaded end which is either bent at right angles to the body of the bolt or in a U-shaped hook.

Two types of hook bolts.

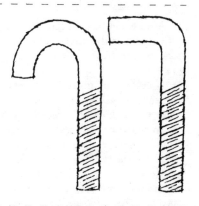

Hook Spanner Wrench

This wrench is used for special jobs. For a description of the different spanners and their uses refer to the section on *Wrenches*.

Horse

This is another name for a sawhorse. See *Sawhorse*.

Horsepower or H.P.

This is a standard unit of measure of power. One horsepower is equal to 33,000 pounds lifted one foot in one minute. It is also equal to 550 foot-pounds per second. In electrical terms, 1 H.P. is equal to 746 watts.

Automobile engines or motors are evaluated by horsepower ratings. According to the Society of Automotive Engineers, the horsepower of a car equals the square of the bore (measured in inches) multiplied by the number of cylinders, the product is divided by 2.5. As a formula, it is expressed:

$$H.P. = \frac{D^2 \times N}{2.5}$$

Hose Adaptor

A hose can be connected directly to a pipe or the mixer-outlet of a deck faucet by means of a hose adaptor.

Unless you make permanent connections to the hot and cold water supply lines, it is necessary to use an adaptor to connect a portable dishwasher or clothes washing machine to the kitchen unit. These adaptors screw on or screw into the outlet and some even clamp on the outside. The opposite end of the adaptor has the standard hose thread to make the connection to the hose.

In place of a regular hose cock, you might have a plumbing system where a valve is used to control the flow of the water and a pipe extends to a convenient place for the hose connection. These adaptors are made with one end in the form of a plumbing nipple or coupling to connect with the water pipe. The copper tubing adaptor has one end

which can be soldered to the tubing. The opposite end of both adaptors are made with the standard hose thread.

Hose adaptor has one end with standard hose threads for connecting to the hose. The other end is threaded like a coupling (as shown in this photograph) or as a plumbing nipple.   P & G Supply Co.

A hose adaptor can be attached to the mixer-outlet of a deck faucet. Here the adaptor is used with a pressure relief vacuum breaker valve connected to the hose from the dishwasher.

Hose Clamps and Couplings

Hose clamps are used to secure menders when repairing garden hose or to fasten a hose to an unthreaded nipple. An example of the second use is in a car joining the radiator and the motor block.

Hose couplings are used to join the ends of garden hose together and to fasten one end either to the hose cock or the other end to a nozzle or sprinkler.

Compression couplings (left half of photograph) are used for vinyl plastic and reinforced plastic garden hose. The male and female couplings (upper left) are slipped over the hose and the cone-shaped threaded inserts are "screwed" into the hose with a special key (lower left). A hose clamp and mender type of coupling (upper right) are used primarily for rubber hose but can be used with some types of reinforced plastic garden hose. The grip or teeth type of hose coupling (lower right) is used for rubber hose. While they can be used with reinforced vinyl garden hose, they generally will not stand up with all vinyl hose. The fitting toward the center (lower right) is a splicer to join two sections of hose permanently. The one in the corner (lower right) is a male coupling.

Hose clamps come in many different sizes and are tightened around the hose by means of a nut and bolt. All that is needed is a screwdriver to tighten the bolt head; the nut is kept in place by a lip on the edge of the clamp.

There are several types of hose counplings, each designed for different kinds of garden hose—rubber, vinyl and reinforced vinyl. The couplings are secured to the hose by:

1. a hose clamp set over the hose into which a mender type of coupling has been inserted.

2. teeth which are forced over the outside of the hose after the coupling has been forced into the hose.

3. compression fittings wherein the coupling is slipped over the end of the hose and a threaded cone-shape insert is forced inside the hose to make the coupling secure.

See *Couplings*.

Hot Water System

See *Heating System ABC's*.

Hot Water Tank

There are two ways to heat the hot water needed in the home. Either there is a tankless hot water heater, wherein the water is heated in coils connected to the main heating system, or there is a hot water storage tank. The water in the tank can be heated by a separate heating element, making it completely independent of the house's heating system, or the hot water can be stored in the tank but heated by the house's heating system.

A hot water storage tank is more commonly used even though many newer homes with central heating are built with the tankless hot water systems. Understanding how a hot water storage tank works will enable you to maintain the system more efficiently.

How the System Works

Hot water storage tanks come in various sizes. How large a tank is installed depends upon the size of the house, which is used as an indication of the size of the family. If you have a hot water storage tank that is about the right size for your home or maybe a little too small, you have undoubtedly found that a protracted use of hot water will result in cool, and possibly cold, water eventually flowing through the pipes. You, therefore, have to stop using the hot water until the heater can warm a new supply of water.

Let's see how the system works by following the flow of water from the cold water supply pipe through the heating process to the hot water outlet pipe to the faucets.

A—The cold water usually en-

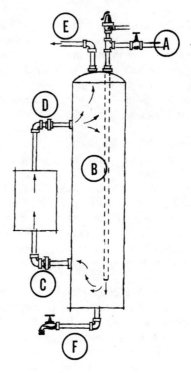

Hook-up of hot water storage tank.

ters the tank, if it's an upright model, through the top of the tank. There is, generally, a shut-off valve on this line so that the flow of cold water can be cut off if the tank needs repairs. Usually, a safety valve is also connected along this line. It's a run-off type of valve which permits water to flow into the tank if it gets too hot.

B—The cold water enters the tank but remains within a pipe, called the cold water tube, which brings the cold water down inside the tank to the lower section. Permitting the cold water to enter directly at the top of the tank would cause it to cool the hot water al-

ready in the tank. Note that the hot water outlet pipe to the faucets is practically next to the cold water inlet pipe.

C—The cold water settles along the bottom of the tank and enters a pipe about one-fourth the way up from the bottom of the tank. This pipe leads to the heater. This heater can be a special heating unit separate from the house's heating system or it can be connected to the house's system.

D—After being warmed in the heater, the water continues to flow upward and enters the tank again. Hot water normally rises and therefore flows to the top of the tank. As more hot water is accumulated, the level of hot water drops lower and lower until all the water in the tank is heated. When the bottom level of the hot water reaches the inlet pipe to the heater, it repeats the trip—gets heated and goes back into the tank.

E—The hot water outlet pipe to the faucets is connected to the top of the tank. Therefore, as you turn on the faucet, in the kitchen, bathroom or laundry, the hot water accumulated in the top of the tank flows through this pipe. As water leaves the tank, more cold water enters and starts the heating circulation trip.

F—All tanks have a drain cock connected to the bottom. This valve is normally closed. It is opened only to empty the water out of the tank when repairs have to be made or the system is to be closed down while the family is away on a vacation during the winter.

To Make Repairs

If the tank is in need of repairs, you could shut off the supply of cold water to the tank by closing the shut-off valve on the cold water supply line. Also shut off the heating unit, wherever possible.

boiler or tank repair plug

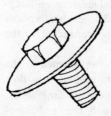

You can drain the tank by opening the drain cock at the bottom. It is best to let the water cool a while, unless there is a leak. Be careful if you use plastic garden hose to drain the tank by connecting to the drain cock. Hot water will weaken the plastic and may ruin the hose. If you have a rubber hose, use it instead. You can also reduce the amount of water to be taken out, if you open the hot water faucets in the house to remove the hot water in the pipes. It is best to open the hot water faucet at the lowest part of the system, possibly the one near the laundry tubs, if you have them in the basement.

If there is a hole in the tank, it can be repaired by using a boiler plug. There are two types. One has a sheet metal screw at one end and is screwed into the opening by using an open-end wrench to turn the head. A washer helps plug the leak. The other type, used for bigger holes, is similar to a toggle bolt and the nut grips the inside of the tank as the bolt is tightened with a screwdriver. Once the repair is completed, you can refill the system: see how-to later in this section.

If You Go Away

If you live in an area where there are freezing temperatures in the winter and you plan to go away for a week or longer, you have two choices. You can leave the hot water system in operation or you can shut it down.

If you shut the heat off, it is necessary to drain the pipes and the tank. Otherwise, there may be a freeze and as the ice expands in the tank, it may crack the tank or the pipes. Drain the system as you would for making repairs. Furthermore, you should also shut off the cold water supply to the house. After you do that, you can empty the cold water supply line to the tank by opening the shut-off valve on the cold water inlet line. Leave that valve and the drain cock valve open while you're away.

Starting the System Up

To start the system up after making a repair or after you have returned from a trip during cold weather, you should:

1. Shut the drain cock.
2. Open a hot water faucet at the sink or a tub.
3. Open the cold water shut-off valve at the inlet pipe.
4. Let the cold water flow into the tank and wait until water starts to flow out of the open faucet.
5. With the system full, you can now shut off the faucet.
6. Open the remaining hot water faucets in the house until the air is removed from the line. As soon as water starts to flow evenly, shut each faucet.
7. Turn on the heating unit.

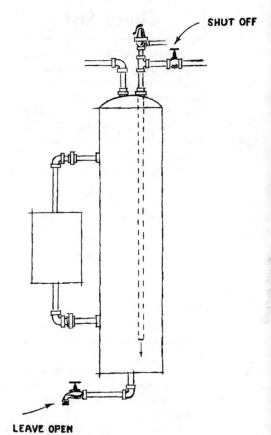

SHUT OFF

LEAVE OPEN

"Hot" Wire

This term is used in electrical work to identify the conductors carrying the current as distinguished from the ground wire. In all wiring circuits, the black wire is the "hot" wire. In special circuits, the red and the green also carry current and are considered hot wires.

House Maintenance— Check List

A systematic check of the house and its equipment should be made at regular intervals in order that defects may be noted and measures taken to correct them. In making this survey, the following check list of items for possible repairs and improvements may be helpful.

See *House, Structural Parts*.

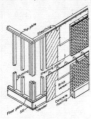

Foundation Walls

1. Masonry walls for cracks or broken portions that may require filling.

2. Mortar joints to see if pointing is needed.

3. Walls for leaks that may require dampproofing.

4. Eaves or tops of walls for leakage and to see if repairs or coping are needed.

5. Masonry walls for efflorescence or scum that may need removal.

6. Stucco walls for cracks, discoloration, or damaged portions that may need pointing, cleaning, or replacing.

7. Frame siding for loose or decayed boards or open joints that may need repair or replacement.

8. Painted surfaces to see if blistering, cracking, or peeling has occurred and if repainting is needed.

9. Wall surfaces to see if they need repainting or replacement.

10. Grading around foundation for proper drainage.

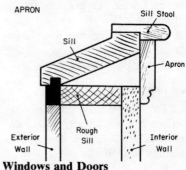

Windows and Doors

1. Window caps to see if new flashing or repairing of existing joints is required.

2. Holes or cracks around window frames to see if calking or repair is needed.

3. Windows for broken glass panes that may need replacement.

4. Putty around panes to see if reputtying is necessary.

5. Screens to see if repair or repainting is needed.

6. Storm doors and windows to see whether they need repair or repainting and if additional ones should be provided.

7. Blinds and shutters, to see if repairs are needed.

8. Awnings to see if repairs or replacements are necessary.

9. Balconies and railings to see whether they need repairs or painting.

10. Windows to determine whether additional ones should be installed.

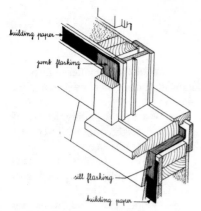

building paper →
jamb flashing
sill flashing
building paper

Roof, Flashing, Gutters, Downspouts

1. Shingle slate, or tile roofing to see whether repair or replacement of broken, loose, or missing units is necessary.

2. Metal or roll roofing for cracks, open joints, or worn coatings that might need repair or the application of waterproofing materials or paint.

3. Flashing for rust or defects and to determine whether repair, replacement, or repainting is necessary.

4. Gutters or conductor pipes for leaks and to see whether they need repainting or replacement.

5. Skylights for leaks or defects that might require glazing, flashing, repairing, or repainting.

6. Trapdoors, scuttles, or other roof openings, for leaks that might need flashing, repair, or repainting.

7. Chimney for defects and to see whether pointing or replacement of brick is necessary.

8. Need for chimney cap or chimney pots.

9. Chimney draft to see whether it is effective or may require lengthening of the chimney or installation of metal hoods.

10. Lightning arrestors.

11. Downspouts to see whether splash blocks need to be provided at outlet end or whether downspouts should be connected to a drain line.

Porches and Steps

1. Column bases for possible decay and need for repair or renewal.

2. Balusters to see that none are broken, loose, or missing.

3. Railings and posts to see that none are broken, loose, need repair or strengthening.

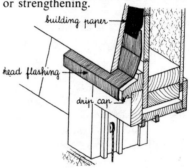

building paper →
head flashing →
drip cap →

4. Floor boards to see that none are decayed, broken, or loose and need repair.

5. Floor supports for decay and to see whether they need replacement or strengthening.

6. Steps to see that none are broken, loose, or worn and need repair.

7. Advisability of installing latticework to screen spaces under the porch.

8. Advisability of enclosing porches with glass or screening.

9. Floors to see whether they need refinishing or repair.

10. Masonry for open joints or cracks that might need pointing.

11. Floor tile for loose tile or other masonry material for damage that might need repair.

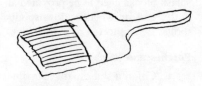

Garage

1. Advisability of installing insulating material.
2. Roof for cracks, open joints, or worn coatings that may need repair.
3. Doors, for adjustment.
4. Windows, for replacement of broken panes.
5. Advisability of laying concrete floors.
6. Advisability of installing heating equipment.
7. Inside and outside surfaces to see if painting is necessary.

Grounds

1. Walks and driveways; to see whether they need repair, replacement, or whether additional ones are necessary.
2. Fences, trellises, and latticework that might require repairing or painting.

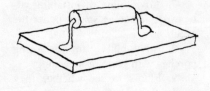

Basement

1. Foundation walls for large cracks or broken places that might require filling.

2. Walls for smaller cracks or mortar joints that might require pointing.
3. Walls and ceiling to see if they need brightening with new and lighter paint coatings.
4. Walls and floors for leaks that might require waterproofing or provisions for drainage.
5. Wood sills and walls for joints between them which might require calking.
6. Floor joists at the sills for spaces or holes around pipes that might need firestopping.
7. Floor joists for sagging and warping that might require additional support or bridging.
8. Basement floor for cracks or disintegrated places that might need repair or resurfacing.
9. Need for additional partitions to provide space for special purposes.
10. Unfinished walls and ceilings to determine desirability of finishing them.
11. Floors for painting or installation of asphalt tile.
12. Storage facilities such as shelves, closets, cupboards, and bins.
13. Advisability of constructing basement garage.

Heating and Ventilating

1. Smoke pipes or flues to see whether cleaning is necessary.
2. Boiler coils or baffles to see whether they require cleaning.
3. Grates to see if they are warped or broken and need replacement.
4. Fire box to see if cracked, and whether repairs are necessary.

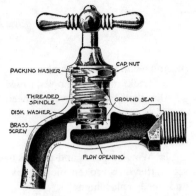

5. Boilers for cracks or leaks that might need repair or new parts.

6. Chimney masonry for cracks that might require pointing.

7. Woodwork adjoining pipes and heating system to see that fire protection is adequate.

8. Coating on boilers to see whether patching or recovering is needed.

9. Heating pipes to see whether repairs to covering are needed.

10. Advisability of installing automatic stokers, ash conveyors, or similar labor-saving devices.

11. Radiator valves for leaks that might require repacking.

12. Radiators to see that they are painted properly to increase efficiency.

13. Need for installation of additional radiators.

14. Need for radiator covers and radiator tops.

15. Thermostatic heat-control system to see that it is operating properly.

16. Air conditioning and need for humidifiers.

17. Advisability of building new or additional fireplace.

18. Advisability of installing an ash dump for fireplace.

19. Need for installation of room-heating device in existing fireplace.

20. Fireplace screens, and irons and similar equipment to see whether repair or replacement is needed.

21. Gas or electric log to see that it is operating properly.

22. Fireplace hearth, fireback, and dampers, for possible repair.

23. Mantel or fireplace front for possible remodeling.

24. Ventilating devices in kitchen and need for additional ones.

25. Walls and ceiling for installation of insulating material.

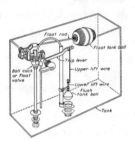

Plumbing

1. Drains to see that they are open.

2. Faucets for leaks that might require new washers, tightening, or new parts.

3. Flush valves in water closets to see whether they need repair or replacement.

4. Covering for water pipes and advisability of taking other precautions to prevent freezing.

5. Water-pipe fittings to see whether additional shut-off cocks or valves are needed.

6. Water-heating equipment to see that it operates properly.

7. Piping for possible repair or replacement.

8. Fixtures for repair or replacement.

9. Advisability of installing ad-

ditional bathrooms, lavatories, and toilets.

10. Advisability of providing toilet and shower in basement.

Lighting and Power

1. Wiring to see whether rewiring is needed.

2. Exposed wires to see that insulation is not worn or damaged.

3. Appliance cords to see whether they need to be replaced.

4. Electrical outlets to see whether additional convenience outlets, such as floor and base plugs, are needed.

5. Supply of fuse plugs for fuse box.

6. Chimes, buzzers, and doorbells to see whether repairs or additional installations are needed.

7. Advisability of installing transformers for bells to replace batteries.

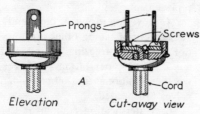

Prongs — Screws

Elevation   A   Cord

Cut-away view

Doors and Windows

1. Doors and windows to see whether they need refitting, adjustment, or repair.

2. Doors for advisability of re-

placing wood panels with glass.

3. Locks, chains, or bolts, to see whether they are defective and need repair or replacement.

4. Supply of extra keys for various locks.

5. Window cords and pulleys to see if they are broken or defective and need replacement.

6. Window latches or other window-fastening devices to see if they are broken or need replacement.

7. Window sash and doors to see if cracks around them need weather-stripping.

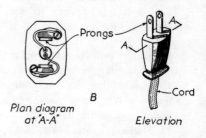

Prongs

A

Cord

Plan diagram at "A-A"   B   Elevation

Walls and Ceilings

1. Plaster for cracks or holes that may require patching or replastering.

2. Advisability of installing more partitions, either temporary or permanent, to provide additional rooms or closets.

3. Partitions for removal to afford additional space.

4. Doorways for width and to see if plastered arches or similar larger openings should replace them.

5. Walls and ceilings for refinishing or redecorating and need for painting, papering, or installation of wall tile.

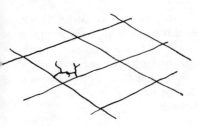

Floors

1. Floors to see that they do not creak and whether they need renailing, additional supports, or joists stiffened by bridging.

2. Need for refinishing.

3. Advisability of laying new flooring over old.

4. Floor coverings to see if they need repair or replacement.

5. Baseboard and molding for shrinking and settling, to see if adjustment or replacement is needed.

6. Tile for repair or replacement.

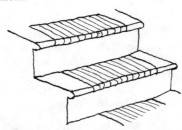

Stairs and Stairways

1. Stairs to see that they do not creak or need strengthening.

2. Treads on stairs to see if replacements are needed.

3. Rubber or composition treads for slipperiness.

4. Basement stairs to see whether additional supports or repairs are needed.

5. Railing on basement stairs to see that it is structurally sound.

6. Advisability of changing closed stairways to open ones by the removal of wall on one side.

7. Posts and railings for stiffness and need of replacement.

8. Method of access to attic and advisability of providing disappearing stairs.

Attic

1. Walls, floor, or underside of roof to see whether insulation is needed.

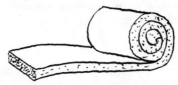

2. Ventilation and need for installation of louvers or additional windows.

3. Mortar joints in chimney to see whether they require repointing.

4. Chimney and side walls for cracks between them that may need filling.

5. Studs at floor line for firestopping.

6. Possibilities for changing attic space into finished room or rooms.

7. Need for additional partitions.

8. Flooring for stability and smoothness as well as need for refinishing.

Miscellaneous

1. Lining of existing closets and need for additional closets.

2. Need for additional shelves, bookcases, and cupboards.

3. Advisability of providing clothes chute, telephone cabinet, or other built-in conveniences.

For more efficient results and longer life of the housecleaning equipment, it should receive good care. Mops, cloths, and similar household aids should not be put away, after the cleaning operation, without being washed or cleaned.

Mops

The string mop which you use for washing the floors must have a hot soapsuds bath at least twice a month. Rinse it in clear water until all suds are out, ring out excess moisture, and hang it outdoors in the sun to dry.

The dry mop for the floor should be cleaned immediately after each time it is used. Take it outdoors, and shake the dust out thoroughly. If you are a city dweller and cannot do this outdoors, you can get the dust out through the small attachment on your vacuum cleaner. Another way to clean it indors is to put the head of the dry mop into a paper bag, shake thoroughly; remove the mop and you'll find the dust settled in the paper bag.

If your floor mop is cellulose sponge (rather than the regulation string mop) after each use remove the sponge from the handle, wash it in warm soapsuds, rinse in clear water. Then replace it in the handle, and squeeze the excess water from the sponge by pressing the handle down very hard.

When mop is not in use, do not stand it up. Instead, hang the mop on a hook in the wall. Bore a hole near the top end of the stick, run a wire or string through the hole, and use that to hang the mop stick on the hook.

Dust Cloths

At frequent intervals wash the dust cloths in warm soapsuds. Rinse in clear water. Hang outdoors in the sun to dry.

After each washing of the cloth, or before using a fresh cloth, you may want to oil-treat it. This is done by making a solution of 1 pint hot water and ¼ cup lemon oil. Dip the cloth into it, then squeeze out excess moisture, and hang it up to dry. This oil-treated cloth should be kept in a covered metal box or a jar, when it is not in use because it may be a fire hazard if left exposed. Cloth used on metalware needs a washing in warm soapsuds after each use. Rinse in clear water, and hang up to dry.

Cellulose Cleaning Sponge

The small hand sponge (which you use to clean the sink, drainboard and table tops, and other kitchen things) needs to be washed in warm soapsuds after each use. Rinse in clear water. Squeeze out excess moisture. Once a week sterilize the sponge by washing it in boiling water.

Wax Applicator, Floor

After each use wash the applicator in warm soapsuds. Rinse in clear water, shake out excess mois-

ture, and hang up to dry. The reason for the soapsuds bath is to prevent hardening of the wax which remains on the applicator.

The wax applicator should be hung up when not in use.

Hush Tube

This is part of the flush-tank inlet supply assembly. The cold water necessary to fill the tank flows through this tube after leaving the valve assembly, downward into the tank.

There are many types of flush-tank units; some are quieter than others. It may be an ordinary pipe or it may be fluted in order to control the noise of the water flowing into the tank.

See *Toilet Tank Repairs*.

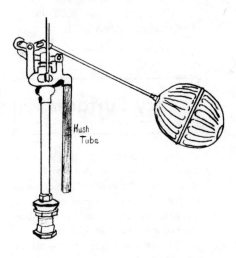

A hush tube.

Hydrometer

Use a hydrometer for testing the battery in your automobile. It should be given good care to prolong its life and use.

Cleaning

Wash body and float with soap and water. Use care when washing float to keep from injuring the markings. Battery acid deposits which do not yield to soap and water, can be removed with a solution of hot water and soda.

Care in Use

Provide a well-protected container positioned in a handy place. Handle with extreme care and replace to storage position when not in use. Clean grease from bulb and tip with carbon tetrachloride or soap and water. Flush with water and wipe dry.

Store in a cool place protected from direct sunlight. Wrap float in lens tissue paper and pack hydrometer securely to prevent damage.

Icy Surfaces

Icy surfaces constitute a menace. It is essential that ice be removed in order to avoid accidents to persons or injury to the house. To prepare yourself against the dangers of ice, you should have:

- rock salt or some chemical for the removal of ice
- an ice chopper, a long-handled tool with a square cutting edge
- an electric resistance cable if you live in extremely cold areas
- a blow torch or heat lamp for emergencies.

Roof Care

Unless steep-pitched roofs are provided with suitable snow guards, the snow is liable to slide off and injure persons or cause damage to property, especially after a heavy snow. Sliding snow and ice can rip a gutter away from the edge of the roof, can accumulate in the gutter, blocking the flow of water and causing seepage through the roof and walls, or crash down on shrubs used for foundation planting.

On flat or slightly-pitched roofs, there is a danger of an accumulation of snow which may clog the gutter and prevent the normal flow of water down the downspout.

There are several ways to keep your roof and house protected from the dangers of snow and ice. There are roof guards, made of metal, which are installed along the edge of steep-pitched roofs. These units have metal points which are nailed into the roof and calking is applied to keep the holes sealed. Or the units can be nailed or screwed into the roof, depending upon the type used.

Gutters can be protected from an accumulation of ice by using an electric resistance cable. See *Gutters and Downspouts*. This cable can also be used over portions of the roof to melt the snow as it falls.

Stairs and Walks

Accumulation of ice on stairs is particularly dangerous. If you live in a cold region where you have frequent snow in the winter, try to eliminate the stairs by building a ramp walk. But if you have stairs, use hand rails during snows and freezing rains.

You can remove ice from stairs by an electric resistance cable, chemical removers or an ice chopper. Be careful when using the

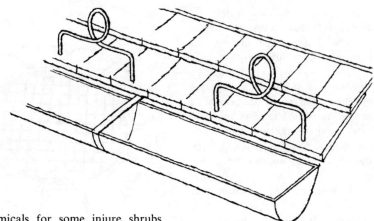

chemicals for some injure shrubs and lawns.

Walks and driveways can also be cleared of ice by the use of chemicals and an ice chopper. In some newer homes, piping is run under the walks and driveways and connected to the hot water heating system. A separate circulator pumps

Snow guards are necessary on steep-pitched roofs.

the hot water through these pipes, installed under the concrete, to melt the snow as it falls and to prevent the accumulation of ice.

Impedance

This is a radio or Hi-Fi measurement of the opposition to an electrical current and is measured in ohms.

Incinerator

In many areas, a convenient and safe way must be found to destroy trash. In most areas, removal of fallen leaves in the fall is also a problem. While the leaves can be saved for a compost heap, you might find yourself with too many for comfort. A handy incinerator is the answer.

If you plan on building an incinerator, choose a location away from the house where the smoke will not be annoying and where fire will not be a danger. There are commercial units available and, in some cases, your outdoor fireplace can be used as a substitute.

Here, however, are two simple incinerators you can make quickly and inexpensively. One is made of concrete block on a poured concrete foundation. One block is left out along the bottom course to provide for the draft. See *Concrete* and *Concrete Block* for how-to details.

The other easy-to-make incinerator consists of half of a 55 gallon oil drum buried in the earth. It should be buried so that about 1" extends above the soil level. You can add a few flagstones or solid concrete blocks around the perimeter.

In both instances, an iron grate is necessary over the top of the incinerator. It will keep small, burning pieces of paper or dry leaves from flying out of the unit. You may be able to pick up the right size grate from a second-hand dealer or junk yard.

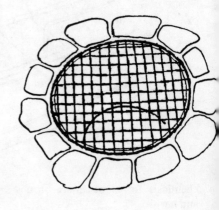

Half of an oil drum can be used for an easy-to-make incinerator.

A concrete block incinerator.

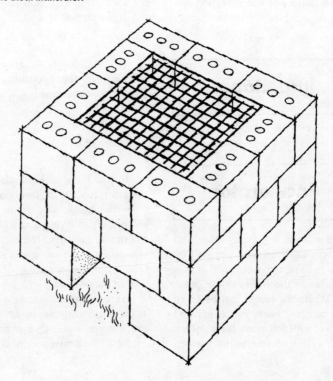

Increaser

This is a plumbing fitting which has one end larger than the other in order to increase the size of the pipe opening. It is similar to a reducer but used where you want to connect a larger pipe.

An increaser or reducer—it is used to join a smaller pipe to a larger one.

Indicators

This is a name sometimes used for special gages, particularly those used to measure speed or pressure. See *Gages.*

Insects

Most insects are unwelcome guests. Whether it is the mosquito that hums in the night while you try to sleep, the ant that finds its way into the pantry or the flea that came in with the dog, the Japanese beetle that eats away the roses, harmful insects must be destroyed. Insects cause considerable damage and annoyance.

Many chemical sprays and powders are available to combat different insects. DDT has proved to be one of the most effective insecticides and is available in dusts, sprays and aerosols. However, the indiscriminate use of DDT over the past several years has given rise to some strains of insects which are resistant to the chemical. If DDT does not work, then it is necessary to try some of the others to do the job.

While DDT frequently does an effective job against insects, certain precautions are necessary when it is handled by humans. Do not spray DDT near foods; keep it away from pets—canaries, dogs, cats; keep it out of reach of children; don't use it if you have a tendency toward allergies. See *DDT Hazards.*

How To Use DDT

There are two forms of liquid DDT available. One is a residual spray; it is applied on a surface and kills the insect if it crawls over the sprayed area. The other is a space spray which is released into the air

Insect	Type of DDT To Use	Application
Ants	5% solution or 10% powder	Heavy[1]
Bedbugs	5% solution	Light[2]
Fleas (on animals)	10% powder	Light
Flies	5% solution	Light
Mosquitos	5% solution	Light
Roaches	5% solution or 10% powder	Heavy
Weevils	5% solution	Heavy

[1] For a heavy application of a spray, spray all the liquid that will remain on a surface without dripping or running. For a heavy application of a dust, apply sufficient powder to form a film.

[2] For a light application of a spray, use only enough liquid to moisten the surface. For a light application of a dust, apply only enough to form a faintly visible film.

as vapor; this is quick-killing and usually is made with other chemical insecticides added to the DDT.

In powder form, this type of insecticide should contain at least 10% DDT to be effective. It is best dispensed with a small hand dust gun.

Garden Insects

When Spring blossoms forth after a long, bleak Winter, no one welcomes it more heartily than the amateur gardener. But unfortunately, the insects awaken at the same time the garden does, and they begin their annual attack on flowers, trees, shrubs and vegetables. The care you give your garden may end as wasted effort if you fail to keep close watch for destructive pests.

There's nothing more discouraging than to discover that the leaves and growing tips of your prize roses, for example, are beginning to curl, crinkle and look black and sickly. Close examination reveals scores of tiny green and black insects—

aphids—and on the unfolding buds, too!

No less discouraging is the havoc wrought by soft brown scales and other scales on many of the most popular ornamental plants. These insects lie dormant during the Winter on branches of shrubs and trees. When Spring arrives, they jump into action, laying their eggs by the thousands. Soon baby crawlers emerge and begin to move about on the plant, sucking the plant juices as they go and excreting a sticky substance which settles on leaves and branches and in which develops a disfiguring black fungus.

Multiply these cases many fold —for there are scores of different kinds of harmful bugs in the average garden—and you get an idea of how important this problem is to "green thumb" Americans.

Until recently, the problem was complicated by the fact that most insects required a different chemical control, which meant not only repeated sprayings, but waiting for the

Beneficial garden insects: left, praying mantis; right, ladybug.

damage to occur in order to know which chemical to spray. You might find aphids on the roses and spray for these. A short time later you might find that the chemical did not kill the green worms chewing holes in the leaves. And having controlled this condition, you might find that the foliage was changing from green to brown. This would require a third chemical.

Recent chemical developments are simplifying pest control in the garden considerably. Different chemicals are being combined and new ones are being added. One of the most effective, recent chemicals is malathion, described by the U.S.

All-purpose garden pesticides control a wide range of insects and diseases. Here it is being applied as a spray.

Some common insects that attack vegetables.

Aphid

Striped cucumber beetle

Potato beetle

Squash bug

Mexican bean beetle

Corn ear worm

Tomato horn worm

Cabbage worm

Department of Agriculture as "one of the safest insecticides to handle." Malathion combines a high insect-killing power with a high degree of safety to humans and animals. This new chemical will also kill flies that have become resistant to DDT and related insecticides.

Another advantage of malathion, when used on vegetables, is that it virtually disappears from most crops in about a week, thus enabling the gardener to pick them much earlier than usual after spraying, and without danger of contamination.

A few of the better known insects which this chemical will con-

Photographs courtesy of Monsanto
Chemical Co.

A garden pesticide must reach the criti-
cally important undersides of leaves.
Here it is being applied with a specially
designed dust-gun. Note the upstream of
the ejected pesticide.

trol are: aphids, spider mites, scales, leafhoppers, Japanese beetle adults, thrips, mealybugs, Mexican bean beetles and lace bugs. You can use it on such ornamentals as the rose, chrysanthemum, gladiolus, phlox, delphineum and many other flowers; on rhododendron, boxwood, holly and other broad-leaved evergreens; on spruce, juniper, arborvitae and other narrow-leaved evergreens; on a host of deciduous shrubs including spirea, forsythia, privet, snowball, and euonymous; in your vegetable garden on beans, tomatoes, cabbage, broccoli, onions, carrots, peas, potatoes, squash, beets and other crops; on such fruits as apple, pear, peach, cherry, plum and grape; and on ornamental trees such as birch, magnolia and lilac.

Check the label of an insecticide you wish to buy to see whether it has malathion in it. Although no single spraying program will control all insects, spraying or dusting several times from early May through July should give good results. Follow directions closely, for too much of almost any insecticide may damage plants in certain stages of growth. Be sure to cover all surfaces of the plant as evenly as possible, and check your duster or spray gun periodically to make sure that it's in good working order. Should it rain soon after using, apply it again, for rain will wash off most of the material.

A word of caution—Not all garden insects should be destroyed. There are some that feed on the harmful insects and do no damage themselves. These include the praying mantis, ladybug and the lace-

wing fly. And if you encourage birds in your garden, they will be a big help in controlling harmful insects. See *Bird Houses* and *Bird Baths And Feeders*.

For information on lawn insects, see *Lawns*.

Other Controls

In addition to chemicals to get rid of the insects, you can take certain preventative measures so that insects do not invade your home. Screens on your windows will help to keep flies and mosquitos out. Door closers that automatically close the screen, or for that matter any door, will help to keep flying insects out.

There are preventative sprays in

the garden to keep insects from injuring your lawn or ruining your vegetable garden. For how to combat Japanese beetles and other lawn and garden insects, see *Lawns—Insect Control*.

Also see *Decay—House Structure* for information about termites.

How To Fight Flies and Mosquitoes

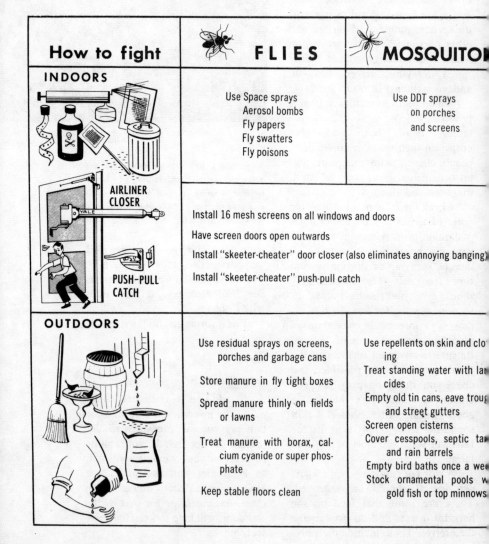

How to fight	FLIES	MOSQUITO
INDOORS	Use Space sprays Aerosol bombs Fly papers Fly swatters Fly poisons	Use DDT sprays on porches and screens
AIRLINER CLOSER PUSH-PULL CATCH	Install 16 mesh screens on all windows and doors Have screen doors open outwards Install "skeeter-cheater" door closer (also eliminates annoying banging) Install "skeeter-cheater" push-pull catch	
OUTDOORS	Use residual sprays on screens, porches and garbage cans Store manure in fly tight boxes Spread manure thinly on fields or lawns Treat manure with borax, calcium cyanide or super phosphate Keep stable floors clean	Use repellents on skin and clothing Treat standing water with larvicides Empty old tin cans, eave troughs and street gutters Screen open cisterns Cover cesspools, septic tanks and rain barrels Empty bird baths once a week Stock ornamental pools with gold fish or top minnows

Chart courtesy of Yale & Towne

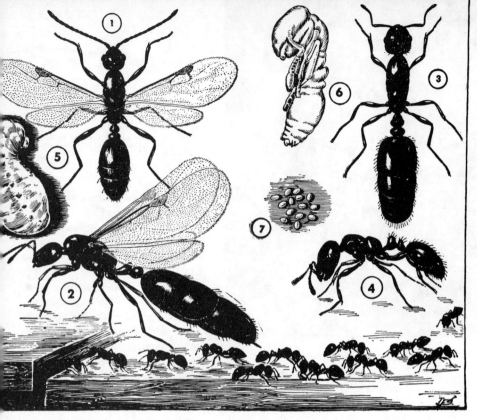

*The black ant; 1 and 2, winged king and queen; 3, queen after losing wings;
4, female worker ant; 5, larva; 6, pupa; 7, eggs laid by queen.*

Grasshopper outbreaks in the United States.

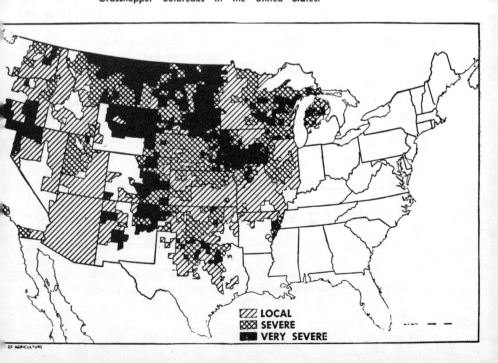

LOCAL
SEVERE
VERY SEVERE

OF AGRICULTURE

The Mexican bean beetle can do lots of damage in your vegetable garden.

Photograph courtesy of American
Cyanamid Co.

chinch bugs, sod worms, webworms, Japanese beetle grubs.

DDT is effective against a wide variety of insects and has largely replaced some of the older chemicals like arsenate of lead.

Lindane is the effective ingredient of BHC. It kills on contact and when taken internally by the insect.

Malathion is a comparatively new chemical which is effective against a wide variety of aphids and mites, including red spider.

Oils are frequently treated so that they will mix with water. They are then used as dormant as well as summer sprays against scale insects.

Parathion is extremely effective and extremely dangerous. Use only if other chemicals have failed and follow instructions closely.

Pyrethrum is non-poisonous but not always effective. When combined with rotenone the combination is called P-R mixture.

Rotenone kills slowly but stops feeding quickly.

Insecticide Ingredients

Following is a list of the most-used ingredients in insecticides. Since many commercial preparations are now combinations, it is well to know just what each of the active ingredients will do.

Bordeaux Mixture is used primarily for leaf spots and blights, but is also effective in repelling flea beetles. The actual killing ingredient is copper.

Calcium Cyanide kills ants, rats, mice, moles, etc.

Chlordane is most effective against insects which infest lawns;

Insulating Varnish

Special varnishes are available, which can be brushed on over wires, coils and electrical contacts to make the surface a non-conductor of electricity. The varnish is a substitute for an insulator made of fiber, rubber, ceramic or plastic.